FRENCH SUBSTANTIVE LAW

KEY ELEMENTS

AUSTRALIA
LBC Information Services
Sydney

CANADA and USA
Carswell
Toronto

NEW ZEALAND
Brooker's
Auckland

SINGAPORE and MALAYSIA
Thomson Information (S.E. Asia)
Singapore

FRENCH SUBSTANTIVE LAW

KEY ELEMENTS

By

CHRISTIAN DADOMO
Maîtrise en droit, D.E.A. (Strasbourg)
Senior Lecturer in Law at the University of the West of England, Bristol

and

SUSAN FARRAN
B.A. (Hons.), L.L.B., L.L.M. (Natal and Cantab.)
Principal Lecturer in law, University of the West of England, Bristol

LONDON • SWEET & MAXWELL • 1997

Published in 1997 by
Sweet & Maxwell Limited
100 Avenue Road
Swiss Cottage
London, NW3 3PR

Computerset by Tradespools Ltd, Frome, Somerset
Printed in England by Clays Ltd, St Ives plc

No natural forests were destroyed to make this product: only farmed timber was used and re-planted

ISBN 0 421 52550 9

A CIP catalogue record for this book is available from the British Library

Preface

The topics included in this book have been selected because we think that they raise interesting and sometimes controversial points concerning French law. Some of them have developed from comparative legal studies at undergraduate level on courses taught at the University of the West of England, others have their foundations in courses included in the Faculty's programme of continuing education for solicitors, others come from occasional papers. Consequently, this book does not purport to be an exhaustive treatise on the whole of substantive French law. Instead, we have sought to concentrate on those areas which appear to us to raise aspects of French law which are either unique to the French legal system, or raise particular difficulties for the common law lawyer. We hope that these topics will provide insight for the student, practitioner or general reader, into some of the complexities of French law.

C. Dadomo
S. Farran

Bristol, July 1996

Contents

Table of Cases

All references are to page numbers

Table of Statutes

All references are to page numbers

Table of Codes

All references are to page numbers

Table of Abbreviations

A.J.D.A.	*Actualité Juridique de Droit Administratif*
Cass.	*Cour de cassation*
Cass. civ.	*Cour de cassation, chambre civile*
Cass. crim.	*Cour de cassation, chambre criminelle*
C.C.	*Conseil constitutionnel*
C.Civ.	*Code civil*
C.E.	*Conseil d'Etat*
C.E. Ass.	*Conseil d'Etat, Assemblée plénière*
C.E. Sect.	*Conseil d'Etat, Section du contentieux*
C.P.	*Code pénal*
D.	*Recueil Dalloz*
D. Chron.	*Recueil Dalloz, chronique*
D.S.	*Recueil Dalloz Sirey*
EDCE	*Etudes et Documents du Conseil d'Etat*
Gaz. Pal.	*Gazette du Palais*
G.A.J.A.	*Grands Arrêts de la jurisprudence administrative* (Long, Weil, Braibant) 10th ed. 1993
G.D.C.C.	*Grandes Décisions du Conseil Constitutionnel* (Favoreu & Philip) 8th ed. 1995
Ord.	*Ordonnance*
R.D.C.C.	*Recueil des decisions du Conseil constitutionnel*
R.D.P.	*Revue de Droit Public et de la Science Politique*
Rec.	*Recueil Lebon (du Conseil d'Etat)*
RFDA	*Revue Française de Droit Administratif*
T.A.	*Tribunal administratif*
T.C.	*Tribunal des conflits*
S.	*Recueil Sirey*

Introduction

The Classification and Categorisation of Topics in French Law

Public Law and Private Law

Traditionally French law is divided into public and private law. The reasons for this are largely historical. Roman law, on which much of French law is based, was divided into public and private law. Indeed it appears to have been Ulpian, a Roman Jurist, who first used the distinction in around 200 A.D. Certainly this distinction is found in Justinian's *Digest* and *Institutes*, which, as parts of the *Corpus Iuris Civilis*, was to provide the foundations of legal study and the emergence of legal science in the twelfth century in Europe. The development of legal science maintained this division on the basis that relations between individuals and relations between the State and its subjects gave rise to special problems and needed differences in approach, not least because the nature of the interests involved could not be weighed equally. In fact public law was relatively undeveloped in Roman law compared to private law, largely because it was difficult to impose respect for the law on the State itself. It was not until the nineteenth century, under the influence of the "Age of Reason" and when doctrines on the "rights of man" became influential, that public law started to emerge as a subject worthy of study, particularly once the idea became popular that no-one was above the law—least of all the monarchy—and that the State should be organised in conformity with reason and so as to safeguard the rights of man. The need to bring the State and particularly the officials of the State within the control of the law has increased not only because of the emergence of democratic political structures but also because of the wide range of discretionary powers conferred on these officials, the exercise of which impinges on the daily lives of individuals.

The distinction between public and private law can be based on a number of models. First there is the substantive distinction, which is based on the simple idea that public law is the law applicable to the State and to administrative officials. If the State is involved in legal relations then the applicable law is public law. Public law, therefore, deals with the relation of individuals with the State and with the organisation of the State. Private law, on the other hand, is the law which deals with relations between private individuals. Applying this criterion, civil law and commercial law fall into private law, while constitutional law and administrative law are public law. However the distinction is based on a false premise, because the State may, and indeed often does, intervene in the relations between private individuals. Indeed, if one considers that all law emanates from the State, then all law is public.

A second way of distinguishing between the two is on the grounds of the formal distinction based on the concepts and techniques used. For example, private law recognises contracts based on the voluntary will of the parties, whereas public law knows only unilateral acts because the State and the individual cannot be said to be equal. Thus, the unilateral act is a manifestation of authority. According to this model, although the State and its officials may participate in contracts, these are different from private law contracts.

Conceptually, private law is based on a notion of rights while public law is based on the notion of legal authority or the exercise of public power. A private individual may act in any way which is not prohibited, whereas a public authority may only act in a way which is permitted, that is within the powers conferred on it. Following this model to its logical conclusion, criminal law would be regarded as private law, although in fact it is regarded as public law under the previous model because it involves the individual and the State.

A third model is the functional model which focuses on the operation of procedural rules. Public law operates to protect the general interest or the interests of the public—without defining whose these are—whereas private law rules operate to protect the interests of the individual. However, even here this distinction is not absolute. Often private interests are protected because in the long run this is for the general good. For example, contracts may be enforceable because to allow individuals to freely break their contractual undertakings could lead to disruption in public order.

Although historically private law and its study and development preceded public law, even in the field of private law there were historical differences in terms of origins. Within the private law codes not all the legal rules or institutions originated from Roman law. Indeed the French Civil Code draws quite heavily on Canon law, particularly the institutions of marriage and filiation, and also customary law—for example, matrimonial property regimes. Other aspects reflect the contemporary beliefs of the period of codification, thus the law on property and inheritance reflect the ideas of the Revolution of 1789.

In French law the distinction between public and private law is important because of the procedural aspects. The *Cour de Cassation* deals with private law issues, while the *Conseil d'Etat* is reserved for public law ones. In a class of its own is the other public law court, the *Conseil Constitutionnel*, created under the 1958 Constitution. However, the procedural aspect is not conclusive. Although there are special administrative courts, not all disputes involving the State will come before these. Some will go before the ordinary courts of law which will also hear private law disputes. These administrative courts create problems in the categorisation of law because not only do they have to take cognisance of private law from time to time, but administrative law may be applied in a civil or criminal court. Moreover, constitutional law questions are not dealt with in the administrative courts. Today the question may be not so much whether an issue is one of public or private law, but whether it is one of administrative law or private law.

LOCATING THE MAIN SOURCES OF LAW

The main sources of French law can be divided into authoritative primary sources of law and subsidiary, persuasive sources of law. Within the first category are legislation and custom, while the second category includes the decisions of the courts and legal writings. When referring to sources of law, the starting point will generally be the relevant code. This will indicate whether there have been subsequent statutory modifications and in the annotated versions reference will be made to cases which illustrate how certain provisions may be interpreted and also refer to certain academic commentaries on the application of the law.

USING THE CODES

There were five original codes: the *Code Civil* (1804), the *Code de Procédure Civile* (1806), the *Code de Commerce* (1808) and the *Code d'Instruction Criminelle* and *Code Pénal*, both of 1811. Since 1939, a number of "new" codes have appeared including the *Code de la route* (Highway Code); *Code de la nationalité* (Nationality Code); *Code des loyers et propriété* (Housing Code); *Code des douanes* (Customs Code); *Code fiscal* (General Tax Code); *Code rural* (Rural Code); *Code des mines* (Mining Code); *Code de la sécurité sociale, de la mutualité et mutualité sociale agricole* (Code of Social Security); *Nouveau code de procédure pénale* (New Code of Criminal Procedure); *Code administratif* (Administrative Code); *Code de l'environnement* (Environmental Code); *Code des sociétés* (Code of Company Organisations); *Code de l'urbanisme* (Town Planning Code); *Code de la santé publique, de la famille et de l'aide sociale* (Public

Health, Family and Social Services Code); *Code de la construction et de l'habitation* (Construction and Dwellings Code); *Code de l'expropriation* (Expropriation Code); *Code du travail* (Labour Code); *Code de l'organisation judiciaire* (Code of Judicial Organisation)—which is attached to the Code of Civil Procedure; *Code des postes et télécommunications* (Post and Telecommunications Code).

In private law the code most often referred to is the *Code civil*, while in public law this will either be the *Code administratif* or the Constitution itself.

In using the Codes, it is important to note that the location of subject-matter may be different from what one might expect from one's own system. It is, therefore, necessary to consult the index of the applicable code, which will be located at the end of the code. This point can be illustrated by considering the contents of the Civil Code. This Code is divided into three Books, and prefaced by an introductory title. The first Book (Articles 7–515) includes such topics as: (1) the enjoyment of civil rights, (2) the acquisition and loss of nationality, (3) the law relating to the status of French nationals and foreigners, (4) the relevance of domicile, marriage and divorce, legitimacy, adopting and disappearance of status, and (5) the regulation of paternal power and guardianship. The second Book (Articles 516–710) deals with the nature and definition of property—but not transactions relating to it—while the third Book (Articles 711–2281) is concerned with obligations of various sorts, and includes the law relating to succession, contract, capacity, debt, delict, matrimonial property law, special contracts, quasi-contracts and quasi-delicts, partnership, loan, deposit, agency, securities, and prescription. Some of the Codes, such as the *Code de procédure pénale*, the *Code du travail* or the *Code de l'organisation judiciaire* (which itself is part of the *Code de procédure civile*) are futher subdivided into *Législation* (*e.g.* Art. L 111–1 C. *Trav.*), *Décrets en Conseil d'Etat* (*e.g.* Art. R *1* C.P.P.), *Décrets* (*e.g.* Art. D *1* C.P.P.) and *Arrêtés* (*e.g.* Art. A *1* C.P.P.).

The amount of detail given in any one article will vary depending on the area of law concerned and the date of the code. Many of the Articles in the Civil Code are worded in a very general way and in order to understand their scope considerable reference to cases and commentary may be required. By contrast the provisions in procedural codes or the criminal codes may be more specific. When searching for an article it is important to check whether or not that article has been replaced by a new one. The old article will have the word *ancien* indicated before it, or *abrogé* after it, with an indication of the Act by which it was abrogated. Abrogated or old articles appear in italics. Any Act modifying an article is indicated in brackets immediately after the article, for example (L. 22 Sept. 1942). Acts are always referred to by date.

FINDING CASE LAW AND COMMENTARIES ON THE CODES

In an annotated edition of any code there are references to decided cases. The citation of the cases will depend on the court being referred to. Decisions of the Court of Cassation can be found in the *Bulletin des arrêts de la Cour de cassation*. This is published in two series, one dealing with civil cases, the other with criminal cases. The former can be found in the *Bulletin Civil*—cited as *Bull.* or *Bull. Civ.*—and the latter in the *Bulletin Pénal*. Decisions of the *Conseil d'Etat* are found in the *Recueil Lebon* (cited as *Rec. Lebon*). General case reports, commentary on these and academic articles can be found in *La Semaine Juridique*. This is divided into four parts—usually but not always in one volume—*Doctrine*, *Jurisprudence*, *Textes* and *Sommaire*. Notes on cases are indicated by the reference *note* followed by the name of the writer. Case decisions from regional courts will be indicated by the location of the court and the date, for example Bordeaux 27 fév. 1979. If the court is a specialist court then this will be indicated, for example *Trib.com*. Nantes 8 oct. 1981.

A reference frequently cited and used extensively by practitioners is the *Juris-Classeur Pérodique* (cited as J.C.P.). This is an encyclopaedia of commentary on all the articles, which is regularly updated. Another useful publication containing cases and commentary is the *Gazette du Palais*—cited as *Gaz. Pal.* This appears in two volumes and a reference will give the year, volume and page. Dalloz-Sirey publishes a collection of articles and commentaries under the title *Chronique* (abbreviated to *Chron./Chr.*), *Jurisprudence* (J)—case law—and *Législation* (L).

In French law collections of case decisions are also found in textbooks rather than journals or official publications. These are collections of "*grands arrêts*" (leading cases), for example: *Les Grands Arrêts de la Jurisprudence Civile*, by Capitant, Weill and Terré; *Les Grands Arrêts du Droit Criminel*, by Pradel and Varinard; *Les Grands Arrêts de la Jurisprudence Administrative*, by Long, Weil *et. al.*; *Les Grandes Décisions du Conseil Constitutionnel*, by Favoreu and Philip; *Les Grands Arrêts du Droit de l'Assurance*, by Berr and Groutel, etc. The main law journals are: *Revue de Droit Public* (R.D.P.); *Revue Française de Droit Constitutionnel* (R.F.D.C.); *Revue Francaise de Droit Administratif* (R.F.D.A.); *Actualité Juridique de Droit Administratif* (A.J.D.A.); *Revue Internationale de Droit Comparé* (Rev.Int.Dr.Comp.); *Revue Trimestrielle de Droit Civil* (Rev.Tr.Dr.Civ.); *Revue Trimestrielle de Droit Commercial* (Rev.Tr.Dr.Com.) and *Revue de Science Criminelle et Droit Pénal*

Comparé. It is also not unusual to find references to collections of conference papers or to doctoral theses.

The style of judgments varies according to the court. Judgments of the *Cour de cassation*, for example, will have a long and discursive discussion of the legal points involved, whereas the actual decision may be expressed in quite a short formula. A *tribunal*, on the other hand, may have a longer judgment punctuated by numerous points introduced by "whereas". One of the difficulties for the reader versed in another legal system is that there may be a number of "*attendu*" or "*considérant*" between the start of the judgment and its conclusion. However, the decision, which appears at the end of the *dispositif*, is generally indicated by the words *par ces motifs*. Any article raised in a case must be based on law—either an article of a code or a statute.

The structure and terminology—even once translated—of a French court decision are rather different from English case reports. For a start the reports are shorter and no dissenting opinions are given. The case will start by indicating the name of the court, which is followed by the reference number of the case, the date of the decision, and the title of the decision—which will indicate the main subject-matter. The order of these matters varies from one court to another. The relevant law is referred to by "*Vu*"—these are the "*visas*", the applicable legal considerations. The relevance of these to the case before the court is indicated by "*considérant*". These statements—the *considérants*—indicate the legal reasoning which will inform the decision, which is indicated by the word "*décide*". The ruling is then divided into articles. Sometimes the ruling will be indicated by the words "*Par ces motifs*", these indicate the *dispositif* of the court. Finally the report will indicate the composition of the court and who appeared before it.

LOCATING AND UNDERSTANDING STATUTES

Legislation is found in the *Journal Officiel* (J.O.) which is published daily. It is also now available on CD Rom and LEXIS. The report of legislation indicates the ministers and governmental department responsible for introducing the measure, and refers to any relevant preparatory measures or resolutions concerning the projected law, reports and discussions. The title of the Act is its number and date, followed by a short indication of its subject-matter. Acts are divided into Parts, sub-divided into Titles. Within the Titles are Articles, which run consecutively through the Act. Sometimes the Titles are further divided into Chapters. At the end of the Act are the names of the President, and the relevant ministers. *Décrets* are also referred to by number and date, followed by a brief indication of the subject-matter. However, the actual *décret* is preceded by reference to other relevant *décrets* and *ordonnances* prefixed by "*Vu*", and then the new *décret* is introduced by the word "*Décrete*". This is divided into Sections, sub-divided into articles.

There are no strict rules for the interpretation of statutes. While the first approach will be to ascertain the literal meaning of the words, this will not be used if to do so makes a nonsense of the law. In this case, resort may be had to the logical approach, whereby the context and the relation of a particular law to the whole body of rules is considered. This approach is quite often adopted in private or administrative law, but not in criminal law.

Unlike an English Act of Parliament, there is no section giving a definition of the various terms used in the statute. Sometimes the law may be interpreted by adopting an historical approach and taking into account the debates surrounding the legislation, the reports at the time, etc. This approach will not always, however, be suitable, for example in the case of fiscal or penal law, or where there is no relevant historical background—which is often the case with *décrets* and *ordonnances*.

Finally a teleological approach may be adopted, or, as it is sometimes called, a social approach, whereby the interpretation followed is the literal analysis best suited to the prevailing contemporary view of social welfare and justice. This has had to be done in some cases to bring the Civil Code up to date with the twentieth century and to take into account the growth of administrative law and the role of the courts. Nevertheless, the teleological approach cannot be followed if to do so would contradict the literal or logical application or ignore the historical context altogether.

Part One
Private Law

Chapter One
The law of obligations

INTRODUCTION

(A) THE LAW OF OBLIGATIONS GENERALLY

The law relating to obligations falls under that area of private law known as *droit civil*. The fundamental source of the law is the *Code civil*, promulgated on March 21, 1804. This, however, must be read in conjunction with subsequent legislation, decisions of the courts, and elaboration by commentators. The Civil Code deals with the law of persons, the family, property, obligations and enforcement of debts. There is necessarily some overlap between these different areas. Moreover, before considering some particular aspects of the law of obligations it is first necessary to understand certain concepts which are fundamental to this area of French law. These are the distinction made between *droits personnels* (personal rights or rights *in personam*) and *droits réels* (real rights or rights *in rem*); the meaning of the concepts of *patrimoine*; and the distinction between *actes juridiques* and *faits juridiques*.

As has been indicated in the general introduction, civil law is primarily concerned with claims between individuals. This means persons who are the subject of subjective rights. Those rights may be exercisable by persons themselves, or require respect on the part of others. For this purpose, "persons" includes both *personnes physiques*[1] (natural physical persons), and *personnes morales*[2] (artificial or legal persons—such as companies).

The subjective rights which may be exercised and enjoyed are divided into two categories: *droits patrimoniaux* and *droits extra-patrimoniaux*.

---

[1] There is, as in many legal systems, a distinction between being human and having legal personality, and even conferment of the latter may not mean full legal capacity.

[2] These need not necessarily be composed of individuals, but may include groups or other collectivities which are attributed with legal rights—*e.g.* associations, trade unions, clubs, etc. Not all collectivities or groups will be regarded as *personnes morales*, notably the family.

(B) FUNDAMENTAL CONCEPTS

Droits patrimoniaux

Droits patrimoniaux are rights which have an intrinsic market value. In law they are relevant in the context of sale, exchange, gift, etc. These rights can be further divided into *droits réels* (real rights) and *droits de créance* (rights of credit).

Patrimoine

Patrimoine can be understood either in the non-legal sense, as a person's fortune, or, in a more juristic sense, as the collection of rights and obligations which one person may transfer to another in exchange for financial consideration. As such, *patrimoine* consists of the totality of rights and obligations, present and future, attaching to a person, regardless of any changes in the actual composition of the property. In French law this notion of *patrimoine* is inseparable from the idea of legal personality attaching to a natural or legal person. *Patrimoine* is therefore indivisible and intransmissible, and is integral to the life of the holder.

There is consequently, in French law, a close relationship between property rights and contractual rights. The sum total of a person's rights and obligations will form part of the *patrimoine* of that person, provided such rights and obligations have a pecuniary value—whether this is active (that is a credit) or passive (a debt). Not all rights and obligations will, however, have a pecuniary value. These will therefore be extra-patrimonial, although they will still form part of a person's legal personality.

This assimilation of patrimony with personality finds academic support in the classical school of legal reasoning first propounded by Aubrey and Rau.[3] Its critics, influenced by the German school of thought, distinguish between different categories of property, and support a *théorie d'affectation*, by which property is classified according to the ends to which it is directed. This has the advantage of giving coherence to a wide range of assets and liabilities but fragments the person and his property.

The classic theory of *patrimoine* means that changes in the actual composition of property can be accommodated—provided there is still some pecuniary or economic value—and both active and passive rights can be included. This relates closely to both contractual rights, for

---

[3] See G. Marty and P. Raynaud *Droit Civil* (Sirey, 2nd ed., 1972) pp. 465–466.

example the ability of a person to enforce active rights against passive rights, and claims in tort—again the right to enforce active rights usually to gain some kind of pecuniary return (for example compensation). Although this idea of *patrimoine* only includes that which has an economic or pecuniary value, this is interpreted very broadly, so that all rights with financial potential—for example the right to sue for breach of contract or to claim damages for nuisance—are included.

According to French legal theory, everyone who has legal personality has patrimony. Thus, although a minor may have limited legal capacity, the fact that he or she has legal personality means that the law recognises that there must be legal provision for the *patrimoine* of a minor.

Within the broad umbrella of *patrimoine* different rights can be distinguished. In the contractual text the nature of the rights which arise are different from those concerning torts. Where there is a consensual agreement between two or more persons, then certain reciprocal obligations are created (*droits de créance*). One person enjoys the active or positive aspect of the relationship, while the other bears the passive or negative aspect, *la dette*. These two sides of the agreement presuppose that there is a legal relationship or nexus between the two parties which gives them rights against each other. The obligations which arise may concern the payment of money, an obligation to do something, or to refrain from doing something. Of course, similar obligations arise in the context of delict (tort), particularly as French law recognises negative and positive obligations.[4] The difference in delict is that the obligation is general until a victim emerges.

Extra-patrimonial rights cannot be given a direct or immediate economic value. Their prime purpose is the protection of the person. However, as the protection of a person has both moral and physical aspects, for example bodily integrity and reputation, some of these apparently extra-patrimonial rights may have an intrinsic economic value in as much as they can be exploited for gain, or given a value if abused—for example in the case of defamation, or where a person attracts sponsorship, or merchandising rights because of their personality, looks, etc.

The division between these various rights is not therefore clear cut. A particular grey area is that of family rights where some rights may be deemed to be extra-patrimonial—such as the exercise of parental authority over children—while others will be deemed to be patrimonial—for example the management and control of property belonging to minors, property rights deriving from a matrimonial property regime,

[4] E.g. there is a positive duty to rescue a person in danger, provided the rescuer can do so without endangering his own life. Failure to rescue carries a criminal sanction.

rights under the law relating to reserved shares in a deceased estate, etc. Moreover while family rights include personal rights within the context of private and family life, these may also have patrimonial aspects, for example the right to one's image, to one's name and honour, the right to physical integrity. Most of these rights are acquired automatically and not as the result of agreement. The recognition of them by the law is therefore defensive rather than positive, allowing the owner of the right to claim the legal right to sanction the actions of others. Once this happens and money compensation is paid, these personal rights cease to be extra-patrimonial.

It is evident that the concept of *patrimoine* can include both real rights—that is rights to property itself—and personal rights. Nevertheless, French law distinguishes between such rights, although, again, this distinction will not always be rigid. There are for instance some rights which are hybrid, for example usufruct,[5] and others whose classification is controversial, notably the right of a tenant or leaseholder.[6] There are also rights which are described as *droits réels in faciendo* that is personal obligations which attach to a thing. In such circumstances if the property is transferred to a third party it remains encumbered by the obligation attached to it.[7]

While the range and variety of possible personal rights seems to be unlimited, there is some support for the view that real rights, because they can be raised against anyone, should be limited. However in practice most real rights are subject to requirements of publicity—for example all rights relating to land must be registered—so that third parties are less likely to be detrimentally affected. Moreover, as personal rights can also affect third parties—in as much as they must respect them—the dangers of uncertainty created by an unlimited class of rights could be equally applicable in the case of personal rights. It is, however, rare to find decisions in which new real rights are upheld, although one way round this is to argue that the rights claimed are personal or hybrid.

---

[5] See Chapter Two, Topic Two, below.

[6] The debate, which is one of longstanding, was revived during the nineteenth century in the writings of Troplong. The relationship between the person who grants a rent (*bailleur*) and the person who rents the property (*locataire*) is personal, arising in contract, but—particularly where the property is immovable property—the *locataire* has direct powers, not dissimilar from those of usufruct—which are considered as real rights. These powers have been enhanced by the protection of special laws in recent times, and so the problem of definition has been exacerbated. See B. Starck (ed) *Introduction au Droit* (Litec, Paris, 3rd ed., 1991) pp. 463–466.

[7] A common example is where property is encumbered by a mortgage.

Droits réels

Droits réels are rights which a person exercises directly over things, without requiring any further legal framework, for example the right of ownership, or the right of passage over a servitude. The main characteristics of such rights are that the holder has the right to follow the property (*droit de suite*) and a preferential claim over it against other claimants (*droit de préférence*). These rights are considered in greater detail in Chapter Two below.

Droits de créance

Droits de créance are rights which arise as a result of law or contract and which are exercisable against another person as a consequence, for example the right to claim a sum of money or to undertake work or to claim compensation for damage.

Droits personnels

While *droits réels* are rights over a thing (*in rem*), *droits de créance* are rights with respect to another person—to do or to refrain from doing (*in persona*) and are also referred to as *droits personnels*. However, this term can be confusing because it also, and more frequently, refers to *droits extra-patrimoniaux*, whereas *droits de créance* are clearly *droits patrimoniaux*, like "real rights"—*droits réels*.[8]

Droits extra-patrimoniaux

There are rights which are non-commercial in the legal sense, but which are protected objectively by the law. Such rights include the right to physical integrity, life, freedom, political rights, the right to exercise a profession, etc. It is these rights which are *droits personnels* in the strict sense, in as much as they attach to the person.[9] Such rights may attract *patrimonial* consequences, in as much as compensation for physical or

---

[8] E.g. a person who rents a house has a *droit de créance* against the landlord as regards peaceful occupation and enjoyment of the property, whereas the person who occupies property which he owns has a *droit réel* over the property itself.

[9] A distinction needs to be made between *droits fondamentaux*, as far as they relate to civil liberties or human rights. The latter fall into the area of public law, but the distinction is not always clear, *e.g.* freedom of expression may find protection in private law in so far as an artist or author has legally enforceable material and moral rights over his work or creation. The main difference is that a court will only adjudicate a claim to a subjective right if it believes it to be well-founded (Art. 30(1) N.C.P.C.).

moral harm may be awarded. It is also true that some of these rights may acquire the characteristics of *droits patrimoniaux*, for example the use and exploitation of a name, image, or title.[10]

Les actes juridiques

French law recognises two sorts of rights or obligations. Acts attracting legal consequences, that is a manifestation of will which complies with certain legal rules and which is intended to have legal consequences, and facts giving rise to legal consequences, that is circumstances to which the law attaches consequences often regardless of will or intention.

Typical of the former are bilateral contracts, or unilateral acts such as the creation of a will. However a distinction can be drawn between acts which are deeds—*negotium*—and documents—*instrumentum*.[11] More usually *actes juridiques* are understood in the sense of deeds (*negotium*). In private law such acts may be onerous, where there is an exchange of obligations, or free, as in the case of a gift; they may involve acts of administration, conservation or alienation; they may be carried out *inter vivos* or on death. The gravity of the act, its value and the object of it may all influence the legal rules which govern it.

In order for such acts to be legally valid certain rules have to be complied with. The fundamental concept underlying the enforceability of such acts, however, is the consensual nature of them—the fact that they are based on the voluntary exercise of consent to create obligations.

Les faits juridiques

The other form of obligation which arises is that which occurs as a result of certain occurrences to which the law attaches consequences. For example, the birth of a person is an occurrence to which the law attaches legal consequences, as is death. Other occurrences may require some form of conscious effort—although not necessarily intention—for example, possession of a thing, or guardianship of an animal which causes harm. The nature of the *animus* required will vary according to the requirements of law, from situations where fault may be implied—for

---

[10] Nor can it be said that the two categories are distinguishable by their transmissibility or non-transmissibility on death. Descendants of a deceased may have the right to defend the deceased's name, while some real rights such as a usufruct are not transmissible at death.

[11] These may be used as evidence either of an *acte juridique* (e.g. sale), or a *fait juridique* (e.g. a statement concerning an accident). The distinction is not altogether clear as constitutional law statutes, regulations and indeed the Constitution itself are regarded as *actes juridiques*.

example, cases of strict liability for defective products—to cases where intention must be established for liability.

There are two meanings attributable to this concept. In the wider senses *faits juridiques* are all those aspects of social life which attract legal consequences—whether these relate to the creation, transmission or extinction of rights. In the narrower sense, and by contrast with *actes juridiques*, they consists of facts themselves—for example birth—or actions—such as injury—which by their existence set in motion the creation, transmission or modification of rights. *Faits juridiques* may be voluntary or involuntary. Even where they are voluntary, but the effects they produce are not desired, they remain *faits juridiques*. Similarly involuntary actions may have natural or accidental consequences. For example, birth and death are involuntary events with legal consequences. Fire, war and flood are also involuntary events with legal consequences. Voluntary events are distinguishable from *actes juridiques* in as much as in the latter case both the act and the consequences are desired, whereas in the former case, although the act may be voluntary—in as much as it is not the act of an automaton—the consequences are not desired.

Faits juridiques can be further divided into those which are legal—that is they give rise to positive obligations enforceable in law—and those which are illegal or contrary to the law, in as much as they attract legal sanctions—*délits* or *quasi-délits* (delicts and quasi-delicts)—and consequently raise issues of civil liability and capacity, either for one's own wrong-doing or that of another.

(C) THE OPERATION OF THE LAW OF OBLIGATIONS

The interaction of these different concepts can be clearly seen in the law of obligations. The term "obligations" can be understood in two senses. First, in a general sense, it refers to anything which is subject to legal consequences and sanctions. Secondly, and in the more usual and technical sense, an obligation is a legal nexus between two people, by virtue of which the one (*débiteur*) is bound to do or to refrain from doing something in respect of the other (*créancier*). There are thus two sides to an obligation. One is active, positive, and is a benefit, the other passive, negative and a burden. Both aspects affect the *patrimoines* of the parties on either side.[12]

[12] In Roman law, from which this notion of obligations derives, the legal claim established by the obligation extended to personal, corporeal security for the obligation, non-performance of which entitled the creditor to seize the debtor: J.P. Gridel *Introduction au Droit et au Droit Français* (Dalloz, 2nd ed., 1994) p. 114.

The law of obligations operates to maintain a balance, so that if one person is enriched or impoverished by another, an obligation arises to redress the balance between the parties. This impulse to maintain an equilibrium either derives from agreement—as is the case in contract—or from the operation of law—as is the case with delict or tort. Thus, if one person benefits from the activities of another, he may have an obligation to exchange something in return. Similarly if a person causes harm to another by his actions, there is an obligation to make reparation for the harm. In the first case the obligation is incurred voluntarily, in the second it is incurred involuntarily.

Not all obligations are enforceable in law although they may be binding on the conscience (*obligations naturelles*), others are only partially enforceable. For instance, a gift which is promised but not evidenced in a formal document may not be enforceable through an action for breach of contract. Conversely if a gift is received the donor can claim it back if the recipient is deemed to be unworthy.[13]

Where the civil law makes obligations enforceable, it effectively imposes a *lien* over the assets or *patrimoine* of the person who is liable to carry out the obligation. A careless motorist must therefore compensate his victim; a purchaser must pay for the goods transferred to him. Consequently an obligation, or its corresponding right, commences as a personal right but can be transformed into a real right.

The purpose of the law in the context of obligations is to determine what is just in the arena of social relations, hence the primary concern with private law. Where obligations are assumed, the nature of the law and its extent is primarily determined by the parties themselves. The law is only concerned to ensure that the freedom to incur obligations is not abused so as to lead to injustices. Where the obligation is not assumed voluntarily however, the law is more prescriptive.

---

[13] *E.g.* if a husband receives a gift from his wife and he then commits adultery, the wife may demand the gift back on the basis that the underlying rationale of the gift has disappeared. Similarly a gift of money to an adult child may be claimed back if the child is found to have received it on false grounds—*e.g.* by claiming to be a penniless student when in fact he had a job.

TOPIC ONE
CAPACITY

Legal personality has two aspects: the more abstract general dimension which relates to extra-patrimonial rights, such as honour, aspects of private life etc., which are inherent to being human, and a more concrete dimension which is to do with a person's place in society and which confers on each individual his or her personal identity. Within this second aspect are two concepts: *l'état*—status—and *la capacité*—the ability of a person to exercise rights and incur liabilities.

With these two aspects in mind, it can be stated that every person has legal personality consisting of a collection of non-patrimonial characteristics which are personal to them and which have legal significance. These include characteristics relating to identification—name, date and place of birth, fingerprints, signature, etc.; characteristics determining legal status, such as nationality, marital status, domicile, etc.; and in a wider sense characteristics relevant to their professional or political status.[14] In French law it is possible to differentiate between the *état personnel* of an individual—which includes aspects such as name, sex, date of birth, place of birth; *état familial*, which is concerned with parentage, marriage and affiliation by marriage—for example in-laws, cousins and step-parents; and *état civil*. This last, which incorporates elements of *l'état personnel* and *l'état civil* is a formal, official statement of legal recognition of a person's status, made by a public authority. As a person changes their status so this official document is changed and updated.[15]

Nevertheless, despite these different aspects a person's status is essentially indivisible and, therefore, like a person's *patrimoine* represents the sum of the parts: unalienable, because it is determined by law and not by will; and permanent in as much as a person cannot get rid of it.[16]

---

[14] The notion of status is a composite of many aspects. This is partly the result of Roman law influence. In Roman law a person's status depended on the degree of freedom they enjoyed, whether they were a Roman citizen or not, and their family status—*i.e.* whether they were legally free—*sui juris*—or subject to the domination of another—*alieni juris*. Although all these features have disappeared from French law, the idea of status as a composite of different aspects relating to an individual has remained.

[15] To the extent that it is now possible for a transsexual to have his or her new sex recorded on the document, following the ruling of the European Court of Human Rights against France in the case of *B v. France* March 25, 1992, and a decision by the Court of Cassation on December 11, 1992, overturning its former line of reasoning.

[16] It has been said that the status of a person is like the body's shadow, the two cannot appear or disappear without each other. Therefore, unlike certain rights and obligations it can neither be acquired or lost after a long period of time. An exception to this general principle was introduced in an Act of January 3, 1972, whereby the right to establish filiation is lost after thirty years.

(A) LEGAL CAPACITY

Whereas a person's status may vary depending on all the different aspects which make it up, the question of capacity is much less individual. All legally recognised persons are capable of having rights and incurring obligations, although not all persons will have unlimited capacity. In this respect French law distinguishes between *incapacité de jouissance*, which is the inability to enjoy certain rights, and *incapacité d'exercise*, which is the inability to exercise rights which may be enjoyed. The legal situation differs depending on whether the person claiming the right is a natural person or a legal person.

French law recognises *personnes physiques*, *personnes morales*—physical natural persons and legal persons (such as commercial organisations, institutions such as a hospital, etc.).[17] Not all legal persons have the same characteristics, but they do all have a name, a domicile or place where they are located, legal status (*état*) and *patrimoine* (either assets or debts or both). The law of obligations ignores the characteristics of the persons it governs, so that whether a person is a physical person—a human—or a fictitious legal person—*personne morale*—the law is the same. The law starts from the premise that all persons have full legal capacity, except where the law declares them incapable.[18] This topic is primarily concerned with natural persons.

The capacity of a person relates to their legal ability to exercise various rights and incur obligations and liabilities by which their legal personality is affirmed.[19] Legal capacity can take many forms, it may be civil, commercial, criminal or political. However, civil capacity is fundamental in determining the extent to which a person can participate in the legal world—for example it determines a person's ability to act as a witness, to marry, to enter contracts, to incur liability for harm, to write a will, to succeed to property, etc. Without civil capacity, a person cannot have political or commercial capacity.

French law, similar to other legal systems, restricts or excludes the legal capacity of certain persons, be these natural or fictitious persons. A person who is *incapable* is one who in law does not have the capacity to

---

[17] There are also societies and foundations which are neither natural persons nor legal persons, not dissimilar from unincorporated associations or public trusts in English law. These may have limited capacity but will suffer from a number of disadvantages, for example they cannot have any *patrimoine*.

[18] In the realm of contract see, *e.g.* Arts. 1123 and 1124 C. *Civ*.

[19] There is a distinction between capacity and competence. The latter is limited in application to the exercise of administrative and judicial powers: F. Terré *Introduction Générale au Droit* (Dalloz, Paris, 1994) p. 257.

undertake all legal acts, particularly contracts.[20] Incapacity may be determined by the ability to act—taking into account maturity, understanding, etc.—or by the nature of the act itself.[21] As indicated it is possible to distinguish two sorts of incapacity, that of *incapacité de jouissance*—whereby a person is absolutely incapable of certain acts because they cannot be the holder of the right under consideration—for example, a girl under 15 cannot marry—and *incapacité d'exercise*—where a person has the right but their capacity may be determined by what it is they want to do. In this latter case, the incapacity may be general or specific. Therefore, in some acts, the person who is incapable may be assisted by another, for example a tutor or guardian, and indirectly be able to exercise certain rights or obligations.

Here the law also distinguishes between acts of preservation—for example the preservation of property, *acte conservatoire*; acts of administration, *acte d'administration*; and acts of disposition, *acte de disposition*.[22] In the first case the person lacking capacity—deemed to be *incapable*—may act, while in the second case a representative is required, because of the diversity of actions available and the possible liability which may be incurred. In the third case, the representative may not act without further authorisation or intervention, for example the intervention of a judge or family council. There are also circumstances in which statutory limitations are placed on capacity for very specific undertakings.[23]

It should not be thought that incapacity only relates to those who need to be protected from their own youth or mental inability. Certain persons will lack capacity to undertake certain acts because of their position of authority or influence. For example, there are a number of restrictions relating to gifts and sales where the incapacity is based on the danger of undue influence, for example there are restrictions on gifts between spouses; a tutor may not purchase the property of a minor; public servants may not acquire public utilities, etc.[24] Similarly persons may be declared

---

[20] In this sense incapacity only relates to the author of an act, not the object of it (Art. 1124 C. *Civ*.).

[21] Similarly, incapacity may be absolute or partial, *e.g.* certain public utility companies may not receive gifts without administrative authorisation (Act of July 1, 1901).

[22] The question of capacity also has procedural implications. In principle everyone with legal personality has the right to seek the assistance of the law. Non-emancipated minors, or adults under tutelage, require a legal representative—*curator ad litem*—except in cases where the action is of direct personal application, *e.g.* a request by an adult to terminate tutelage, or an action to establish the paternity of the natural child of a mother below the age of majority.

[23] For example, while the age of voting for most purposes is 18, for certain civic posts, such as deputies or senators, it is older. Similarly there are various age limits for eligibility for certain posts.

[24] These are referred to as *incapacités de suspicion* rather than *incapacités de protection*.

incapable because of some sanction attached to them, for example a criminal may not benefit from his act; a bankrupt may not engage in commercial undertakings, etc.

(B) MINORS

Minority affects both the right to enjoy certain rights and the ability to exercise them. The age of majority in France is 18, at which point, in the case of civil or private law acts, incapacity ceases.[25] Minority may also cease on emancipation by marriage or judicial ruling. This latter will be made by a *juge des tutelles* in the case of a person under the age of 16, after an interview with the minor and following a request either from the child's parents, or one of them, or from the wider family if the minor is *en tutelle* (subject to a tutor or guardian). Before a minor can be emancipated by marriage, he requires the assistance of those persons whose consent is required both for the marriage itself and for the agreements which relate to marriage, for example the choice of matrimonial property regime. If such assistance and consent is not acquired then the marriage may be a *nullité relative* as far as the property consequences of the marriage are concerned.[26]

Emancipation confers on the minor virtually full capacity to contract or so sue.[27] However, an emancipated minor may still be restricted in his commercial or civic capacity.

Unemancipated minors are subject to parental authority.[28] This concept—which is strongly influenced by the Roman law origins of French law[29]—is directed at protecting the minor, promoting his legitimate interests, controlling his person and administering his property.

The parental control of the actual person of the minor is manifested in

---

[25] Art. 388 C. *Civ*.

[26] The actual act of marriage will not necessarily be null because a minor acts for himself and not through a representative to conclude a contract of marriage (Art. 1388 C. *Civ*.).

[27] Arts. 481 and 1124 14. C. *Civ*.

[28] The foundation for this is found in Art. 371-2 C. *Civ*., which specifically refers to the father and mother of the child, thereby excluding all others, *i.e.* the State, welfare services, other relatives, etc. The presumption is that when the child is legitimate and the parents are not divorced or separated, they act together, so the decision of one is deemed to have been made with the consent of the other. Where in fact there is disagreement, then a *juge aux affaires familiales* will have to intervene. Since 1993, even where the parents divorce there is a presumption that parental authority continues to be exercised jointly (Act No. 93-22 of January 8, 1993).

[29] Roman law distinguished between the natural father of *genitor* of the child and the *pater*—the person who exercised parental authority over the child. Even today the law may distinguish between the two, *e.g.* where filiation is not established.

a number of ways,[30] the most important of which are to protect the child's security, health and moral welfare.[31] Therefore the parent has both a right and an obligation to look after the child, to watch him and to provide for his education, although this duty—*la garde*—will naturally vary according to the age and circumstances of the child. In this respect the parent is assisted by the operation of criminal and public law, as well as being subject to sanctions for any failure to observe this duty.

La surveillance of the parent consists in the daily upbringing of the child, his health, physical and psychological welfare and attending to his daily needs and care. Neglect, deprivation or abuse render the parent liable in civil or criminal law.[32] In this respect the parents have almost total control over the child and may prevent the child from doing things of which they disapprove, open private correspondence and restrict the child's contact with certain persons. An exception to this last point relates to grand-parents, and in the case of divorce, access to the other parent where this has been approved by the court.[33]

Parents are also responsible for the education of their children in the broadest sense. They must respect the legal requirement that children attend school until the age of 16, but are also responsible for the cultural, philosophical, moral, religious and professional orientation of their children.

Parental responsibility not only places responsibilities on the parents but it also makes them liable for certain actions of the minor. Under Article 1384-4 C. *Civ*. parents are held jointly liable for any torts committed by their child who is living with them and whom they have in their *garde*. This responsibility persists even if the minor is not actually living with them all the time—for example he has run away or is at boarding school—but ceases if the minor is on holiday with a third party or at a summer camp. The only way in which the parents can avoid liability is if they can establish that because of the minor's age, the nature of the activity and harm, the circumstances and in the absence of any

---

[30] *E.g.* the parent(s) choose the child's names—although this is subject to control in France—and give him a surname.

[31] *Sécurité, santé* and *moralité* (Arts. 371-2 and 375 C. *Civ*.).

[32] There are two main sanctions available against parents, one is to relieve them of parental authority, the other is to subject them to certain educative measures, *e.g.* and advice from health and social welfare services. The latter is sanctioned by a *juge des enfants* while the former can be ordered by a *juge pénal*, if the matter has arisen in a criminal context, or a *juge civil* if the matter has arisen in a civil context—*e.g.* where the minor is a victim of tortious conduct.

[33] The courts have had to interfere from time to time with the rights of parents to withhold medical treatment or sustenance from their children on the basis of religious or philosophical beliefs.

shortcoming in surveillance or education, they could not have prevented the harm.[34]

Tutelage

Where a child does not have parents, or a parent, to assume parental control—for example because they are dead—then the minor is placed under tutelage.[35] This affects both the person of the minor and his property. The responsibility for this lies with a number of organs. First, there is the family council—*conseil de famille*—consisting of four or six members of the family, or close friends or neighbours who are able to consider the best interests of the minor.[36] Secondly, there is the tutor himself. This will be a person outside the family council, either designated by the last-dying parent—for example in a will—or appointed by law according either to proximity in terms of relationship—*tutelle légale*—or as nominated by the family council—*tutelle dative*. The most important role of the tutor is to administer the minor's property, to pay and recover debts, and administer it profitably. In this role the tutor acts with the authorisation of the family council and sometimes the court. Thirdly, there is the subrogate tutor chosen by the family council, and finally there is the *juge des tutelles*. This is a judge of the *tribunal d'instance*, who exercises general jurisdiction over the tutors and the legal administration of the affairs of minors within the court's jurisdiction. He will call together the family council and preside over it if necessary. In emergencies he will make decisions in place of the council and where they cannot agree will cast the deciding vote. Although the distinction in different types of incapacity can still be clearly seen in the case of minors, in recent years greater participation of minors in certain decisions affecting them, and certainly in procedural matters,[37] has developed.

In certain circumstances a minor will totally lack capacity—for example a minor under the age of 16 cannot make a will,[38] and a man

---

[34] Following a decision of the Court of Cassation of May 9, 1991, there appears to be a jurisprudential swing towards holding not only parents liable but any person who has assumed responsibility for a minor—*e.g.* by taking them on holiday or organising an educational course.

[35] See Art. 427 C. *Civ*. This may also happen because a parent, although living, is unable to manifest any intention—perhaps due to absence or mental incapacity.

[36] The family council is responsible for day-to-day matters concerning the minor, *e.g.* education and maintenance, and it is the family council which must consent to the minor's adoption, marriage or emancipation. The family council's consent is always required for actions relating to rights which are non-patrimonial.

[37] See *e.g.*the new Arts. 388—1 *et seq*., C. *Civ*.

[38] Arts. 903 and 904 C. *Civ*.

under 18 and a girl under 15 cannot marry.[39] In other situations, although the minor lacks capacity, a parent or guardian can act on the minor's behalf.

Contractual and non-contractual obligations

Capacity varies not only according to the minor's age, but also according to the nature of the act. In particular there is a distinction between contractual and non-contractual obligations. Contractual obligations are based on the presumed voluntary will of the parties. There is an implied requirement of good faith, breach of which can be relied on to reach a just result. It is necessary for the legal system to incorporate certain measures to protect persons who voluntarily assume obligations without being fully aware of their consequences. This does not mean that the law will intervene to redress every incident of imbalance between contracting parties, but French law presupposes a minimum level at which a person can be held liable for contractual obligations. Article 1124 specifies that those considered incapable of contracting are unemancipated minors and protected adults, further defined under Article 488.

However, in non-contractual obligations, increasingly minors are being held liable for any harm they cause to others, the determining factor being not simply age, but the ability of the minor to be aware of his or her actions.[40] There is, however, a distinction applied in French law to the situation where the minor causes harm and where he is the victim of harm. In the former case the requirement of fault—particularly under Article 1382—may mean that the minor is not held liable. However, the approach of the courts has been to limit non-liability to mental incapacity.[41] Some problems arise concerning liability under the other related Articles of the Civil Code, particularly under Article 1385, where the guardian of a thing is usually liable for any harm it causes, regardless of fault. It may also be the case that the parents of a child are held liable, either under Article 1382, because they were objectively at fault—even if the child lacked sufficient mental understanding to be at fault—or under Article 1384, because they had the child under their control.

Where minors are victims of damage, then any contributory negligence is judged objectively. The result may be reduced compensation to

---

[39] Art. 144 C. *Civ*.

[40] This development has been largely developed by the courts.

[41] Under the Act of July 5, 1985, in road traffic accidents those excluded from liability because of contributory fault include the physically handicapped, persons over 70 and those under 16.

the victim, even though the victim was not capable of discerning the consequences of his act.

In contract the minor's capacity is more restricted—partly because any contractual undertaking may impinge on property interests. A non-emancipated minor is considered to be insufficiently aware of the consequences of the act to be capable of binding him or herself contractually. Therefore, any minor must be represented by parents, a legal administrator or a guardian. Any contract entered into by a minor without the assistance of a representative is null without the need to prove anything other than the fact that the minor acted without assistance. Consequently minors cannot undertake commercial acts or engage in any commercial profession,[42] nor may they be associated with others in a commercial organisation or business enterprise (for example *associé en nom collectif, associé commandité dans la société en commandite*).

There is some academic debate as to whether such nullity is based on the principle of *lésion* or lack of proper form. The doctrine of *lésion*—which is only applicable in the case of onerous contracts—is based on the idea of prejudice suffered by one contracting party as a result of inequality of benefit/detriment within a bilateral contract.[43] Under Article 2052 C. *Civ*. a contract may not be set aside either because of an error of law or because of *lésion*, because the agreement between the parties is the foundation and source of the law between them. On the other hand, it is inequitable to enforce a contract where one party suffers a substantial prejudice as a result of the imbalance between the obligations of the parties to the contract. *Droit commun* (that is customary legal principles) dictates that where an agreement is evidently grossly unjust or inequitable, it seems that a court may set it aside on the ground that it is to be presumed that the parties intended to achieve equivalence between their respective obligations under the agreement and that where there is an imbalance this must be redressed.[44] Although the Civil Code makes several references to *lésion*, at no point is it defined in the Code. One answer is to focus on the concept of intention, which may be justified because in the Code those Articles relating to *lésion* are

---

[42] Art. 487 C.C. and Art. 2 of the C. *Com*.

[43] Generally the imbalance relates to the disproportionate value of the bargain, and the difference between that due under the contract and a just price—*prix juste*. Thus, a low price may be of advantage to the purchaser but amount to *lésion* suffered by the vendor. It should be noted that *lésion* applies to the moment when the contract is concluded, rather than at a later date when an imbalance may give rise to the doctrine of *imprévision*.

[44] The idea originates from Canon law during the Middle Ages, and was based on the perceived moral need to prevent one party being scandalously enriched at the expense of another (see H. Roland and L. Boyer, *Introduction au Droit* (Litec, Paris, 3rd ed., 1991) pp. 10–11.

situated among those relating to consent, and also because the essence of contract is the expression of will—*volonté*—of the parties, which those deemed *incapable* are thought to lack. This theory adopts a subjective approach, starting from the principle of equality of bargaining power. The contract can only be rescinded or the price increased or reduced on the basis of *lésion*, if it can be established that there has been an "error of will"—*un vice du consentement*—either due to age, infirmity, mistake or fraud, which has resulted in inequality of bargaining power at the time of the agreement, which in turn has led to prejudicial effects. However, it can be argued that the doctrine of *lésion* is not so much based on the idea of error in consent but on lack of equilibrium between the obligations of each side.[45] This is a more objective approach, which focuses on the underlying *cause* of the contract. The danger with this line of reasoning is that it would allow adults with full capacity to invoke the doctrine. However, while the provisions and location of these in the Code suggest a subjective approach, the case law of the courts indicates a more objective approach,[46] in order to achieve an equitable and just result.

The counter-argument, favoured by those adopting a more individualist approach, is that the agreement should stand, judges should not have the power to interfere with agreements voluntarily entered into, and the notion of equilibrium does not require absolute balance—for example a contract of work may be agreed whereby the employer obtains a much greater advantage than the employee, because the latter is paid a very low salary for the job.[47] A contract which meets the formal requirements should be enforceable and may not be revised or declared a nullity, even if it is a "bad bargain".[48] If contracts can be upset by third parties, then contractual security is undermined. The anti-*lésion* lobby argue that the value of the contract is not the sole consideration, qualitative considerations as well as economically quantitative factors need to be taken into account.

---

[45] This imports an objective dimension into a subjective legal arena, which upsets the fundamental idea that the law of contract is the law stipulated by the parties to that contract.

[46] See, *e.g.* decisions of the Court of Cassation of December 28, 1932, April 21, 1950, and October 19, 1960.

[47] If the return is regarded as derisory then the court may set aside the transaction or allow recission, *e.g. Cass Civ. 1*, May 4, 1976.

[48] A situation in which *lésion* is available is where a vendor has sold immovable property for less than seven-twelfths of its value (Art. 1674 C. *Civ.*). In such a case the vendor may have the sale declared null and rescind the contract. This must be done within two years from the date of sale. Alternatively, the purchaser may make restitution to the vendor of the market price, less one-tenth. However, this does not apply where a purchaser has paid an excessive price for property, nor in the case of other property such as movables, jewels, pictures, etc. *Lésion* also applies in the case of co-owners and partners where a division of assets is made.

However, the Civil Code does allow rescission in certain circumstances (Article 1118 C. *Civ.*) notably in the case of unemancipated minors (Article 1305 C. *Civ.*) and protected adults.[49] This Article has a twofold effect: it allows only a limited class of persons to invoke the doctrine and it only allows rescission of certain types of contract on the basis of *lésion*.[50] Thus, an adult with full capacity cannot rely on *lésion* except where expressly provided in the Code or a subsequent law.[51] In principle an unemancipated minor lacks the legal capacity to enter into juristic acts such as contracts. Therefore, whether nullity is based on inequality of legal status or failure to comply with the fundamental requirements of a valid contract, the contract cannot be enforced against the minor. If the act is an administrative one which the minor's legal representative would have been able to undertake alone, then it seems that the doctrine of *lésion* may apply on moral grounds, the victim of the contract being the *incapable*—the legal representative not acting for himself but for the minor. This line of reasoning has been primarily developed through case law. If, however, the act is one which the legal representative could only have undertaken with reference to another person or institution involved with the protection of the minor—such as the family council or a family judge—then the act is null due to lack of form.

Parental control of property

A minor's incapacity, particularly in the case of contractual obligations, but also, although to a less extent, in non-contractual obligations, is closely related to the lack of control which the minor has over his own property. Although the incidence of tutellage is relatively rare, it is this institution which has been instrumental in forming the law relating to parental control of a minor's property.[52] Indeed it is possible for a judge to order that a tutor of the minor's property be appointed—*tutelle aux biens*—even if the minor has parents. The patrimony of a minor is administered by his parents or, if there are none, by a judge. This latter procedure is used particularly where the child's parents are dead or

---

[49] Either under curatorship (Arts. 510–3) or wards of court (Art. 491– al. 2). There is a slight difference in legal approach, in as much as where the act is one of administration which an adult under a curator could have accomplished without assistance, the court may refuse to apply *lésion*, and instead adjust the bargain (Art. 513-3 C. *Civ.*).

[50] Where a contract is rescinded on the grounds of *lésion* the nullity is relative rather than absolute.

[51] See, *e.g.* the Acts of July 8, 1907 and March 10, 1937 and of March 11, 1957.

[52] Similar rules apply in the case of incapable adults and those who are missing.

divorced, or the child is a natural child. In such cases, a single parent may administer the child's estate except for those specific acts where the authorisation of a judge is also required. A minor, because of his personal incapacity, is deemed to be unable to undertake certain property transactions.[53] He cannot, for example, purchase a car or arrange a loan or credit purchase, or be a party to any agreement which has the object of exploiting his photograph for publicity purposes.[54]

A minor's property incapacity extends to include gifts. A minor is unable to consent to a gift.[55] Even if consent by an authorised person is given, some gifts are absolutely prohibited in order to protect the minor from undue influence and to prevent certain possible abuses—for example gifts from a minor to his guardian are absolutely prohibited.[56] A minor over the age of 16 is, however, capable of disposing of all that part of his estate which a major would be similarly capable of disposing of, by will,[57] and the whole of his estate if he does not have any parents or ascendants up to the sixth degree living.

A minor also has to be protected against accepting gifts which may be onerous or conditional in some way. This does not mean that the minor may not receive any gifts. Testamentary gifts subject to a charge, for example, may be accepted by the tutor or legal administrator of a minor. Other gifts may be accepted once the additional consent of the family council or *juge des tutelles* has been obtained. Similar considerations will apply where a minor inherits part of an estate which includes both *l'actif et passif* (assets and debts). Where a minor is left a legacy free of any charge, then the mother or father of the minor may consent to its acceptance.[58]

(C) THE INCAPACITY OF CERTAIN ADULTS

Prior to 1968, the law relating to incapable adults was to be found in the provisions of the Civil Code and an Act of June 30, 1838, concerning the internment of mental patients. As a result three possible regimes

---

[53] The nature and range of these have largely been developed through case law.

[54] This last example may be modified if the minor is approaching majority (*Cass. Civ.* 1, March 27, 1990).

[55] The only exception is where a minor gives his wife a gift under a contract of marriage—prior to the marriage—with the authorisation of those persons whose consent is necessary for the marriage (Art. 1095 C. *Civ.*).

[56] See Art. 907 (a)(1), (2). Where a gift is given contrary to the restrictions, it can be set aside within a period of five years and so is subject to *nullité relative* rather than *nullité absolue*.

[57] Art. 904 C. *Civ.*

[58] Art. 935 C. *Civ.* See also Arts. 461 and 463.

existed. The most extreme was that of *interdiction judiciaire* whereby the adult was entirely represented by another and deemed to be utterly incapable—on the grounds of madness, dementia or imbecility—of acting for himself at all, even if the adult had lucid intervals. This regime of complete representation was ordered by a civil court and placed the adult in the same position as regards capacity as a convicted criminal, who was also denied any rights. The second possibility was the nomination of a *conseil judiciaire* by the court for an adult who was feeble-minded. Under this regime the adult was prevented from undertaking transactions relating to property without assistance. The third possibility was the appointment of a provisional regime to assist the adult while temporarily detained in an institution (*l'administration provisoire*). Under this the administrative acts of the committed adult were carried out by a member of the staff of the institution. Consequently virtually every adult undergoing psychiatric care was under some kind of regime.

The law was reformed in 1968,[59] with considerably more attention being paid to medical advice and expertise and greater emphasis being placed on the need to balance the rights of the individual with considerations of public security, and more discretion being afforded to the judge.

Committal to a psychiatric hospital is now governed by an Act of June 27, 1990. It is recognised that any committal interferes with the daily freedoms of the individual concerned. At the same time the public have a right to be safeguarded against those individuals who may cause harm. As far as capacity is concerned the law distinguishes between different forms of hospitalisation, for example voluntary submission to treatment by the adult, hospitalisation at the request of a third party supported by two medical opinions and committal as a result of procedural measures—for example in the context of public order disturbances.

Under Article 488 C. *Civ.* the presumption is that all adults—that is those who have obtained the age of majority—are fully capable of all civil acts. Nevertheless the Article also provides that a regime of legal protection may be applied to an adult if there is an alteration in his personal faculties which renders it impossible for him to look after his own interests. This includes not only inability to understand what he is doing but also if he becomes profligate or very extravagant or intemperate, so that he places his own or his family's needs and considerations in danger. In such a case adults may be placed under two different regimes:

---

[59] Act of January 3, 1968.

tutellage or curatorship.[60] The former is for those adults who are handicapped either because of an impairment of their mental faculties, or serious physical impairment, which make it impossible for those adults to act in their own interests. These adults need someone to act on their behalf and in their place. The latter is for those adults who place themselves at risk. They are deemed to be partially incapable and in need of assistance. They may undertake daily administrative acts by themselves but not more serious acts involving the alienation or acquisition of property or obligations. In these cases the act is carried out by the adult himself but is not enforceable or valid without the assistance of the curator—usually by a signature attesting the consent of the curator.

La tutelle des majeurs

La tutelle des majeurs is the most restrictive of the two regimes. It results from an order of the court based on one of the grounds stipulated in Article 488 C. *Civ*. and following a request from an authorised interested party. The effect of this regime is that all acts of the adult are null from the moment of the order. Any transactions entered into before the order may be set aside if the circumstances giving rise to the order were generally known at the time, otherwise third parties have a two-month period from the order before it can be raised against them. This regime can be ended by a court order. While it exists, the organisation of the regime is similar to that of the tutellage of minors. The main differences are that the tutor will be the spouse, if there is one, or a descendant chosen by the family council, or another. In the case of adults, the tutor may be a legal person—which is not possible in the case of minors.[61]

Certain personal acts may be carried out by such an adult—for example marriage—with the consent of his parents or family council.

In certain circumstances a judge may appoint a person close to the incapacitated adult to handle his affairs without judicial supervision, removing the need for a family council and tutor. For example, if the adult is married under a community of property regime, his wife may administer his affairs. Similarly, if the adult has little property and leads a very simple life the court may allow a charity or institution to act as tutor.

---

[60] There is a third type of protection available called *loi sauvegarde de justice*. This is a procedural measure which entitles certain adults to claim the right to recission on the grounds of *lésion*—which is not normally available to adults—and the action for a reduction of price. This protection can be claimed by adults who have suffered a medical impairment of their faculties, and must be pleaded in court.

[61] This is particularly important in the case of a mentally handicapped adult, whose parents may well wish to make provision for him after their deaths by entrusting his welfare to a specialist establishment.

A judge may also use his discretion to authorise the exercise of certain rights, either with or without assistance. The beginning and end of any tutellage must be accompanied by sufficient publicity for the benefit of third parties.

Curatelle

Curatelle is a less restrictive regime in terms of its operation and applicability. It is directed at assisting the adult and is not required for certain acts. The *curateur* will be the spouse or another person—natural or legal—who assists in all those acts which, in the case of tutellage, would require the intervention of the family council. These are primarily those involving capital, and would include, for example, obtaining a credit card at a bank. Because the role of the curator is to assist, he or she cannot act without the adult in question. Acts undertaken without the requisite assistance may be annulled if this is requested by the curator or the incapable adult. Even if the adult is permitted to act unassisted, he may apply for rescission or reduction if the transaction appears to be prejudicial to him. With the assistance of his curator, the adult can make gifts. He does not, however, need his curator's assistance to make a will—although, of course, he can only dispose of that part of his estate which is not reserved for his heirs.

It is clear that the status and capacity of an individual, far from being something which is fixed and unalterable, will vary and change over a lifetime. Moreover, the legal response to different aspects of capacity has not remained constant, but has adapted and evolved to take into account aspects such as the increasingly early maturity of children, advances in psychiatric medical knowledge, as well as the increase in the availability of insurance against various liabilities.

TOPIC TWO
THE UNDERLYING REQUIREMENTS FOR A VALID CONTRACT IN FRENCH LAW

A contract is a particular type of *acte juridique* which gives rise to mutual obligations between the parties. In this respect the Civil Code makes a clear distinction between obligations gendered by agreement[62] and those which are not based on agreement.[63] The enforceability and legal status of contracts in French law derives from the fundamental principle of *autonomie de la volonté*—that is autonomy of the will.[64] According to this principle, it is the parties to the contract themselves who are best placed to decide their contractual obligations. This autonomy is somewhat tempered by the evolution of certain *lois impératives* relating to specific contracts.[65] Generally, the courts cannot interfere with contracts validly entered into, unless some ground relating to the fundamental requirements for a contract can be found, for example duress inducing consent, or an immoral *cause*.

This principle forms the basis for the formation of the contract, because encapsulated within it are issues relating to capacity, the *consentement* (do the parties wish to be bound to each other in a contract), the *objet* of the contract (what the contract is directed at), the *cause* (why do they wish to incur these obligations).[66]

(A) *CONSENTEMENT*

There must be agreement between the two (or more) contracting parties that they wish to be mutually bound. Relevant to this is the principle that everyone is free to contract, or not to contract, and to choose with whom they wish to contract. Thus contractual consent must be freely and consciously given.[67] Therefore, the mere existence of consent or agreement, although a necessary condition, is not sufficient

---

[62] See Art. 1101 Ci. *Civ*.

[63] See Art. 1370 C. *Civ*.

[64] This concept was at the height of its fashion towards the end of the last century. However, the modern concept is distinguishable from that of the *laissez-fare* school of thought in as much as the free will of the parties is curbed by those restrictions thought to be necessary in the public interest. Essentially the contractual obligation is based on the will of the parties. This will is, therefore, both the source of the obligation and what determines the rights and obligations under the contract.

[65] These are distinguishable from *lois supplétives* which the contracting parties can exclude.

[66] All of these are included in Art. 1108 C. *Civ*.

[67] If it is not and there is *vice de consentement*, the contract may be annulled.

unless it can be established—in the case of dispute—that it is free from any flaws based on mistake, fraud or violence.[68]

Consent is manifested by offer and acceptance. In order to avoid problems of whether or not there is consent certain rules apply: the offer—or *pollicitation*—must be manifested externally in some way[69]; it must be sufficiently precise so as to be capable of acceptance, although it may be made to a specific individual or the public at large.[70] The offeror is not bound by his offer, and may revoke it until it is accepted, even if it has been communicated to the other party. However if the offer is stipulated to remain open for a certain period of time, the offeror may not revoke it within that period.[71]

Acceptance may be express or implied, but silence cannot amount to acceptance; there must be some form of manifestation of the will of the accepting party. Any acceptance must coincide with the terms of the offer. If this is not the case then it will amount to a counter-offer.[72]

Once the contracting parties have agreed, the contract is formed, even if the contract has not been reduced to writing,[73] although in certain cases the nature of the contract requires writing in order to be valid as to form.[74]

If the offer is made by the display of goods then the contract is completed when the buyer places the goods in his basket, provided he has the requisite intention to buy. The display of the goods is evidence of the sellers continuing intention to sell. It is therefore seen as an offer—probably to the public at large—rather than an invitation to treat.[75]

---

[68] See Art. 1109 C. *Civ*.

[69] Although it seems that an offer may be express or implied, *e.g.* by conduct.

[70] In this case the offeror may reserve the right to refuse to contract with certain persons.

[71] The established case law indicates that even where no period is stipulated an offer should remain open for a "reasonable period of time". The legal rationale for holding the offeror bound to his offer in this way is not clear. It may be based on the unilateral juridical act of making the offer—binding the offeror in contract—or it may be based on a duty not to revoke—tortious liability for breach of good faith. It can equally be argued that to allow the offeror to revoke his offer unreasonably is an abuse of rights.

[72] If the disagreement is simply about peripheral matters the contract may nevertheless be regarded as formed.

[73] Not all contracts need to be reduced to writing, although this is far more prevalent than in England. Such writing may take the form of an *acte authentique* or *sous seing privé*, invariably drawn up by a *notaire*.

[74] Writing serves two purposes: evidentiary, which is important for enforceability, but failure to comply with writing will not render the contract void; and formal, where failure to comply with the form will render the contract void. Writing serves to make the contract certain, it has a publicity function—including a fiscal dimension in certain cases—and acts as a caution as far as the contracting parties are concerned.

[75] On the other hand if the goods are not displayed but merely advertised this may not amount to an offer.

If the contract has been concluded by post there are four possibilities to consider in French law. The first, which is based on the principle of *émission*, is *le système de la déclaration* whereby the contract is formed the moment that the offeree (*l'acceptant*) writes the acceptance. The second, *le système de l'expédition*, is that the contract is formed the moment the letter is posted. The third is that there is no contract until the offeror is aware of the acceptance of the offeree, that is of receipt of the letter. This is the *système de la réception*. The final possibility is that there is no contract until the moment when the offeror is aware of the contents of the letter—*le système de l'information*. Unfortunately French law is not consistent as to which of these applies, sometimes favouring *émission* and sometimes *reception*.[76]

Essentially French law adopts a subjective approach. In the case of dispute the questions of fact are solely within the *pouvoir sovereign du juge du fond*.[77]

(B) *OBJET*

From the Civil Code it is not altogether clear what is meant by *l'objet*. Article 1108 C. *Civ*. refers both to the *objet du contrat* and the *matière de l'engagement*. The *objet* of the contract is also the *objet* of the obligation, thus the *objet* of the contract in the sense of its aim, may be confused with its effect. It is the legal relationship which the parties wish to engage in. It must exist—or be capable of determination[78]—and it must be both certain and legal.[79] If the *objet* is one which is not recognised in law—and this is not limited to those contracts covered by the Civil Code—then the contract is absolutely null.[80] The contract has to be considered not

[76] The response of the courts is that the moment at which a contract conducted by correspondence is concluded is largely a question of fact depending on the circumstances of the case. The contracting parties may, of course, stipulate which theory they wish to adopt. In the case of revocation of the offer, the moment of acceptance is vital and uncertainty as to when this is can obviously affect whether or not the revocation is valid.

[77] Such cases will rarely go on appeal to the Court of Cassation unless the judge has made fundamental mistakes in interpreting the facts.

[78] Destruction of the subject-matter of the contract will destroy the *objet* thereby rendering the contract null, even if the parties were in good faith. Similarly a contract of agency in which the mandate of the agent is not stipulated is also null. The same reasoning applies if the *objet* is impossible. A contract for future performance, *e.g.* the sale of a building which has not yet been constructed, is valid provided the *objet* is certain.

[79] Art. 1126 C. *Civ*. stipulates that every contract must have as its *objet* something which the parties are obliged to give, or that one party is obliged to do or to refrain from doing something. In this context the word "thing" does not necessarily denote something corporeal.

[80] French law distinguishes between relative nullity and absolute nullity. The latter applies here, because the purpose of the law is not to protect the contracting parties but based on considerations of public order.

only from the perspective of the contracting parties but in the context of public order, good morals and society at large. It also has to be considered in its entirety.[81] However, if there is a mistake about the *objet*, the contract is not null unless the mistake goes to the heart of the *objet* of the contract.[82] In order to be valid, the *objet* must respect the necessary principle of equality or equilibrium of obligations—otherwise the doctrine of *lésion* or *imprévision* may apply. The question of whether the *objet* is illegal or contrary to public order overlaps with the requirement of *cause*.

(C) CAUSE

In French law all lawful agreements which are seriously intended are valid contracts. The formation of a contract will depend on the parties, who are intending to contract, reaching an agreement through offer and acceptance; but for the contract to be valid there must, in addition, be a lawful *cause* (Article 1108 and 1132 C. *Civ.*). This concept originated from Roman law.[83] At first Roman law only recognised as enforceable contracts which complied with established forms—usually procedural and governed by the purpose of the contract—there was therefore no question of whether consideration or *cause* was required because a bare contract—*nudum pactum*—was simply one which was not recognised as enforceable. Gradually emphasis and insistence on the form was undermined by allowing certain defences and allowing the court to look behind the form in order to take into account elements such as illegality and unjust enrichment. Under the influence of the Glossators,[84] the idea that a bare agreement was unenforceable was taken to mean that

[81] *E.g.* taken separately, the payment of a sum of money and the transfer of blood by a blood donor to a donee are not illegal. Taken together, *i.e.* the payment for a blood transfusion, the contract is illegal.

[82] This means that the mistake must go to the substance of the contract and is so fundamental that had the mistaken party been aware of the error he would not have entered the contract. The mistake may refer to the subject-matter of the contract or to its essential qualities, including errors of law—*e.g.* that the vendor was owner when he was not. See Art. 110 C. *Civ*.

[83] *E.g.* under Justinian all agreements were actionable if they took the form of a *stipulatio*, but other agreements were only enforceable if they were "real" contracts (either nominate or innominate) and consensual. In all real contracts the obligation arose from the delivery of property or performance or a promise, not from mere agreement. The recognised categories of consensual contracts were purchase and sale, hire, partnership and agency.

[84] As to the Glossators, see Dadomo and Farran *The French Legal System* (Sweet & Maxwell, London, 2nd ed., 1996) p. 4.

something more was required.[85] This element was termed *causa*, although it was still not entirely clear what this consisted of in the case of consensual contracts—as opposed to contracts requiring execution or delivery. Canon law, however, recognised that promises, whether supported by anything additional or not, ought to be kept—this was a matter of good conscience. Mutual declarations were based on good faith and therefore valid and enforceable (*pacta sunt servanda*). Even Canon law had to recognise that certain promises should not be kept, for example if they were immoral, or arose from fraud or mistake, or were simply not intended to be enforceable at the time they were made. Consequently Canon law also had to distinguish between non-enforceable agreements and those which were enforceable. To do this the term *causa* was also used. Effectively this placed a check on the idea of unrestricted autonomy of the will, while at the same time excluding too much inquiry into the intentions and motives of the contracting parties.

The modern development of the concept of *cause* was influenced by Domat, who distinguished four categories of agreements: (1) the reciprocal exchange of a thing; (2) reciprocal performance; (3) performance given in exchange for a thing, and (4) gratuitous undertakings. In the first three of these there is clearly an undertaking of one party based on the reciprocal undertaking of the other. In the fourth category the undertaking of the donor is based on a reasonable and just motive—which could be as nebulous as the pleasure of giving.[86] Pothier refined this classification, distinguishing only two classes of contract—those which were onerous and those which were gratuitous.[87] These two historical aspects come together in the Civil Code, where one finds that a contract based on a *cause* which is illegal—that is prohibited by law or contrary to good morals or public order—is not enforceable.[88]

The classical explanation of *cause* as it appears in the Civil Code, is that it is the immediate and direct end which impels the contracting party to enter into the contract.[89] The *cause* of the obligation can be

---

[85] This may have come about by a mis-reading of the works of Ulpian, or because there was already some dispute as to whether in Roman law *causa* meant no more than any ground or foundation for an action or a juridical reason which amounted to a special or essential element of a contractual obligation.

[86] In this last category there is some confusion between motive and *cause*. It is on account of the latter that the contract is enforceable—hence the enforceability of the contract of gift, but also the fact that a contract of gift can be rescinded if the reason for giving disappears.

[87] In gratuitous contracts it is the benevolence of the donee which is sufficient as the *cause*.

[88] Art. 1133 C. *Civ*.

[89] This can be described as the "why" of the contract. Thus, every contract requires the basic elements of consent, capacity, an object which is certain and which constitutes the subject-matter of the contract and a *cause*. In this respect motive is distinguishable, *e.g.*

found in the nature of the contract. In bilateral contracts, for example, the *cause* of the obligation lies in the existence and the performance of the obligation of the other party, because each party is both creditor and debtor. In unilateral, real contracts, such as deposit, loan, pledge, the debtor who has received the thing must return it, while the creditor has handed over the thing in anticipation of its return. In other unilateral contracts, for example a promise to pay a sum of money, the *cause* may lie outside the obligation itself—for example the obligation to pay for a damaged car arises from the liability to compensate. *Cause* relates, therefore, to the reason for assuming the obligation, rather than the contract as a whole. It is therefore both the efficient *cause*, in that it has an objective sense by generating the obligation, and it is the final *cause*, in that it has a subjective sense, which is the end to be achieved.[90]

The objective or abstract meaning of *cause* is constant for certain types of contract, while the subjective sense differs from one person to another. For example, the objective *cause* of the purchases and sale of a car is the exchange of money for the object; the subjective *cause* may be to acquire a status symbol, to invest a sum of money, or to learn to drive. In consensual contracts *cause* lies somewhere between these two ends. The subjective or concrete *cause* will vary depending on the circumstances of each particular contract, and so the objective or abstract *cause* of that type of contract may be modified.

The concept of *cause* has not received universal acclaim among French writers. There is a school of "anti-causalists",[91] which has expressed the view that the theory of *cause* is ill-founded and useless in practice, particularly when applied in the context of gratuitous contracts. In these *cause* becomes confused with motive or intention. The latter is a separate requirement for a valid contract. If there is no free intention then the contract is void for lack of consent—regardless of *cause*. In onerous contracts, the place of *cause* may be taken by the formalities required for particular contracts, for example the transfer or the handing over of the thing, or performance rendered. If the formalities are not complied with, or performance not made, there is no obligation for the other party. In these contracts the failure of the object of the contract would be sufficient to annul the contract, there is no need to rely on *cause*. The notion that the obligation of one party, in a reciprocal

---

the motive for purchasing an item may be to enhance status or present a certain image, whereas the *cause* is directed at acquiring the thing.

[90] In this respect *cause* does not necessarily equate with "bargain", and so can include not only gratuitous promises, but also contracts which in English law would be regarded as unenforceable because they are based on moral consideration or past consideration.

[91] *E.g.* Laurent, Planiol and Baudry-Lacantinerie.

contract, is the *cause* of the obligation of the other party, confuses effect and *cause*. It is the bilateral contract which gives rise to this effect and therefore it cannot be held that the *cause* is an essential element to the contract. One of the main problems in justifying the retention of *cause* is that it comes in that part of the Civil Code which deals with formation of a contract and not in that part relating to enforcement.

Despite this criticism, the notion of *cause* was rehabilitated in the 1920s in French law by writers such as Capitant, Maury and Josserand, and remains part of the French law. The concept of *cause* gives the courts power to examine the enforceability of a contract beyond the mere formalities. To this end, two aspects of *cause* have been developed: the material and the psychological. The material aspect brings *cause* closer to the object of the contract, for example in a bilateral contract, the *cause* of the obligation is the object of the other obligation, in particular the performance of that obligation. The psychological aspect brings *cause* closer to consent. By consenting to be bound to an agreement the parties have a purpose which must be licit and moral. This enables the courts to bring into play fundamental principles of good morals and public order to either uphold the enforceability of contracts or find that they are immoral.

The concept of *cause* also enables the courts to determine whether rescission is available where one party has not fulfilled his obligation. This rescission is based not on the lack of formalities surrounding the contract—because the contract is valid in that sense—but the failure of the *cause*.[92]

Effectively, retention of the concept of *cause* provides a way in which contractual liability can be limited, particularly where the licitness of a contract is in issue. In this context the classic meaning of *cause*, which separates it from the motive or purpose behind an obligation, is undermined.

(D) FAILURE OF CAUSE

Where there is no *cause* or that which exists is illicit, then the obligation can have no effect.[93] Classical theory treated the contract in both situations as absolutely null, but the more modern approach is to

[92] Even here there is some confusion. *E.g.* French law refers to "false *cause*" or *erreur sur la cause* (Art. 1131 C. *Civ.*) which may be relied on in cases of mistake, but this is superfluous in as much as absence of *cause* will mean that the contract is unenforceable any way, as will the existence of an illegal or immoral *cause*.

[93] A *cause* may be illicit, even if it is not contrary to law, if it is contrary to good morals or public policy.

distinguish between the two situations. Where the *cause* is illicit then the contract is an absolute nullity, because of the need to protect the public interest. Where there is no *cause* (absence of *cause* or a mistake as the *cause*) the contract is relatively null. In such a case either party may seek to have the contract declared null, but in the case of an illicit contract no restitution can be claimed unless the contract is gratuitous or the party claiming restitution can show that the turpitude rests largely or wholly on the other party.

It can be argued that *cause* is an historical relic which emerged as a compromise between the extreme formalism of Roman law and the extreme liberalism of natural law. Certainly the requirement for *cause* has not been retained in all Civil law systems.[94] However, *cause* does meet some of the concerns found in any legal system relating to the enforceability of contracts: (1) it is relevant to the seriousness of the promise; (2) it provides justification for entering into the obligation; (3) it is in addition to any evidentiary requirements—which may be falsified; and (4) it provides a means whereby transactions of suspect or marginal value can be avoided.

[94] E.g. in Canada, Germany, Brazil, Switzerland and Japan.

TOPIC THREE
FORCE MAJEURE AND *IMPREVISION*

As has been indicated in the context of minor's contracts[95] and the doctrine of *lésion*, French law is reluctant to allow a contracting party to escape from contractual obligations which have been voluntarily assumed. At the same time the underlying concept that a contract should be based on equivalent obligations does allow the possibility of reviewing a contractual obligation where there is a serious imbalance between the respective obligations of the parties. The question therefore arises whether one party can avoid contractual obligations by relying on circumstances beyond their control, and which have arisen after the formation of the contract.

In French law, the contract represents the legal obligations agreed by the parties and it will be rare that either party can avoid their side of the obligation without being in breach of contract. However, there are circumstances in which non-performance of the contractual obligation will be excused. This may arise if the parties to the contract agree to renounce any obligations incurred under the contract; or where the object of the contract is replaced by another; or where the two contracting parties become merged. For example, if a tenant purchases the freehold of the apartment he is renting. The obligation may also be cancelled out by the operation of *compensation*, whereby the debt owed by one person is offset by the same debt, or a debt of similar value, owed by the other person.

Article 1147 C. *Civ.* indicates that a *débiteur*—a party owing a contractual obligation—will be held liable for damages if he fails to perform his contractual obligations, unless this non-performance is justified by external factors—*cause étrangère*—which cannot be imputed to the debtor. The Article does not specify what these external circumstances or factors may be and it has been for the courts to indicate the scope of the Article. There is scope, therefore, for French law to recognise the doctrine of frustration in limited circumstances in which non-performance of obligations may be acceptable.

Two doctrines are considered here, those of *force majeure* and *imprévision*. The doctrines are primarily of relevance in the case of contractual obligations, although *force majeure* can also apply in cases of

[95] See Chapter One, Topic One, above.

delict,[96] and *imprévision* is relevant in the context of administrative law. The two doctrines are distinguishable and should not be confused with the situation where non-performance of a contractual obligation is attributable to the contracting party.

(A) *FORCE MAJEURE*

Article 1148 C. *Civ*. expressly provides for the possibility of *force majeure*—or *cas fortuit*.[97] *Force majeure* refers to circumstances beyond the contracting parties' control or power to prevent, which render performance of the contract impossible.[98] It consists of three characteristics: (1) irresistibility; (2) unforeseeability; and (3) externality.[99]

Irresistibility is understood to mean a force which is superior to that of man, making the execution of the contractual obligation totally impossible. This does not mean that only events which are natural phenomena will be considered: man-made occurrences are also relevant. The essence of the irresistibility lies in the contracting party's inability to do anything about the turn of events. This applies both to the events themselves and their consequences.[1] This aspect is judged in an abstract sense, the judge's task being to consider whether any person placed in the same situation as the contracting party would have been similarly unable to overcome the obstacles presented.[2]

Mere difficulty in meeting the obligations will not suffice, unless those

---

[96] *E.g.* where a rail signal fails to work due to mechanical fault and an accident results, this has been held to be *force majeure* (*Cass. Civ*. 10.6.1965). Similarly the presence of oil in puddles on the road (*Cass. Civ*. 28.10.65). However, tortious liability for damage occasioned by events which could have been foreseen will not be protected by *force majeure*—*e.g.* erosion to castle walls (*Cass. Civ*. 17.3.1993) or very bad weather predicted by the meteorological office (*Cass. Civ*. 17.4.1975).

[97] Although the Article appears to distinguish *force majeure* from *cas fortuit*, the case law has not done so and both terms are regarded as referring to the same concept. The terms are used interchangeably at various points in the Civil Code (see, *e.g.* Arts. 1302, 1882, 1929 and 1934)—see C. Larroumet *Droit Civil* (Economica 2nd ed., 1990) p. 753.

[98] *E.g.* the destruction by fire of a factory in which goods subject to a contract were being produced. It should be noted that war in itself is not regarded as *force majeure*, although it may give rise to other circumstances which are. Similarly an administrative declaration of a state of emergency will not by itself establish a *force majeure*.

[99] *Extériorité, imprévisibilité et irrésistibilité*.

[1] *E.g.* outbreak of war may make the execution of contractual obligations more difficult, but will not necessarily make them impossible. Similarly, the destruction of a company's premises, while unforeseeable as an event, did not necessarily have the consequences of making business impossible: *T.G.I.* Paris, 16.1.1989.

[2] Therefore interruption of the electricity supply in exceptionally cold weather could only be raised as a *force majeure* by the supplier if such weather was so unknown or rare in that particular region as to make it impossible for the supplier to take steps to maintain the supply: *T.G.I.* Angers, 11.3.1986.

difficulties are not only serious but insurmountable. Similarly, the fact that the burden of executing the contract has become more onerous than was originally foreseen does not qualify as *force majeure*. There are two exceptions to the defence of *force majeure*. The first is where, for instance, a defendant has already been summoned to pay a debt; *force majeure* will not defeat the proceedings although payment may be suspended.[3] The second is in the case of road traffic accidents, where the victim will still be able to bring a claim even if the cause of the accident was due to *force majeure*.[4]

Unforeseeability means that the event must have been absolutely fortuitous. If it could have been foreseen, or even suspected, and the individual could have adopted measures to avoid or prevent the problem, then this aspect will not be met.[5] A recurrent problem which has arisen in this context is the issue of strikes. During the 1960s the courts adopted a very restrictive approach and refused to allow that strikes could amount to *force majeure*. This approach has been modified following decisions of the *Chambre Mixte* of the Court of Cassation, in 1983,[6] so that now it will depend on the circumstances.[7] This aspect is judged objectively from the perspective of the reasonable man—*in abstracto*—but some reference may have to be made to the actual facts of the case—*in concreto*.[8] The relevant moment at which this characteristic must be appreciated appears to be the moment at which the contract is concluded, rather than when it is entered into.[9] However, the issue may also be relevant in the case of ongoing contracts—for example the supply of utilities such as electricity.

---

[3] *E.g.* bankruptcy will not automatically cancel the debt.

[4] See the Act of July 5, 1985, No. 85-677, relating to the victims of road traffic accidents. While this primarily relates to the victims of tort, it is also relevant to cases where accident victims are being transported under a contract. In neither case can the driver of the vehicle avoid liability on the grounds of *force majeure*—other extenuating circumstances may be admitted, such as the fault of the victim. It should be noted that this Act was accompanied by measures requiring compulsory third party insurance.

[5] Non-performance on account of strikes, which prevent employees from reaching their place of work, may amount to external factors under Art. 1147 C. *Civ.*, while not satisfying the requirements of Art. 1148.

[6] February 4, 1983.

[7] A less lenient approach is taken in the case of theft when this possibility is foreseeable—*e.g.* when transporting money or valuables—and preventable.

[8] *E.g.* the courts have held that a strike may be foreseeable, *Cass. Civ.* 18.5.89—concerning SNCF strikes in which the court held that the railway authorities had not considered whether there were ways of defusing the situation.

[9] If, however, a person assumes contractual obligations either knowing or suspecting that he will be unable to fulfil them, he will not be exonerated from the obligations by then relying on *force majeure*.

The externality of the event means that it must have come about through no action—direct or indirect—of the contracting parties.[10] It must be not only outside the circumstances of the particular contract but also outside the parties' sphere of activity.[11] Therefore, defects in products or vehicles used to carry out obligations cannot amount to *force majeure*, nor can the actions of employees, the poor construction of buildings, or the interruption of production processes due to liquidation of assets. Similarly, the intervention of administration authorities in the carrying out of a business—for example because a trader is acting outside the terms of his licence—will not amount to *force majeure* even though they are external to the contracting party.

These three elements should be read together, so that it may be the case that the circumstances make the performance of the obligation absolutely impossible, even though they are not strictly external to the contracting parties' activity. To insist on each element being established separately could lead to inequitable results—an example is where the long-term illness of an employee prevents his return to work, or a sudden strike stops a business from operating.[12] Indeed at one stage the case law tended to merge the two aspects of *irrésistibilité* with *impossibilité*,[13] on the grounds that if an event could be foreseen it would be possible to take steps to avoid it.

The doctrine is strictly interpreted in French law, and the circumstances must be such that performance of the contract is absolutely impossible in both a legal and physical sense. This will be a question of fact, so the matter rarely comes before the Court of Cassation. This concept includes both natural occurrences and human conduct. In neither case will all eventualities be regarded as *force majeure*. In the former, for example, avalanches, sudden violent thunderstorms or fallen trees may be recognised provided these are not normal or foreseeable occurrences in the circumstances. In the latter, the disruption caused by demonstrators to the transport of goods may amount to *force majeure*,[14]

---

[10] If the intervening event is brought about by unpredictable and unpreventable behaviour of a victim, liability cannot be avoided on the grounds of *force majeure*, although contributory negligence or fault may be raised.

[11] If the obligation is to be carried out by an intermediary or agent of the contracting party, then the defence of *force majeure* will not be available for non-performance even though this is external to the contracting party.

[12] A strike will not always amount to a *force majeure*, because the employer is responsible for relations with his employees and the strike might be both foreseeable and preventable.

[13] See C. Larroumet (n. 97, above) p. 756.

[14] See, Bordeaux, 6.6.1977. Although if such demonstrations could be foreseen—*e.g.* in the case of the transportation of veal calves—then such a claim would fail.

but changes in public taste, or the introduction of new products on the market, or the intervention of administrative officials will not. *Force majeure* only applies to impossibility, it does not apply where there is a fundamental alteration in the nature of the obligation. The relevant impossibility is measured by referring to the express provisions of the specific contracts and considerations of reasonableness. Thus, impossibility may include economic and practical considerations.

(B) CONSEQUENCES OF *FORCE MAJEURE*

Force majeure can have a number of effects on the normal consequences of a contract: for example, the running of prescription may be suspended if a debtor is unable to pay due to forces beyond his control—such as a postal strike or transportation strike—which has prevented the debtor from acting. In such a case the suspension lasts as long as the event causing the impossibility. This line of reasoning, developed by the courts, is contrary to the clearly stated provisions of Article 2251, according to which there can be no interruption to the running of prescription unless expressly provided so by a written provision. This jurisprudential approach is distinguishable from the effect of exceptional circumstances such as war or political events which paralyse normal life—as in 1968. In these sorts of circumstances, special laws impose a moratorium on the implementation of any orders for the payment of a debt, either for a stipulated period or until a further edict indicates that claims may operate as normal. Similarly the fine payable for delaying to comply with a judgment of a court—*astreinte*—may be modified by the judge (under a law of 1972), if the debtor can show that failure to comply with the judgment is not due to fault on his part, but to an outside cause.

The general consequences of *force majeure* are twofold: first, and most importantly, the debtor is released from the claims of the creditor.[15] He is therefore liberated or exonerate absolutely from any obligation. The only exception to this may be where the impossibility is only temporary and execution of the obligation is possible after a reasonable delay. The consequence of *force majeure* may operate in either contract or tort. Thus, in a tortious action, the tortfeasor who has caused the harm is relieved from having to pay compensation. In contract, the contractual obligation is extinguished. At one stage the law distinguished between contractual and non-contractual obligations, holding that in the case of the latter absolute exoneration would not apply absolutely in the case of

---

[15] This is total exoneration from liability whereas other external factors may amount to only partial exoneration.

force majeure if the defaulting party was at all to blame. This approach was criticised as being illogical in as much as the characteristics of *force majeure* were incompatible with notion of fault on the part of the defaulter; either the harm was caused by occurrences outside of the defaulter's control, or they were not. Where *force majeure* is established, then no damages are recoverable for the non-performance of the contract.[16] If only part of the contract is rendered impossible, then the rest of the contract must be carried out. If the circumstances giving rise to the *force majeure* are deemed to be only temporary, then the contract may simply be suspended.

Secondly, and less often, *force majeure* has the effect of safeguarding a party in the case of delay or proof. For example, the case law recognises that if a debtor or an owner of property is prevented from exercising his rights because of *force majeure*, the operation of any time-limits in exercising such rights will be suspended.[17] In the case of proof, for example of title to land, Article 1384 C. *Civ*. dispenses with the need for written proof from a party who has lost his paper documents of title as a result of *force majeure*.

(C) *IMPREVISION*

Imprévision, like *force majeure*, concerns factors which are external to the parties, rather than attributable to them. Unlike *force majeure*, however, it does not make performance of the obligation impossible, only more onerous or difficult for the *débiteur*. Moreover, the events need not be unforeseeable, simply unpreventable. The essential aspect of *imprévision* is that it upsets the equilibrium of the obligations owed by the parties. In particular *imprévision* is a concept influenced by the canonists and post-Glossators, and is fundamental to the idea of achieving equivalence of obligations. Today it appears to be a public law concept which emerged in the administrative courts at the turn of this century. Its application is primarily in the context of ongoing contracts in which successive performance is required, but where change of circumstances has made the obligations of one party unequal to those of the other party.[18] The legal issue is whether the *débiteur*—who is losing out under

---

[16] Arts. 1147 and 1148 C. *Civ*. The court may order the equitable adjustment of contractual rights and obligations if impossibility is pleaded. Also, under Art. 1184, rescission is available in respect of performance already given—which means that in many cases the breach of contract caused by *force majeure* will be settled out of court.

[17] This is based on the maxim that *prescription* cannot run against a person who is prevented from litigating.

[18] In particular it applies in the context of contracts of lease where, *e.g.* a lease might be agreed for 15 years at a rent of FF1,000 per month, but during the period of the lease devaluation is such that this becomes an unrealistic sum.

the arrangement—can apply to have the original contract revised by the court.

The development of the doctrine is a result of considerable jurisprudential debate, central to which was the case of *Canal de Craponne*, in which the Court of Cassation had held that a judge could not modify the agreement of parties to a contract in order to take into account present circumstances or so as to achieve a more just result.[19] The decision of the Court of Cassation was based on Article 1134 C. *Civ*. which clearly stated that the contract represented the intentions of the parties, and a court could not interfere with these except on recognised grounds, such as illegality.

In 1916, the *Conseil d'Etat* adopted a different line of reasoning in a case concerning Bordeaux Gas,[20] holding that the tariff charged to gas users could be modified if the current tariff was out of line with economic circumstances. Further application of the doctrine emerged in the context of a line of cases concerning public excavation works, in which the land being excavated proved to present particular problems and greater risks to the contractor. These unforeseen circumstances were treated by the *Conseil d'Etat* as insurmountable obstacles which gravely disturbed the economy of the contract. As a result the remuneration to the contractor was justifiably increased, even though this meant a modification of the original contract.

The period of inflation which followed the First World War provided an opportunity for the Court of Cassation to reconsider its approach, but it refused to depart from its previous line of reasoning.[21] Partial relief was afforded through jurisprudential use of the doctrine of *lésion*, whereby present prejudice caused by an agreement concluded in the past resulting in unequal benefit to the parties, might entitle the prejudiced party to an adjustment of obligations. However, legislation was required to obviate the rigour of the Court of Cassation's approach.

---

[19] Decision of March 6, 1876. This case, which related to a contract originally entered into in 1560 and 1567, concerned an arrangement to provide water for irrigation. During the nineteenth century, due to monetary devaluation and the rising costs of the operation, the company undertaking the work requested a re-adjustment of the price. The court at Aix-en-Provence had agreed to this.

[20] 30.3.1916 *Gaz de Bordeaux*.

[21] Support for the Court of Cassation's approach can be found in arguments favouring the need for certainty in private contracts, the risk of contracts being adjusted whenever there is an economic crisis, and private contracts being rendered unstable by the intervention of a third party. Moreover, there is nothing to stop the parties to these types of contracts from including in the contract the possibility to periodically review its terms. See, *e.g.* the discussion in H. Captitant *Les Grands Arrêts de la Jurisiprudence Civile* (Dalloz, 10th ed., 1994) pp. 410 *et seq*.

Such legislation took two forms: temporary measures and permanent ones. The former were particularly used to take into account the problems caused by the 1914–18 War. These included the *Loi Faillot*, which permitted the resolution—rather than the revision—of a contract entered into before the War, if one of the contracting parties suffered from hardships and prejudices which could not have been envisaged at the time of contracting. Other laws related to landlord and tenant agreements—particularly rents—salaries, and trading licences.[22] Similar measures were adopted after the Second World War.[23]

(D) THE PUBLIC LAW—PRIVATE LAW DIVIDE

There was therefore a jurisprudential conflict between the two courts, which in turn represented a difference of approach between public law—notably administrative law—and private law. This is explicable if the nature of the different contracts are considered. In private law only those who are party to the contract—generally a limited number of individuals—are affected by them, whereas in public law, particularly in the case of the provision of basic utilities, there is a wider public interest to serve. In the former case the intention of the parties and the terms of their agreement are paramount. In the latter case, administrative contracts serve the interest of the general public and they may, therefore, be more easily adjusted in order to continue to serve the public more effectively. A public service contract which is not economically viable is not in the public interest.

The nature of the contracts which led to the development and general recognition of the doctrine should not be overlooked, nor the fact that as an arm of the public power the *Conseil d'Etat* was particularly well placed to protect the public interest. Moreover, the additional cost incurred in paying a modified sum to the contractor of public works was met by the public power involved.

(E) APPLICATION OF THE DOCTRINE OF IMPREVISION

The doctrine of *imprévision* applies where the contract is one for future performance and is not speculative, and where the circumstances have changed to such an extent that a reasonable person could not have foreseen the new circumstances.

Its application is wider than that of *force majeure* and enables the

[22] See, *e.g.*: those of March 9, 1918, April 1, 1926, July 6, 1915, June 9, 1927, April 8, and July 12, 1933.

[23] See, *e.g.*: Acts of April 23, 1949 and June 9, 1941.

courts to consider the general public interest. The theory is based on Article 1135 C. *Civ.* relating to good faith in the performance of contracts. This permits an objective approach to the interpretation of contractual arrangements and means that the principle of *pacta sunt servanda* can be modified. However, even in the context of private law contracts, considerations of reasonableness and good faith may assist the party seeking to rely on *force majeure*. Although the event rendering the performance absolutely impossible must arise independently of the will or actions of the party seeking to rely on it, and must be of such a nature that its occurrence could not be reasonably foreseen at the time that the contract was formed, if the party has been reasonably diligent in attempting to overcome the obstacles, and the court is satisfied with the reasonableness of these efforts and the good faith of the party, then it may be satisfied that the event was beyond the control of the party.

The two doctrines provide a good illustration of the separate approaches of administrative and civil law. While the Court of Cassation does not recognise the theory of *imprévision*, the *Conseil d'Etat* does. On the other hand, the *Conseil d'Etat* may modify contractual obligations, while the Court of Cassation or the lower courts may only authorise the supplementation of a contract, not its modification. The equivalent of equitable jurisdiction in English law, seems, in French law, to lie with the *Conseil d'Etat*. This means that if unforeseen events occur, the *Conseil d'Etat* is less constrained in its response.

The Court of Cassation, although reluctant to recognise any doctrine of frustration, may impliedly recognise the doctrine of *force majeure* by construing a contract in such a way that the parties are deemed to rely not only on the manifest intention evident in the contract, but also the dictates of reasonableness which are implied. Thus the Court may intervene by supplementing the contract by interpreting it in a particular way, thereby avoiding any problem of modifying the contract. In practice, this Court will in any case be rarely involved as interpretation of a contract is primarily a matter of fact and not law. The lower courts may also implicitly recognise the possibility of frustration by limiting the applicability of contractual terms to foreseen events supplemented by considerations of reasonableness.

One of the underlying reasons for the conflict of views expressed between the administrative and civil courts over the doctrine of *imprévision*, was the firm belief that the sanctity of a contract ought to be upheld. This principle has been severely tested during periods of monetary devaluation, when debts which had originally been nominal, suddenly escalated in value. The civil courts maintained that the sum payable was that stipulated in the contract, regardless of its actual value in the current economic climate. Despite academic writing which suggested that the courts, in the interests of equity, ought to either revise the nominal value of the contract, or annul the contract entirely, on the basis of *imprévision*,[24] and the fact that some of the lower courts were prepared to do this, the Court of Cassation has continued to reject the theory.[25]

In administrative law, on the other hand, there was less of a problem in admitting the doctrine particularly in the case of public works or services.

[24] One of the criticisms of the Court of Cassation's approach is that it ignores the fact that contracts take place within an economic and social context, and where the contract is for a considerable time, changes in these ought to be taken into account. Moreover the rejection of the theory of *imprévision* is out of line with the Court of Cassation's acceptance of the doctrine of *lésion*.

[25] Some relief was provided by legislation, *e.g.* the Acts of January 21, 1918, May 9, 1920 and April 22, 1949.

TOPIC FOUR
STRICT AND VICARIOUS LIABILITY

Even before the reception of Roman law into civil law systems, the courts administered a penal law which made no distinction between crime and tort. Under Roman law liability for delicts was penal in nature, primarily because it was the function of the public authorities to repress crime and prevent forms of self-help or vengeance. Gradually the principle developed that man should be held liable for the damage caused by his fault. This gave rise to a general action for damages caused *dolo aut culpa* in which the penal element was reduced. The defendant was liable for any wrongful damage, whether to persons or to property. The distinction in the nature of intention between crimes and other delicts led to a distinction between criminal and civil justice. Civil law admitted a more general principle of compensation, an idea which was to find favour with the Natural Law School which advocated the view that the obligation to make good a loss wrongfully caused arose naturally. Prior to 1800 it was generally agreed that there was an obligation to make good any damage caused as a result of intentional or negligent conduct. Gradually this penal element was replaced by the idea of compensation for the victim, rather than criminalisation of the tortfeasor, and by the seventeenth century fault had become the criterion for civil liability, although this penal element was never entirely lost as evidenced by the importance of the concept of fault in attracting liability. Whether other forms of liability existed was not clear. Grotius for example held that they did not, while Pufendorf suggested that there should be liability on the part of anyone who benefited from certain economic activities. Most jurists, however, explained liability in other situations as being warranted by the special circumstances of the case or on the basis of the tacit consent of the parties or on the grounds of an expanded sense of negligence. Pothier and Domat held that fault was necessary for delictual liability, and it was this approach which became incorporated into the Civil Code.

Fault, is an error of conduct judged against the reasonable man. There is, however, a distinction between moral fault and legal fault. Civil liability rests on the latter. In developing the law the judges respond to policy considerations and the demands of a certain order within society. The fault principle provides a mechanism whereby the victim of anti-social conduct is compensated, although the damages awarded may have no bearing on the degree of fault of the defendant.[26] The notion merges the idea of *culpa* and unlawfulness.

The provisions for delictual liability in the French Civil Code distinguish between liability for personal conduct and liability for things. In the case of things, liability is strict and rests on the relationship between the person and the thing—ownership or guardianship. There need be no defect in the thing itself, and the victim need establish nothing other than causation. Causality, not fault, is the crux of liability, and in order to avoid liability the defendant must establish that the cause was something external to the thing. Partial exoneration from liability may be achieved if the defendant can establish that the actions of the victim himself were the cause.[27]

As in other systems, the expansion of delictual liability occurred casuistically, with very little systematisation or abstraction. Policy limitations were more or less apparent, both as to what kind of loss might be recognised, who was regarded as capable of sustaining that loss, and who was excluded from either liability or the right to claim compensation. Unlike the situation in the common law however, French law was not so hampered in the development of contract law. Consequently, a number of areas which might fall under the law of torts in common law, fall under the law of contract in French law. Indeed where there was only one major article providing for the whole of delictual liability, it was in many ways easier to expand the law through the principles of contract, in order to accommodate new situations.

In French law the general principle is that there should be no liability without fault. However, the fault principle has proved inadequate to deal with some of the social and legal demands of the twentieth century, in particular there has been a shift towards the principle of strict liability for accidental damage. The major catalyst for this change was the rapid and widespread process of industrialisation which occurred in the nineteenth century, and the related hazards of an age of coal, steel, electricity and manufacturing of chemicals. The expansion of the railway, and later the car and aeroplane, together with advances in the technology of manufacturing processes, led to increasing accidental damage, in which the prime factor was industrial, mechanical and anonymous. Initially

---

[26] For a discussion of these issues, see A. Tunc, "Tort Law and the Moral Law" [1973] C.L.J. 247 and Hamson [1973] C.L.J. 241.

[27] Partial liability, which was strongly supported by writers such as A. Tunc, was particularly relevant in the case of road traffic accidents prior to compulsory motor vehicle insurance. In a decision of the Court of Cassation in July 1982, it was held that even if the fault of a pedestrian injured in a road traffic accident could be established, this would not have the sufficient characteristic of unpredictability or irresistibility necessary to exonerate the driver of the vehicle.

liability remained firmly based on fault—there were a number of policy considerations at work, not least that governments and powerful interests in society had much to gain from unfettered industrial growth. Consequently Article 2382 C. *Civ*. became a defence in the hands of manufacturing defendant companies.

The *laissez-faire* approach of the law in the nineteenth century protected the right of the individual to self-determination—including taking risks in the work-place or later on the road—and self-responsibility. Such a philosophy effectively excluded not only any concept of strict liability, but also—except where actual fault could be proved—employer's liability for most accidents. There was also reluctance to burden developing industry with the extra cost of accident compensation, particularly at a time when there was a surge in effort to build up French wealth against that of the Prussians. The break-through in the law came via Belgium—where the Napoleonic Code was in force—in a decision in the late 1870s, in which the judge held that the victim of a mining explosion could succeed in a claim against the employer, on the basis that the accident was caused by things under the latter's control. On appeal this approach was criticised as being too revolutionary, but compensation was allowed on the basis of presumption of fault.

In the 1890s a number of cases came before the French *Conseil d'Etat* and the *Cour de Cassation* concerning accidental injury. A leading case was that of *Guissez, Cousin and Oriolle v. Teffaire* (1896) brought by the widow and dependants of a man killed in a boiler explosion on board a tug. The case presented problems because the tug was not a building and so could not be brought under Article 1386—relating to buildings. It was also unclear whether it could be argued that the owner of the tug had the boiler—or more expressly the pipe which exploded—within his control. Two possible approaches were followed: first that Article 1386—liability for falling buildings—could be applied by analogy, and so fault was not required, so that the defendant was presumed responsible unless he could show that the cause of the accident lay elsewhere; or secondly that Article 1384 could be applied by itself to justify the imposition of strict liability, so that fault was presumed unless the employer could show that the boiler was properly maintained and that he was not at fault. Despite the legal hurdles the court found in favour of the plaintiffs.

In 1887 an Act providing for workers' compensation was passed, which to a certain extent removed employment accidents from litigation by the provision of workmen's compensation schemes, and moved claims of this type into the area of social security legislation. This Act incorporated the notion of strict liability on the part of employers. Prior to this, however, the courts had been prepared to hold that accidents in the course of employment—although they fell outside the scope of

Articles 1382 and 1383—came under the implied terms of the contractual arrangements between employer and employee, whereby the employer was obliged to pay the employee for compensation for such accidents and to guarantee the worker's safety, and indemnify him if there was any accident. The only onus on the employee was to show that there was a contract of employment The employer could only avoid liability if he could show *cas fortuit* or *force majeure*.

Nevertheless, the gradual movement towards strict liability continued. Economically the country was strong enough for manufacturers and industry to bear the imposition of new duties of care, and there was a perceived need to keep the growing socialist movement satisfied. In any case certain writers such as Josserand and Saleilles were extremely critical of the inequality of a system of liability based solely on fault. There was also a ground swell of political and humanitarian concern for the rights of workers which was to force changes, as was the advent of the motor car and its increased use.[28] Indeed the increase in car accidents took over where the case law on industrial accidents left off.

To begin with, strict liability was avoided by retaining fault but insisting on higher standards from the defendant. The subjective test of what was reasonable in the circumstances came to be replaced by a more objective test, and the onus of proof shifting from the victim to the defendant. During the 1920s and 1930s the courts were prepared to hold that Article 1384 applied provided the thing was dangerous—whether it was operated by humans or not. Liability in such cases was based on the *garde* (control) of the thing, not the thing itself. This was therefore a presumption of responsibility which could not be rebutted by evidence of lack of fault or lack of evidence establishing the cause of the damage. Liability could only be avoided if there was positive evidence that the damage was due to an event which was unforeseeable and external to the guardian of the thing and the thing itself—for example the act of a third party.

The courts were also prepared to extend the ambit of Article 1386, so that where the owner's negligence or lack of care caused harm to a third party, the owner was liable solely on the basis of ownership, because as owner he was responsible for maintaining the thing in good condition—that is he had the means of doing so—and therefore had the duty to prevent an accident. The courts indicated that Article 1386 C. *Civ.* extended to everything which was incorporated into a building—the

---

[28] At first the French courts seem to have only accepted the principle of strict liability for motor accidents when the car was not being operated by a human being—*e.g.* when the brakes failed to keep the car stationary—maintaining the requirement of fault if there was a driver.

original provision only relating to buildings. In the manufacturing context this meant that all industrial premises and the machines therein could be included.

As far as cars were concerned, they could not be included in Article 1386, but Article 1384 could be applied if the car was not being operated by anyone when the accident occurred.

Article 1382 continued to present problems because the onus of proof rested on the injured party who had to establish that the person who had caused the injury was at fault. However, there has been a gradual shift away from requirements of actual fault, particularly where economic considerations indicated that the defendant could bear the cost of compensation without suffering, as was the case with the railways. This transition was effected by development of the idea of responsibility for the creation of risk, rather than responsibility for the accident itself. In many countries the movement towards strict liability—particularly in the case of accidents—has been achieved through legislation, and this approach had some adherents in France. However, this has not been the case. The movement towards strict liability has been developed primarily through the courts.

(A) STRICT LIABILITY

French law sought a compromise between freedom to engage in any activity and liability for all the consequences flowing therefrom. This has been achieved by the use of presumptions of fault or responsibility. In some respects this has been facilitated by the very broadly worded basic rule found in Article 1384 *C. Civ.* which provides that a person is not only responsible for the damage which one causes by one's own act, but also for the damage which is caused by the act of a person for whom one is answerable or of things which one has under one's control. By the end of the nineteenth century it was held that this provision was not simply a preliminary announcement for liability for animals or buildings—under Articles 1385 and 1386—but had an independent force of its own and was applicable in all cases in which a thing under the defendant's control had caused harm, thereby creating a presumption of liability. It was through this line of development that the protection of workers was first achieved.

In 1930 the *Chambres Réunies* of the *Cour de Cassation* gave the *Jand'heur* decision.[29] The question raised in this case was whether Article 1384 could apply when the vehicle, which had caused the accident, was not being driven by the owner or by an employee, or

---

[29] *Jand'heur v. Les Galeries Belfortaises* February 13, 1930.

whether Article 1382, with its requirement of fault should apply. The Court rejected the view that the vehicle needed human intervention to make it move, in order for a claim to succeed, holding that it was sufficient that the object required a guard because of the dangers it created for others. Whether the car was moving or not there was a presumption that the guardian of the thing was at fault. Therefore the distinction between an accident caused by an object and that caused by a person, was irrelevant. The Court concluded that Article 1384, was not restricted to dangerous things, since liability attached to the custody of the thing itself, and that there was a presumption of responsibility which could only be rebutted by proof of *force majeure* or some other external cause not attributable to the custodian of the thing, mere negation of fault by the defendant was not enough to escape liability. The Court held that the provisions of the Article had to be adapted to new needs, and that the case law had to perform a creative function to meet realities and requirements of modern life which might not have been considered in previous decisions. Later cases held that actual contact between the thing causing the harm and the victim, was not always necessary to establish a causal connection. Eventually, in the case of road traffic accidents, legislation was introduced, and compulsory insurance removed most road traffic cases from the arena of debate.[30]

This extensive interpretation of the original Article of the Code has made it virtually unnecessary for French law to introduce strict liability for a wide range of legal issues. However, before Article 1384 can apply, certain conditions must be met.

First, there must be a thing—this will include every corporeal object but not animals or buildings, the former falling under Article 1385, the later under Article 1386. The thing can be animate or inanimate. Secondly, the thing should not have played a purely passive role in the causation of the harm. If the thing was in its normal place or condition then the Article will not apply. Causation of the harm must therefore be active rather than passive. This does not mean that an inert object may not be the cause of the harm. The distinction lies in the burden of proof. If the thing is passive, then the plaintiff must establish that it was the cause of the harm. If it was active, then the defendant must show that it was not the cause of the harm. Thirdly, responsibility attaches to the custodian or guardian of the thing, not necessarily its owner. The custodian is the person who has the use, management and control of the thing, or the material direction of the thing. Usually the custodian or guardian will be the owner, but flexibility in this concept enables the

---

[30] *E.g.* the Guarantee Fund 1953, and the introduction of compulsory automobile liability insurance in 1958.

courts to find the driver of a stolen car liable rather than the owner, or to exclude a chauffeur. The flexibility of the criteria also allows the courts to place the risks where it is the most just. Where damage is caused by a thing in transit, then the law distinguishes between the carrier, who has control in the handling of the thing, and the person who has control over its construction or composition.

Liability will be excluded in the case of an external unforeseeable event (*force majeure*), the fault of the victim, or unforeseeable behaviour by a third party. It can also be excluded if the interest damaged is not a legitimately protected interest. This line of reasoning—which clearly allows policy considerations to play a role—was used in a series of cases in the first part of the twentieth century to defeat claims by surviving unmarried partners—*concubines*—for compensation for the wrongfully caused death of a lover. Until 1970 it was held by the courts that there was no legal interest at stake here, the claim of the *concubine* being contrary to good morals and public order because of the nature of the extra-marital relationship.

The academic question which surrounds the development of Article 1384, is whether it can be claimed that liability under the Article is still based on fault. Some writers adhere to the theory of creation of risk (*théorie du risque créé*), whereby he who created a risk of harm to third parties through his conduct and seeks to make a profit by doing so, must accept liability for any harm caused, regardless whether he or his assistants were at fault or not—society has an objective social interest in requiring compensation.

Other writers, such as Mazeaud and Tunc, maintain that French law still rests on the principle of fault. The essence of the fault lies in the custodian of the thing letting it escape from his control—*faute dans la garde*. There is support for this view in as much as not every careless act attracts liability, thus not every careless act can be said to give rise to *faute*. The notion of *faute* operates to limit liability, largely by requiring the establishment of the equivalent of a duty of care owed by the defendant to the plaintiff. Retention of the notion of *faute*, which is understood and judged in an objective sense and embodies a sociological element—for example the approval or reprobation of the defendant's conduct by society—provides a vehicle for the exercise of judicial discretion. French law, like other systems, basically requires conduct, causation and damage, in order to attract delictual liability. Policy considerations determine which kind of harmful conduct is actionable, and which range of interests the law regards as protected.

If fault is defined as the failure of the tortfeasor to meet the standards of the *bonus paterfamilias*, then there are conceptual difficulties in extending liability to unavoidable error, partly because the reasonable man is bound to make errors. To base liability on error is contrary to the moral notion of fault. At the same time there is clearly a moral requirement that the victim of an accident is not denied all possible chance of compensation. Focus on fault, however, can lead to delays in obtaining compensation, inadequate or no compensation, expense and uncertainty. The concept of fault is therefore an inadequate mechanism for providing for the phenomenon of accidents.[31] It has been suggested, therefore, by some writers, for example Tunc,[32] that accident compensation should be based on the question of risk rather than fault. Even this approach would not be without its problems. While it might work in the case of road traffic accidents, the assessment of risk versus social value may create problems in allocation. On the other hand, risk allocation may facilitate the spreading of compensation over a number of sources. Yet other writers—for example Zweigert and Kötz—suggest that Article 1384 includes both elements of fault and strict liability. The latter arises if the harm is caused by a defect in the thing, while the former applies in all other circumstances, in which case the custodian may avoid liability if he can show that he was not at fault.

The abandonment of the fault element does not mean that liability is unlimited. French law also uses causation as a device to restrict the possible number of claimants and the extent of the defendant's liability. However, causation tends to be an empirical problem which is left to the judge, and therefore attracts less academic debate.

In deciding a case based on the Articles of the Code, a judge can choose the type of liability on which to base the decision. In this way the law can be expanded or contracted. The role of the Court of Cassation in this respect has been particularly important—for example in determining the way that the irresistible/unpredictable defence is used—and the ambit of the term "things".[33]

(B) VICARIOUS LIABILITY

The justification for imposing vicarious liability is that the person controlling the enterprise and taking the benefit of the labour of others should also shoulder the burden of liability when something goes wrong with that enterprise. Vicarious liability will, however, only arise where

---

[31] See, *e.g.* the comments of Jolowitz [1968] C.L.J. 50, who suggests that in any case where there is insurance, the tortfeasor rarely has to provide the compensation payable from his own resources, so the relevance of fault as a criterion of compensation disappears.

[32] A. Tunc [1972] C.L.J. 247.

[33] *E.g.* in 1983 it was held that things included damage by an electric saw, and in 1984 the scope of Article 1385 was extended to animals.

there is a sufficient connection between the person who actually causes the injury and the person whom the plaintiff seeks to hold liable for that injury; and there must be a sufficient connection between the acts which caused the injury and the defendant or his enterprise.

Article 1384(1) provides that a person is responsible for the acts of persons for whom he is answerable or responsible. This includes employees, minor children, pupils or apprentices. Whether such a person is sufficiently linked to the defendant depends on the nature of the relationship between them, for example was the person dependent on the defendant in the sense that he or she was bound to follow the defendant's instructions or orders in carrying out the task complained of.

The damage must also be caused in the exercise of the functions of employment, apprenticeship, etc. In this respect the courts seem to have been prepared to hold the employer liable, even where the employee was simply using materials supplied by the employer, provided the work was being done on the employer's behalf.

If the person who caused the harm was himself incapable of being held liable—for example, because of mental incapacity or insanity—the employer cannot be held vicariously liable, although he may be directly liable in his own right if there is sufficient causal connection, for example that the employer knew of the employee's incapacity when he appointed him—that is a personal fault in employing a person in the first place.

Where an employer has been held vicariously liable he may seek indemnity from the employee.[34]

---

[34] See, *e.g.* the situation concerning government torts discussed in Chapter Four, Topic Three below.

Chapter Two
Property

INTRODUCTION

This chapter considers the nature and meaning of property, rights relating to property and the alienation and acquisition of immovable property.

Before considering certain aspects of French property law it is necessary first to locate the relevant sources of the law, and secondly to consider some of the key concepts.

(A) SOURCES

French law on property is found in Book II of the *Code Civil* which is concerned with property and different aspects of ownership, and in Book III which deals with the different ways in which property can be acquired. Many of the original Articles in the Code have been amended by subsequent legislation, but judicial law-making has also played a significant role.

Book II of the Code, is divided into four Titles which are subsdivided into Chapters. These former are:

- *Title 1*: (Articles 516–543) the distinction between property: immovables; movables; possession;
  Title II: (Articles 544–577) ownership, of the produce of a thing, over things which are united or incorporated into a thing, both movable and immovable;
  Title III: (Articles 578–636) usufruct, use and occupation, including the rights and obligations of the usufructuary and the termination of the usufruct;
  Title IV: (Articles 637–710) servitudes, their creation and extinction, different types, those created by law and those arising due to location.

Book III is divided into 20 Chapters, much of which overlaps with the law of obligations but relates also to the different ways in which one can acquire and alienate property. It includes among other things:

- *Title I*: (Articles 718–892) the law relating to succession, including the rights of ascendants and descendants, collaterals, the surviving spouse, affiliated children and the State;
- *Title II*: (Articles 893–1100) *inter vivos* and testamentary gifts, including rules relating to formalities, wills, executors and legacies;
- *Title III*: (Articles 1101–1369) the law relating to contracts and obligations;
- *Title V*: (Articles 1387–1581) contracts of marriage and different matrimonial property regimes;
- *Title VI*: (Articles 1582–1701) sale, and the rights and obligations of vendor and purchaser;
- *Title VIII*: (Articles 1708–1831) lease;
- *Title XVIII*: (Articles 2092–2203) mortgages and charges, their characteristics, creation, enforcement and extinction;
- *Title XX*: (Articles 2219–2283) possession and prescription.

(B) CONCEPTS

(1) Real rights

A property right in French law is regarded as a real right—*droit réel*—which confers on the holder a direct power over a thing. This right is regarded as absolute and enforceable against anyone who interferes with its exercise.[1] A real right in this sense has two elements: the person who exercises the right—*sujet actif du droit réel*—and the object—*objet du droit*.

The division of rights into real rights and personal rights finds support from most academic writers—*la doctrine*—but has been subject to an important doctrinal criticism expressed by Planiol at the end of the nineteenth century.[2] According to Planiol—who himself adopted the views of certain nineteenth century German writers—the distinction between real and personal rights was not justified because, as things could not be the subjects of rights, so it was incorrect to hold that a real right was based on the relationship between a person and a thing. The only rights which could be recognised were those between individuals.[3] With reference to property, such persons could either have active or passive rights. In Planiol's view, the active subject of a real right was the

[1] "Absolute" in this sense does not mean unlimited, but that it exists regardless of any personal nexus between the owner of the right and others, and it can be exercised against anyone.

[2] Planiol *Traité élémental du droit civil*.

[3] This theory was termed *personnaliste*.

titleholder or owner of the thing, while the passive subjects were all those persons who were obliged not to interfere with the exercise of the owner's rights.[4] In order to ensure that the owner has a right enforceable against the world, this passive right was deemd to be a universal obligation, protected by the operation of law. The distinction between this theory and others lay in the use and meaning of the term *opposabilité*. The concept of a right *in rem* is based on the idea that the right can be raised against anyone.

Planiol's theory has been criticised on the ground that it was based on a misconception of what is meant by a right which is enforceable against third parties (that is persons with whom there is no previous legal nexus concerning the thing). Critics point out that most personal rights which are protected by the force of law have to be respected by third parties—for example a contract of employment cannot be interfered with by persons outside that contract—it is, therefore, both personal and a right against the world. This concept of *opposabilité* can be understood as the general duty to respect the rights of others, whether these rights are real or personal. The concept also has another meaning, however, and that is the right to a more specific obligation. The obligation represents a debt in the *passif* assets of the debtor's patrimony, whereas the duty to respect the rights of others does not constitute a debt in the patrimonial sense.

Despite the criticism, Planiol's theory achieved a useful clarification of the meaning of *opposabilité*. One distinction which his theory did not sufficiently explain away, was that a real right gives the holder the right to follow the thing into the hands of a third party and exercise a preferential claim over others. This right is not, of course, absolute. For example, the right to claim immovables must be accompanied by the necessary publicity otherwise the right may be unenforceable against others. Similarly, possession of a movable may defeat the claim of an owner.[5] Nevertheless in considering the exercise of real and personal rights it is generally considered that there is a distinction, particularly in the right to follow the property and to establish a preferential claim to it.

(2) Principal and accessory rights

The exercise of real rights can be subdivided into principal (*droits réel principaux*) and accessory rights (*droits réels accessoires*[6]). The most

---

[4] Passive in this sense meant to refrain from doing, rather than bearing any burden. See the use of *actif* and *passif* in the concept of *patrimoine*: Chapter One, above.

[5] See Art. 2279. C. *Civ*.

[6] There are also rights which are partially real and partially personal, such as usufruct, use and occupation, and co-ownership—see Topics Two and Three, below.

important principal right is that of ownership,[7] while the most important accessory right is that of *hypothèque* (lien[8]) and *gage* (pledge or pawn[9]).

(a) Ownership

Ownership (*propriété*) is defined in Article 544 C. *Civ*. as:

> "the right to enjoy and dispose of things in the most absolute way, provided that no use is made of them forbidden by law or regulations."

In French law an owner has absolute title, so that if a person acquires property by prescription—that is possession over a period of time—not only are all other adverse titles extinguished but the person acquiring by prescription has a positive right.

In French law there is no doctrine of estates and so ownership attaches not to a period of time over land—as in England—but to the land itself. Limited rights do exist, for example servitudes or life interests, but there must always be an absolute owner, whose land is temporarily encumbered with these rights.

There is also no distinction between ownership and management because the French law concept of ownership—like the Roman law *dominium*—is absolute. There is no distinction between equitable and legal rights, therefore unity of ownership is a fundamental principle of French law.

Ownership involves a totality of rights over a thing. Right of ownership is exclusive, absolute and perpetual. Strictly speaking the right of ownership can only apply to corporeal things—whether movable or immovable. Ownership cannot be split up: it is a unified concept.

Ownership of immovables depends on title as well as possession.

---

[7] Others are *servitudes* (easements); *droit de superficie* (the right to build or utilise the surface of land—*e.g.* to grow timber; *emphytéose* (mortgage); *bail* (loans for the development of real property, *e.g.* for restoration of old buildings for leasing (Act of May 31, 1990) or for urban construction (Act of December 16, 1964).

[8] This is a real right because it is security against an immovable. Although the debt only confers a personal right on the creditor, once it is secured against property and given the necessary publicity, the creditor has a right which is enforceable against anyone. If the debtor-owner sells the property, the *créancier hypothécaire* can oppose the sale. He has therefore the right to follow the property—*droit de suite*—and a preferential claim over unsecured creditors—*droit de préférence*.

[9] This is a guarantee secured against movable property—for example, jewels, a masterpiece or share certificates. The security is physically placed in the hands of the creditor or a third party appointed by the creditor. If the secured debt is not paid, then the person with the *gage* has the right to sell the thing and has preference over other creditors. He does not, however, have the other aspect of a real right. He cannot follow the property into the hands of third parties.

Therefore, there are legal proofs that the party asserting ownership may produce (for example documents of sale, donation, etc.) and there is the fact of possession (for example occupation, use, enjoyment, etc.). In French law the legal proofs are indicative of title but not conclusive, facts such as possession and occupation may be just as relevant.

If both parties in a dispute over property claim possession, then ownership is given to the most well-defined possession. If both claim title, then ownership is given to the party which registered title first and can show occupation of the premises—in the case of land or buildings. If one claims title and the other possession, then it depends on which arose first. If title existed before possession, then the one with title is deemed to be owner, but if possession arose before title, then the possessor is deemed to be owner despite the other party's claim to title.

(b) *Possession versus détention*

Physical control of property may amount to a presumption of ownership in French law, particularly of movables. However, the law distinguishes between possession and detention.

Détention is the possession of a thing with the permission of its owner (for example lessees, bailees, executors under a will, etc.). The detentor's title recognises the right of another over the thing and therefore the intention is different from that of true possession. According to Article 2230 C. *Civ.*, under detention one possesses for oneself and for the owner.

Article 2228 describes possession as "the detention or the enjoyment of a thing or a right by oneself or by another who holds the thing and enjoys it on behalf of another". It is possible, therefore, for a person to possess both real rights and things. Possession is a fact, ownership is a right.

As in English law, possession over a period of time, may lead to the acquisition of ownership by prescription. The length of time depends on the circumstances, for example if based on just title and in good faith then the period is 10 or 20 years depending on whether the true owner lives within or beyond the jurisdiction of the court where the property is situated. If there is no just title, then the period of adverse possession must be 30 years. The period may be longer if the acquisitive prescription is interrupted, for example by legal proceedings or natural events.

(c) Protection of Possession

The legal protection of possession differs depending on whether the thing is movable or immovable.

Movables

Where the thing is movable, possession creates a presumption of title (Article 2279 C. *Civ.*) to the movables, provided that the possession is accompanied by the intention to possess as owner, that is *animo domini*. This therefore excludes detentors. If neither the defendant nor the plaintiff can produce evidence of title, then the presumption of ownership is in favour of the possessor.

The law distinguishes between the situation where the movable is acquired through voluntary disposition, for example loan or pledge, and involuntary disposition, for example loss or theft. In the voluntary disposition, the true owner has an action in contract for the restitution of the thing, or he may bring an action of revindication if there is no contract or the defendant is insolvent. If the acquirer of a movable from a non-owner, for example a bailee, is in good faith and the disposition was voluntary in the first place, then such a possessor—provided he/she has *animo domini*—may resist a real action of revindication and the original owner will only have a personal action against the bailee. In the case of involuntary disposition, the true owner has an action of revindication against the finder or the thief, unless the chattel has come into the possession of a bona fide third party, in which case the action must be brought within three years and the possessor must be compensated if he/she acquired the thing at an auction, fair, etc.

In respect of movables, it should be noted that transfer of title in corporeal movables is effected by agreement even if the thing is not yet delivered or the price paid. This accords with the principle that possession of movables is equivalent to title. With immovables, title is also transferred by agreement but since an Act of January 4, 1955, there must be publicity of the transaction, effected through the process of registration.

Immovables

The main remedy for the possessor of an immovable is an action called *réintégrande*. It affords a right of action to any person who is violently ousted from possession of an immovable. However, the action is not available against a third party who has come into possession in good faith (excluding an heir of the defendant). This action, which is a personal action, can be brought by persons who have no real rights over the property including detentors.

An alternative action is the *complainte*. This action is available provided that first, the defendant has acted so as to infringe the plaintiff's possession (good faith or title to the property is no defence in this case) and, secondly, the plaintiff must have had legal possession of the immovable for at least a year and his possession must be continuous, peaceful, public and free from defects. This action is a real action and protects those who have legal possession of the property. It is effective against bona fide possessors as well as others.

TOPIC ONE
THE CLASSIFICATION AND CATEGORISATION OF PROPERTY AND ITS SIGNIFICANCE

There is a conceptual distinction between things in general (*choses*) and things in the property sense. In French law the term *biens* is used to refer to those things which are brought into a legal context, the relationship of people—in the sense of *personnes juridiques*—and things.[10] At its simplest the word *biens* signifies those things which can be used by man to meet his needs, either directly or indirectly, through the mechanism of exchange. At a more complex level property rights attach not simply to the thing but to the rights related to the thing. Things are not always treated individually however, they also have importance when considered collectively. A distinction can be made at this point between a universality of things determined by fact—for example a library consists of a collection of books and the sale of that library or collection relates to the whole not to any indvividual item—and universality established by law, in which things are brought together by the active and passive obligations which they give rise to. In French law there is only one *universalité juridique*, which consists of the collection of rights and obligations of a person as they relate to things and that is *le patrimoine*.[11]

The concept of *patrimoine* has been mentioned in the general introduction. The concept was not developed in the Civil Code itself but was expounded by Aubrey and Rau. According to their classical theory, the concept of *patrimoine* only included rights and obligations having a pecuniary value within the economic context, and could only apply in the context of legal or moral persons.[12] *Biens* are the subject-matter of

---

[10] Since the abolition of slavery, people cannot be the objects of ownership and therefore cannot be *biens*.

[11] The legal notion is distinct from the economists' notion, because in law *patrimoine* includes both assets and debts, whereas the economists' notion excludes negative considerations. The legal sense also includes future property, because it is distinct from the actual things which make it up. The legal concept is also distinct from a sociological concept which includes assets such as education, social standing, family characteristics.

[12] This can cause some problems if the classical theory is strictly adhered to because it means that non-juristic persons, such as foundations or research institutes, which may be primarily financed by donations from benefactors, are not regarded as having any *patrimoine*. A criticism of the theory is that it is too narrow and individualistic. If there is an implied lien between the various interests which make up the mass, then this legally coherent whole could equally apply where these interests are directed at a common aim rather than attaching to an individual—this line of reasoning finds support in the German theory of *patrimoine d'affectation*, *i.e.* a legal universality determined by the destination of the property.

droits patrimoniaux. *Biens* (things or goods), can be understood in two ways: (1) a narrow, material sense whereby *biens* are the objects of legal transactions between individuals; or (2) in a more abstract sense, whereby they are means by which a person can secure the benefit of things—for example the rights of ownership, or the rights of creditors. In the latter sense, it is the exercise of these rights, rather than the things themselves, which make up an individual's patrimony.[13] Therefore, in French law property—*biens*—includes both things and rights *in rem*, that is real rights and the objects over which such rights can be exercised. Moreover, *biens* include corporeal things and incorporeal things, for example usufructs, life interests, easements, mortgages, debts, patents, electrical energy, family names, etc. Importantly a person has only one *patrimoine*, so that although some funds may be set aside for commercial transactions and others intended for private needs, creditors can claim against any property falling within the *patrimoine* of the debtor.

(A) THE CLASSIFICATION OF PROPERTY

The legal status of things is far from being uniform. It varies according to the nature and function of things, their purpose and use, their economic significance and the context of their application—for example whether this is commercial or non-commercial. Moreover, the same thing may have different legal characteristics depending on how it is classified. There are a number of different ways in which property may be classified, more than one of which may be applicable to a given set of facts. The classification of property is important because it can determine which rules are applicable to a transaction affecting that property, or even who may be entitled to the property.[14]

One way of classifying property is to divide it into that which can be owned and that which cannot—although it may be exploited. Air, running water, the sea, are not capable of individual ownership but may be owned and enjoyed by everyone.[15]

A further refinement in this method of classification is that some things can be publicly owned—by the State or the *commune* for example—others can be privately owned. Property falling into the first category is subject to strict regulations and may not be dealt with except

[13] Such rights may include the right of exchange, alienation, transmissibility—*e.g.* to heirs on death, to use property to secure a loan, etc.

[14] This is particularly the case in the law applicable to the property rights of spouses, where in the past entitlement to matrimonial property might depend on whether it was movable or immovable, earned or inherited.

[15] See Art. 714 al.1 C. *Civ*.

in accordance with these.[16] Property falling into the second category, however, may be dealt with more freely. This does not mean that all property owned by the State or by public collectives automatically falls within the *domaine public*. For example, the State has the same rights of ownership of National Forestries as a private forestry owner, therefore this property falls into the *domaine privé*, governed by private law. Some property can only fall into the *domaine public* however, for example national roads, airports, ports and harbours, etc., because there is no equivalent in the *domaine privé*. This method of classification is not incompatible with the general notion of *patrimoine*, because it is possible to refer to property which falls into the *patrimoine national*, which is administered by the juristic or legal persons of public law, either within the public domain or within the private domain—for example national forests and ports and harbours. An extension of this, and increasingly relevant today, is *patrimoine commun de l'humanité*, for example the environment in a global sense.

Another way of classifying property is according to its economic significance for consumers. Following this model, things can be divided into those which are consumable or non-consumable—*chose consomptible/non-consomptible*. In this model the presumptive category of the thing is determined by its intended destination. Things which are destined for the market place are *choses consomptibles*. Consequently a house or family car is not a consumable, even if intended for use, and even if it depreciates over time. The significance of this distinction is that non-consumables attract a wider range of property rights and obligations, for example a person in possession of such property may be liable to account for it, must preserve it, and return it to the original owner. A typical example is in the case of a usufruct over a non-consumable, such as a house. The usufructary must return the property in its original condition, whereas if the usufruct is over a consumable it is regarded only as a quasi-usufruct, and the usufructary only has the obligation to return property of the same quality and quantity, or its monetary equivalent.

A further alternative classification model is to divide things into *fongibles* and *non-fongibles*. The former are those things the nature of which is not immediately apparent from their outward appearance, the appearance usually being symbolic. Typical of these are negotiable instruments such as bank notes or bills of lading. *Non-fongibles*, on the other hand, are things the identity of which is immediately apparent and specific to the thing itself. The distinction is significant in a number of

[16] Disputes concerning such property may come before different courts being matters for *droit administratif* rather than civil law.

ways. For example, if there is an agreement to transfer property this is generally based on the premise that the object of the agreeement is certain. If, however, the object of the transfer is only certain as to quality and quantity but not individual identity, then the object of the agreement only becomes certain on delivery or once some identification of the object has been made. This in turn can affect the rights and obligations of the parties to the contract. The distinction is also important in terms of the formalities and legal rules surrounding transfer.

The most common form of classification is according to whether things are movable or immovable (*meubles/immeubles*). This category is extensive, in as much as it can encompass all rights exercised over property and also rights which are real or personal. It also includes intellectual property rights which are considered as movable.

The distinction originated from Roman law, but has acquired greater importance in French law than it ever had in ancient law. During the period of *Ançien droit* (that is before the Napoleonic Code), the distinction between movables and immovables reflected the economic value of things—the greatest value in a primarily agricultural economy being attached to immovables, movables were much less important. Indeed this historical legacy is still evident in the *doctrine* and *jurisprudence* which informs the interpretation and application of the distinction between the two categories. The social and political organisation of the country re-enforced this standard of values. Movables and immovables were subject to different rules, for example when alienated, under matrimonial regimes, and according to succession law.

The classification, which was founded on the physical characteristics of a thing, was based on notions of value. Eventually, the classification was extended to include not only things but rights themselves. For example, certain incorporeal rights became included in the category of immovable property because of their value (for example certain rents, and titles to offices). The distinction remains important because immovables may be the object of certain real rights which do not apply to movables. Different rules regarding possession and acquisition by prescription apply. Formalities for the transfer of ownership are different—any alienation of real rights in immovable property requires publicity. The two may be treated differently in certain matrimonial property regimes. Movable property is generally more freely alienable than immovable in the case of minors, or those with imperfect capacity. The applicable legal rules may be different either because of the physical nature of the thing or because of its value as property.

This distinction between movables and immovables is recognised in the Civil Code. Article 516 states that all things are either movable or immovable.

(B) IMMOVABLES

Under Article 517 C. *Civ.*, immovables are classified into four categories: immovable by nature; immovable by destination; immovable by their object; immovable by declaration.

(1) Immovable by nature

Things which are immovable by nature include land[17]—including all crops,[18] trees and fruit thereon—as long as it is not cut or gathered,[19] and buildings—including any attachments which complete the building (for example water pipes, lifts, etc.[20]).

(2) Immovable by destination

Things which are immovable by destination are things which are physically movable but which by legal fiction are deemed to form part of an immovable. This happens if two conditions are fulfilled: (1) both the immovable and the movable must belong to the same owner; and (2) there must be a relation of "destination". This means that the owner has placed the movable on or in the immovable for the service and exploitation of the property (Art. 524 C. *Civ.*), for example horses, cattle and farm machinery are immovable by destination when placed on a farm,[21] industrial machinery is immovable by destination when placed in a factory, etc. Thus things which are immovable by destination include anything which is exploited for the purpose of the location—for example, beehives, pigeons, blacksmith's tools, agricultural implements. Such things must be indispensable and directly relevant to the

---

[17] See Arts. 518–526 C. *Civ.*

[18] Where immovable property is pledged as security, its value will depreciate once the crop is cut, therefore an additional indemnity will be required to ensure that the loan is secured for its full value. This indemnity can be secured against the harvest itself: Decision of the *T.G.I.* Bordeaux, June 19, 1986.

[19] Crops may, therefore, become movable once cut or gathered, while part of the same crop may still be immovable. The sale of a standing crop has been deemed to be the sale of a movable by anticipation: *T.G.I.* Montpellier, June 23, 1927.

[20] Examples of things which are immovable by nature include a cold chamber constructed of bricks and stones and incorporated into the soil (decision of the Court of Angers, December 1, 1964); electricity pylons (*Cass. Civ.* May 4, 1937); wind or water mills (Art. 519 C. *Civ.*). However, a thing which attaches to the soil by its own weight, or which can easily be removed, is not an immovable by nature.

[21] If animals are delivered to a non-farmer they are not considered to be immovable, but movable.

exploitation or enterprise involved, for example essential to production. If they are easily replaced or substituted then they may fail the test.[22]

Although it appears that Article 524 only refers to things which are immovable by destination in the context of agricultural or commercial exploitation, the courts have held that this category extends to commercial enterprises, for example office premises where things are placed in the office for the purposes related to the business.[23] It should be noted, however, that whatever the context, an object which is normally regarded as movable can only become immovable by destination if it is incorporated by the owner himself.[24]

Generally if a thing is to be deemed to be immovable as a result of intention, it will have to become attached so that it is literally immovable with the intention that it is to remain.[25]

(3) Immovable by their object

Some things may be immovable if they are so closely connected with an immovable as to be inseparable (Article 526 C. *Civ.*). These include rights which apply to immovable property, for example real rights less than ownership such as usufructs and servitudes, and rights of action which are directed at vindication of title to an immovable, for example a right of action to rescind a contract for the sale of land, or claims for compensation for damage done to buildings during the war.[26]

(C) MOVABLES

Movables are all *biens* which are not included in the categories of immovables.[27] They may be movable either according to their nature or as determined by law. This category also includes movables by anticipation. These are immovables by nature, which are destined in the near future to become movables by being separated from the land, for example crops, wood for cutting, stone in a quarry.

Movables which are determined by law are rights or actions which,

[22] As happened when considering standard kitchen equipment (*Cass. Civ.* June 8, 1982) or a stock of brandy intended for sale (*Cass. Civ.* December 1, 1976).

[23] *Cass. Civ.* December 29, 1984.

[24] *Cass. Civ.* March 23, 1960.

[25] See Art. 525 C. *Civ. E.g.* statues placed in a niche have been deemed to have become immovable, similarly windows, although both could be detached fairly easily.

[26] Act of October 28, 1946. See also a decision of *Cass. Civ.* of July 10, 1968.

[27] See Arts. 527–536 C. *Civ.*

even if they relate to immovables, are transferable—for example in the course of commercial or industrial transactions.[28]

As in the case of immovable property, things may move from one category to the other. For example the material from a demolished building is regarded as movable, as is that which has been assembled to construct a new building. Because of this fluidity, it may be important to establish which category a thing falls in. For instance, when purchasing a home it is important to distinguish which movables are *meubles meublant*—that is furniture and items which are not deemed to be fittings and fixtures—and which are not.[29]

(D) SIGNIFICANCE OF CLASSIFICATION

The distinction between movables and immovables is important for a number of reasons. First, possession of movables can amount to title, whereas this will not occur so easily with immovables, although titles can be acquired by unchallenged possession over a period of time. Under Article 2279 C. *Civ*. possession of a movable creates a presumption of title. Thus a person who acquires a movable in good faith from one who is not the owner may nevertheless become the owner, while bona fide possession of immovable property—such as a house—acquired from a non-owner, will not confer ownership, largely because of the compulsory publicity which surrounds rights to such property. While the purchaser of a movable has no way of knowing that the transferor in possession was not the owner, the purchaser of immovable property can ascertain whether the transferor has title by consulting the register. Moreover, if there is a dispute, in the latter case the court where the property is situated has jurisdiction to determine the matter.

Although the traditional approach of distinguishing property on the grounds of value has ceased to be the prime consideration, owing to rapid changes in the economic value of things, the distinction is still relevant when considering the legal rules applicable to transactions affecting property. As indicated, transactions affecting immovables have to be accompanied by greater publicity. Generally, only immovable property can be the subject of a mortgage. The sale of immovable property to execute a debt is more complex than execution of a debt secured against movable property, etc. There are also some remedies and actions which

---

[28] See Arts. 529–530 C. *Civ*. *E.g*. according to a decision of the Court of Poitiers of May 21, 1906, money owing for the sale of immovable property is movable.

[29] However, it should be noted that the sale or gift of a house which is stated to be inclusive of all its contents would include furniture but exclude money, debts or other rights pertaining to the property (Art. 536 C. *Civ*.).

are only applicable in the case of immovables. For example *lésion*[30] is available to rescind the sale of immovable property where it has been sold at an unrealistic price, whereas it is not generally available in the case of movables.

The significance of the classification in property in French law lies not only in the way this may determine the rules which regulate transactions relating to that property, but also in the determination of who is entitled to that property. A prime illustration of this can be found in the law concerning matrimonial property regimes. Indeed there is a strong relationship between the law of property and family law. Much property law has evolved within the context of family law—for example the law of succession and marriage.[31]

(E) CLASSIFICATION OF MATRIMONIAL PROPERTY

All matrimonial regimes—the purpose of which are to govern the allocatioin of property between spouses—have the following characteristics: (1) the spouses' property is divided into categories; (2) a system of powers is established; (3) the rights of creditors against the property of a spouse who is not party to the debt is regulated.

French law recognises a number of different possible matrimonial regimes,[32] but all of these consist of a combination of fundamental rules—*le régime matrimonial primaire*—and specific rules pertaining to each particular regime. The most common matrimonial regime is that known as the statutory regime of the *communauté réduite aux acquêts*.[33] Under this regime there are three funds into which all property must fall: the fund of the husband, which consists of his separate property; that of the wife, which is her separate property; and that of the community.[34]

---

[30] See Chapter One, Topic One, above.

[31] Historically this was certainly the case. In more recent times it has become important to also consider public interests, and to adopt a more pluridiscipline approach to an understanding of property law; see A. Weill, F. Terré, P. Simler *Droit Civil* (Dalloz, Paris, 3rd ed. 1985) p. 2.

[32] There is the legal or statutory regime—*le régime de séparation de biens*; total community—*la communauté universelle*; and a dotal regime—*le régime dotal*. It is also possible for spouses to draw up their own regime by contract, provided they do not attempt to exclude any of the elements of the primary regime.

[33] Introduced by an Act of July 13, 1965 and subsequently modified as far as the management powers of the spouses are concerned by an Act of December 23, 1985.

[34] Prior to this reform, the applicable statutory regime—which governed most marriages unless the spouses specifically chose otherwise—depended even more on the classification of property, because only movables and acquisitions during the marriage fell into the community fund. Immovables brought into the marriage or property acquired by way of gift or inheritance remained separate.

This last is particularly important, because each spouse is entitled to half of the property acquired during the marriage, regardless of contribution. Therefore, when the marriage ends—either by death of one of the spouses or by divorce—an itinerary of this fund is drawn up and divided.[35]

In order to decide which property falls into which fund, certain formulae have emerged. First, property may be classified according to its origins. Therefore, any property brought to the marriage by either spouse is deemed to be the separate property of that spouse, whether that property is movable or immovable. Within the same category is any property acquired gratuitously by inheritance or gift during the marriage, unless there is an express indication that it is to fall into the community, or it is given to the spouses jointly, in which case there is a rebuttable presumption that it falls into the community.

As a general principle, property which is acquired onerously falls into the community. However, this general principle is subject to a number of exceptions and modifications. According to the text of Article 1401 al. 1, C. *Civ.* the community consists of acquisitions made by the spouses—either together or separately—during the marriage, as a result of their individual efforts or savings made from the income and produce of their separate property. Thus, any property bought with salary or with income generated from other sources is deemed to fall into the community. However, there is a problem concerning earnings from professional activities prior to this being used to purchase other things. This problem stems from a conflict of classification based on different criteria. Article 1401, which is concerned with the division of property into separate and community funds, indicates that professional earnings fall into the common fund. Article 223, which is primarily concerned with the respective powers of spouses, however, suggests that as each spouse is free to dispose of his or her earnings without reference to the other, such property as wages or salary falls into the separate fund.[36]

There are some exceptions to the general principles which allow acquisitions to fall outside the community,[37] or alternatively a different classification criteria is applied. This alternative approach is to classify

[35] On termination by death this must be done before the deceased's estate can be dealt with, as only part of the community fund will fall into that estate. On divorce the principle of equal division may be modified by court order, or by an agreement between the spouses which is approved by the court.

[36] In a decision of 1978, the Court of Cassation ruled in favour of the interpretation of Art. 1401, but this may no longer be good law in as much as the legal matrimonial regime—particularly the powers of spouses—has changed since then (*Cass. Civ.* February 8, 1978). Similar problems of classification have arisen with revenue produced from separate property (see the decision of the Paris *T.G.I.* of October 19, 1988.

[37] See Arts. 1405–1408. C. *Civ.*

things according to their nature. Thus things which are personal in nature—such as heirlooms, compensation payments for injury, invalidity pensions, artistic or literary works, etc.—will be deemed to be separate property. So will things which are regarded as being essential to the exercise of a trade or profession, unless this is a joint enterprise.[38] However, changing the classification criteria does not provide an infallible solution. Prior to legal reform in 1965, it was considered that some things might have two classifications; one based on the right to the thing itself (*le titre*), and one based on its value. For example, if a spouse participates in a professional partnership, his or her shares are separate but the capital value falls into the community. Therefore, on dissolution of the matrimonial regime, while the right to the share remains personal and separate, the value of that share must be taken into account in assessing the value of the community fund. The Act of July 13, 1965—which changed the statutory matrimonial regime—made no distinction between title and value. Consequently there is some uncertainty as to whether this distinction is still valid.[39]

(F) CLASSIFICATION OF PROPERTY AND SUCCESSION

The classification of property is also significant in the context of succession.[40] This is because although in principle a person's *patrimoine* is personal, and logically ceases to exist at his death,[41] following Roman law, the person of the deceased continues to exist—for legal purposes—in his *l'héritier* (heir).[42] Thus, the heir takes on both the assets and debts of the deceased.[43] This can be disastrous both for the heir and for creditors, who may find their claims against the deceased competing

---

[38] This will be so even if those things are themselves immovable, for example a doctor's surgery.

[39] It seems that some things may still fall into a mixed category, see, *e.g.* decisions of the Court of Cassation (Civ.) of December 8, 1987 and July 9, 1991.

[40] Under French succession law the devolution of the deceased estate is immediate, there is no interim period during which the executor or administrator pays off the debts of the deceased and then distributes the remaining estate.

[41] It seems that some *extra-patrimonial* interest will also continue, *e.g.* rights to privacy, and expressions of the deceased's wishes concerning minor children, his corpse and his property.

[42] If there is a plurality of heirs then they are liable proportionately (Art. 1220 C. *Civ.*), unless the debt is indivisible—*e.g.* a mortgage over a building, or the deceased has imposed the obligation exclusively on one of them, or there is an imbalance between co-owners, or the number of heirs is uncertain.

[43] Some debts of a personal nature are extinguished on death, *e.g.* contracts for personal performance.

with existing claims of the other creditors of the heir.[44] This is because the *patrimoine* of the deceased becomes part of that of the heir, and so two masses become merged. The heir, if he accepts the inheritance, therefore becomes personally liable for the deceased's debts. The significance of this is that an heir has a number of choices. He may simply accept the inheritance—*l'acceptation pure et simple*—in which case his rights and *patrimoine* are retrospectively merged with those of the deceased from the moment at which the succession opened, on the death of the deceased,[45] or he may choose to only inherit if he can have the benefit of an inventory—*sous bénéfice d'inventaire*—whereby he can see the extent to which the *actif* outweighs the *passif* before deciding. Also under this option, the two funds remain separate.[46] If this option is chosen, then the right must be exercised within three months and a decision on the basis of the inventory made within 40 days. At the same time the creditors can request a separation of the two *patrimoines*, in order to have a preferred claim before the personal creditors of the heir.

An understanding of the close relationship between *biens*, *choses*, and *droits* helps to explain why aspects of property law are scattered throughout the Civil Code.[47] It is also important to realise that the study of principal real rights is not exactly the same as the study of property—*biens*—although the two become merged if the term *biens* is understood to mean not just the things themselves but the rights relating to these.[48]

---

[44] Heir(s) include those who inherit on intestacy under the legal devolution of the estate and those who receive the residuary estate under testate succession, but not those who receive specific legacies under a will. However, because French law recognises reserved shares for surviving next-of-kin, a person can only ever dispose of part of their estate by will, that part depending on the number of reserved shares, and hence the size of the reserved portion.

[45] See Art. 777 C. *Civ*. This can be accomplished with relatively little formality (Arts. 778–800 C. *Civ*.). Once made it is irrevocable except for limited circumstances involving fraud or *lésion*.

[46] This is accompanied by considerably more formality because of the effect on third parties (Arts. 793 and 794 C. *Civ*.). It may of course be the case that an heir refuses to accept the inheritance at all and renounces any right.

[47] E.g. in family law and succession, the law relating to prescription, etc., but also rights of credit—which clearly creates an overlap with the law of obligations.

[48] Usually it is these, rather than the thing itself, which are of greatest value. However the Civil Code frequently uses the terms interchangeably which can be confusing.

TOPIC TWO
INTERESTS OTHER THAN OWNERSHIP: SERVITUDES AND USUFRUCTS

In certain situations the absolute and exclusive right of ownership is modified in respect of other persons. This may happen in the case of co-owners; the rights of neighbours; the rights of life-tenants. Generally any diminution of the absolute rights of ownership will be temporary. The exception is in the case of servitudes, which may be perpetual, but which may only have as their object the enhancement of land and may not substantially interfere with the owner's rights of enjoyment.

(A) SERVITUDES

Servitudes are principal real rights. Their purpose and function is to enhance the use and enjoyment of land. As such they may not confer simply personal benefit on the occupier of land. A servitude is defined in Article 637 C. *Civ.* as a charge imposed on an estate for the use and enjoyment of another estate.[49] As with the English law of easements, the exercise and existence of a servitude requires two parcels of land—*fonds de terre*—one of which must be dominant and one servient.[50] Where land is subdivided there cannot be a servitude,[51] nor where the two *fonds* are in the hands of the same person. The servitude must benefit the dominant *fond*, for example a right of way over neighbouring land, or a right to pipe water, although the two plots need not actually be adjacent. The number and variety of possible servitudes is considerable, the governing criterion for their creation being that they must be necessary or useful to the land. The essential element here is the relation between the two parcels of land. It is for this reason that servitudes are classified as real rights not personal rights. They cannot be created simply by agreement between two parties. The fact that the owner of the dominant land benefits while the owner of the servient land must bear the burden is incidental to their being the owners of the two *fonds*. It is unimportant that the identities of

---

[49] The term used is *héritage*. This incorporates both the right itself and the tenements over which it is exercised—*une servitude est une charge imposée sur un héritage pour l'usage et l'utilité d'un héritage appartenant à un autre propriétaire*.

[50] While it is possible to have two separate *fonds* in the case of landlord and tenant, it is not possible in the case of co-ownership—*copropriété*—where one plot is divided into a number of units. There cannot be a servitude over the common parts for the benefit of the different units as there is not the necessary duality of necessary *fonds* for a servitude (*Cass. Civ.* January 11, 1989). Any use of the common parts will therefore have to be agreed by contract conferring personal rights.

[51] Paris, *T.G.I.* June 4, 1970.

the two owners may change. Servitudes pass to the transferees of the land.

Servitudes are created either by a legal document—contract, will or notarial deed—or by the law itself, or as a natural consequence of the locality of the land. An example of the latter case is where lower land has the right to receive water which has accumulated naturally without human intervention, from higher land.[52] Similarly, adjoining neighbours have the obligation to jointly maintain boundaries. Where servitudes are created by law, the servitude is referred to as *servitude légale*. Servitudes cannot be created simply by tolerance between neighbours.[53]

It follows that this real right is necessarily immovable and perpetual unless the owners of the two tenaments agree to suppress the servitude.[54]

Besides those interests created for private benefit, Articles 649 and 650 C. *Civ.* provide for the creation of servitudes for public or community benefit.[55] Among the most important of these are those arising in the context of urban development plans, and include servitudes for the provision of services and utilities, for example gas, water, electricity. These servitudes have an administrative character. Servitudes created for public benefit are distinguishable from private ones, because first, they do not require a dominant tenement, and secondly, they frequently restrict the owner of the servient tenement from certain operations on his land, whereas private servitudes are either obligations to refrain from interference—*non faciendo*—or to tolerate or allow the doing of something—*in patiendo*.

---

[52] Arts. 640–645 C. *Civ.*, *e.g.* streams, rivers or natural run-off. The owner of the higher land cannot interfere with this flow of water, *e.g.* by damming a stream. The Article only applies to rain water or flowing water which is sufficiently strong to amount to a water-course. It does not include springs and natural fountains. Failure to utilise this servitude will not lead to its extinction, although interference by the servient tenement persisting for a period of 30 years may free the servient tenement from the obligation.

[53] The case law has consistently refused to allow the creation of servitudes on this ground. *E.g.* the tolerance of a landlord to allow the tenant of a *café-bar* to sell food did not amount to the right to exploit the property as a restaurant (Paris, *T.G.I.* March 13, 1990).

[54] This, of course, can only be done in the case of servitudes created by will in the first place and not in the case of *servitudes légales*.

[55] It is also possible to have collective, communal servitudes, *e.g.* the right to hunt, rights of grazing and pasturage, and acorn collecting owned by the *commune* or village.

(B) USUFRUCT

(1) Introduction

Although French law has no division of rights equivalent to the common law notion of legal and equitable rights over property, ownership itself consists of three elements: *fructus*, that is the right of enjoyment, the right to keep and take the fruits of a thing; *abusus*, that is the right to use the thing, including consume it or destroy it, alienate it or change it; and *usus*, that is the right to use as owner within the confines of the law.

French law recognises the right of a person, other than the owner, to enjoy things in the same manner as the owner but subject to the obligation to conserve the substance of the thing.[56] The *usufruitier* (usufructary), therefore, has all the prerogatives in practice of the owner, but in law lacks the right to alienate or destroy the property which the real owner has. The powers of the usufructary are, therefore, counterbalanced by the constraints imposed on him.

A usufruct may be created over movables and immovables and is the most extensive of all real rights.[57] A usufruct is essentially a personal right in as much as it is granted to an identifiable individual and ceases with their death or an agreed earlier period, but it is regarded as a real right in law enforceable against third parties who try and interfere with the usufruct. Unless the usufruct is of a house (usage and habitation), it may be assigned, but only for the same length of time as the original grant.

Usufruct is therefore a modification on the absolute character of the right of ownership. It is always temporary and not absolute, although the absolute owner's rights may be suspended during the period of usufruct, for example the absolute owner may not have rights of occupation until the usufructuary surrenders his interest (similar to a life tenant or a licencee).

(2) The nature of usufruct

There is some debate as to whether usufruct is a real or personal right. The reason for this is partly historical. For a long time usufruct was regarded as a personal servitude, that is a real right conferring personal benefit. This idea was abandoned in the Napoleonic Code however,

[56] See Art. 587 C. *Civ*.

[57] See Art. 581 C. *Civ*. In the case of movables, it is notable that usufruct is the only real right which can be conferred over such property. Usufruct can also be conferred over incorporeal property—such as rights—as well as corporeal.

which indicated that a servitude could not include rights and obligations which were personal.[58] The Code adopted, almost literally, the Roman definition of usufruct. The Civil Code and academic writers generally indicate that it is a real right, stemming from ownership. However, whereas ownership is an absolute right, usufruct consists of a number of rights and obligations. The object of the usufruct is a material thing, movable or immovable, belonging to another who is the owner. The usufructary enjoys the two rights of *usus* and *fructus* but lacks *abusus*. He may use the property—provided he does not modify its composition and preserves its integrity—and he may reap the fruits or benefits of that property.[59]

In this respect it should be noted that the usufruct affects the global composition of the property rather than individual component parts. Thus, where there is a usufruct over a herd of cattle, the usufructary must preserve the integrity of the herd, and replace animals which perish. He may, however, have a certain freedom to dispose of individual animals—the component parts. His obligation to restore the property to its owner in the state in which he received it, relates to equivalence rather than identicality. His obligations is, therefore, to conduct himself as the owner would, that is to enjoy and manage the property without exploiting it in such a way as to destroy it entirely.

The debate as to whether usufruct is a real or personal right is complicated by the fact that where the usufruct has the right to civil fruits, such as rents, annual charges, interest on arrears, etc., these are essentially personal rights. They are moreover rights over incorporeal, non-physical property. This dilemma may be resolved by bearing in mind that the object of a right should not be confused with the right itself. All things have two aspects, their composition—*l'universalité*—and the rights which attach to the thing. Both these aspects may be regarded as real rights as far as the law provides. Thus a real right is not a fragment of the object over which the right is exercised but the power that the holder of the right has over the object.[60]

Although servitudes are perpetual, usufruct is extinguished by the death of the usufructary. It is therefore only a life interest.[61] Shorter

---

[58] See Art. 686 C. *Civ*. Even before this the glossators and post-glossators had suggested that the right to enjoy property was one aspect of a complex of rights relating to things.

[59] These may be the natural fruits—such as harvest—or industrial products or civil fruits—such as rent—(Arts. 582–586 C. *Civ*.). If the fruits are consumable and cannot be used without being consumed, then the usufruct may still benefit from them but must restore at the termination of the period of usufruct similar produce or their equivalent value, estimated at the date of restitution (Art. 587).

[60] See the discussion by Frédéric Zenati *Les biens* (P.U.F., Paris, 1st ed., 1988) p. 253–255.

[61] However it does seem possible for an owner to create a second and subsequent usufruct,

usufructs of a definite period may be established by contract or will,[62] or even temporary usufructs of an indefinite period—although these are relatively rare. If the usufructary has donated or sold his right of usufruct, then any third party only obtains the benefit of the usufruct for the life of the original grantee. It follows that heirs will never inherit a usufruct.

During the period of the usufruct the rights of the owner are considerably diminished. Indeed he is described as a *nu-propriétaire* holding, as he does, bare title to the property without any of the advantages of ownership. The right of bare ownership can itself be alienated by sale or donation and, because it is a real and perpetual right, be inherited by the heirs of the bare owner, but, of course, its economic value may be limited, particularly if the usufruct has only just been created.[63] Such a sale will not affet the rights of the usufructary and, indeed, the purchaser takes subject to these rights. The owner only regains the rights of *plein propriétaire* once the usufruct ends.

The utility of usufruct from the perspective of the owner is limited. Although he retains the legal shell of absolute ownership, in practice he is handicapped in his exercise of the rights of owner. At the same time, while the usufructary has the obligation to preserve the property, the arrangement is gratuitous rather than onerous, in as much as unlike, for example a landlord, the owner receives no immediate economic advantage unless the property produces a surplus.

Essentially, usufruct is a device to facilitate the administration of property for the benefit of another. At one time it was particularly useful for dealing with the property of those who were deemed legally or factually incapable of administering their own *patrimoine*. Today it is used more to provide for the surviving spouse, while at the same time accommodating the rights of heirs, primarily descendant children.

(3) Establishing a usufruct

Usufruct may be created by law, or by intention—for example by will or contract. It may also be created by an order of court or as a result of possession.

---

which will take place on the expiry of the first one. Thus, where an owner sells property already subject to a usufruct, he may sell it subject to a second subsequent usufruct for himself: *Cass. Civ.* 3.7.1991.

62 According to Art. 619 C. *Civ*. usufructs granted to legal persons (*personnes morales*) such as companies, may not exceed 30 years. An exception, however, applies in the case of usufructs granted to the inhabitants of a *commune* who may be granted the usufruct of pastures and woods in perpetuity.

63 If the usufructary is very old or in poor health, on the other hand, the economic value may be considerably more because the end of the usufruct is in sight.

(a) *Usufruit volontaire*

In the case of *usufruit volontaire*, the owner of the property creates the usufruct. In such a case the usufruct is rarely onerous. It is possible for this form of intentional usufruct to take several forms. It may be granted to one or several persons, or the grantor may himself become usufructary on alienating the property—that is with a reservation of usufruct. Alternatively the owner may alienate the property to one person while at the same time conferring a usufruct on someone else. If the usufruct is created over immovable property, then it must comply with the necessary publicity in order to be enforceable against a third party.

(b) *Usufruit légal*

If a married person dies intestate, the rights of inheritance of the surviving spouse are defined by law. This provision includes a usufruct over a portion of the estate of the deceased. A legal usufruct may also arise in the case of the administration of the property of minors, for example where a minor has property, the parents will have a usufruct over it until the minor reaches the age of 16. Until this time the mother and father may legally enjoy the income and profits generated by that property.

(c) *Usufruit judiciaire*

Usufruct imposed by a court of law existed in Roman law. This was re-introduced into French law under the law relating to divorce in 1975.[64] Under this Act, on divorce or judicial separation, one spouse can be ordered to pay the other a compensatory sum and to make financial provisions. To this end a judge can order that the recipient spouse have a usufruct of certain property of the other.

(d) Possession

In line with the general principle that possession confers a rebuttable presumption of ownership, usufruct over a movable may be acquired by possession in good faith, despite of any flaw in title. With immovables the usufructary possessor may acquire a valid claim by prescription over a period of ten to 20 years. Even where the usufructary is in bad faith, a usufruct by prescription may be acquired after 30 years.

---

[64] Act of July 11, 1975.

(4) Ending the usufruct

The usufruct may end in a number of ways, the most usual being the death of the usufructuary.[65] It is, however, also possible for the usufruct to end by the merger of the usufructary and the bare-owner—for example by simultaneous sale to the same purchaser; by the expiration of the fixed period if there is one, provided this is before the death of the usufructuary; by the loss or destruction of the object of the usufruct[66]; or by non-usage over a period of 30 years. If the usufruct is granted to a legal person, rather than a physical person, it will terminate after 30 years. Usufruct may also cease if the usufructuary abuses his position, for example by failing to preserve the property. In such a case the creditors of the usufructuary may intervene to seek to have the property, against which their debts are secured, preserved.

The courts in such instances may either order the usufruct to cease absolutely; or allow the owner to reclaim the property subject to the condition that he pays the usufructuary a determined annual sum[67]; or order the usufruct to end and order the usufructuary to pay damages to the owner; or reduce the extent of the usufruct so that creditors of the usufructary will still have something to claim against but at the same time there is less danger that all the property will be lost through the maladministration of the usufructuary.

(5) The relationship between usufructuary and owner

The relationship between the *usufruitier* and the *nu-propiétaire* is one of mutual rights and obligations. The usufructuary must be put in possession of the property so as to be able to exercise his rights of enjoyment. To this end he can use a real action against the owner deriving from the real right of usufruct itself. This entitles the usufructuary to proceed against the owner to prevent or restrain the latter from doing anything to interfere with the right of usufruct.[68] If there is a formal declaration of

---

[65] According to Art. 617 C. *Civ*. this may be the natural death of the usufructuary or the civil death, but this latter concept was abolished in 1854. If there are a number of usufructuaries, then it is the death of the last surviving usufructary which ends the usufruct.

[66] If only part of the property is destroyed, then the usufruct continues over the remaining part (Art. 623 C. *Civ*.). If the usufruct is over a building and the building is destroyed, the usufructary does not have the right to use either the ground or the building materials (Art. 624 C. *Civ*.)

[67] If, of course, the devaluation or dilapidation of the property is due to the owner's own negligence, then he cannot seek this remedy.

[68] See Art. 599-1 C. *Civ*. This action is called an *action confessoire*. The obligation on the

usufruct, then the usufructuary may also rely on this to base an action. If the usufruct has been created as part of an agreement—for example at the same time as alienation—the usufructuary may also have a personal action against the owner. It should be noted, however, that the usufructuary must accept the property in the state in which he finds it at the start of the usufruct.

Because the property subject to the usufruct may deteriorate over time, the usufructuary must draw up a description of any immovables and an inventory of any movables when he enters into possession. The usufructuary bears the cost of this, despite the fact that it is the owner who must, at the end of the usufruct, establish what the initial state of the property was.[69] However, this measure does give the usufructuary some protection against a claim at the end of the usufruct that he has failed in his obligation to preserve the property.

As a precaution against such an eventuality, the owner may require an indemnity or *caution* from the usufructuary as an insurance.[70] This requirement only applies in certain types of commercial usufructs and will not arise in a *usufruit légal* or where it seems unnecessary—for example where the usufructuary is the previous owner. If the usufructuary abuses his position or is declared insolvent, then the owner may seek the assistance of the court in implementing any measures of conservation and call in the guarantee.

From the point of view of the usufructuary, usufruct has two dimensions. It creates rights and obligations between the usufructuary and the owner, and it also confers a real right on the usufructuary, deriving from the actual usufruct itself.

The main characteristic of the institution of usufruct is that it gives the usufructuary the right to use the thing, together with any accessories attaching to it—for example a servitude attaching to land. The only restrictions imposed on the usufructuary are that he may not exercise the right of *abusus*. He must act as a *bon père de famille*, that is as a good owner would act with moderation and care; and he must utilise the property as if he were owner—in particular the methods of exploitation of the owner must be respected.[71]

The usufructuary's rights to any fruits deriving from the property relates

---

part of the *nu-propriétaire* is essentially passive, although active enforcement measures may be taken against him.

[69] In fact, apart from preventing him from exercising his rights of enjoyment over the property until this task is done, the owner has very little sanction over this formality.

[70] This may be secured against the usufructuary's interest and therefore provide a real surety similar to a mortgage.

[71] This may restrict any entrepreneurial activities.

to his possession of the property. Thus, once the usufruct ends, the usufructuary has no right to the fruits, even if he planted them.[72]

The value of the usufructuary to the owner, is that the former administers the property to maximise its utility. It is this role which imposes on the usufructuary the obligation to conserve and preserve the property—for example to maintain buildings.[73] This obligation to administer the property entitles a usufructuary of immovables to either use them personally or to rent them out or use them as security, although in certain cases the consent of the owner will be required—for example commercial premises.

Because usufruct confers a real right on the usufructuary, he can oppose the action of a third party seeking to oust him. As usufructuary he has the right to revindicate his property. He also has a right to compensation if the property is expropriated for public use.

Like any property the usufruct can be alienated, and so the usufructuary can sell or give his usufruct to another, but because it is only for his life he cannot leave it to another on death. Similarly the usufruct may be seised by creditors as an object of credit.

During the usufruct the *nu-propriétaire* must not disturb the usufructuary in his possession or interfere with any of the latter's rights.[74] This principle creates some conflict in as much as because the owner is deriving no profit from the property, it follows that he should not have to bear the costs of any expenses relating to it. However, the property itself is the source of these charges, not the enjoyment—*la jouissance*—conferred on the usufructuary. Moreover, the owner has a vested interest in the long-term conservation of the property. Consequently major expenses for repairs, etc., rest with the owner.

As the owner the *nu-propriétaire* loses none of his rights of action stemming from ownership. He may, therefore, rely on the right to revindicate the property, take steps to defeat or contest a servitude and exercise a range of possessory actions. Above all he retains the right to alienate the property or abandon it.

---

[72] An exception may be in the case of civil fruits, such as rents, which may only be payable periodically, in which case the usufructuary will be entitled to a proportion if these are paid after the date on which the usufruct ends. Essentially the usufructuary is entitled to any fruits which he perceives or becomes aware of because he is in possession.

[73] The usufructuary will be responsible for day-to-day maintenance, but the owner will be responsible for capital maintenance.

[74] See Art. 599-1 C. *Civ*.

(6) The relevance of usufruct

One of the most important applications of the device of usufruct is found in the law of succession. This is an example of usufruct created by operation of law, rather than grant or prescription.

Where a deceased leaves a surviving spouse and issue, the survivor is granted a usufruct. The extent of the property to which this applies depends on the number of successors the deceased left. If the deceased left natural or legitimate descendants, the surviving spouse is entitled to a usufruct over a quarter of the deceased's estate.[75] If the deceased only left collateral relatives, that is brothers and sisters, or ascendants, that is parents, then the survivor's usufruct is over a half of the estate. However, this usufruct only relates to certain property.[76] The difficulty with the application of usufruct in this context arises when there are debts. In principle it is the owner, not the usufructuary, who is responsible for the debts of any *patrimoine*. However, in the case of usufruct, the owner has no interest in managing the property so as to make it profitable. At the same time creditors may not wish to wait until the end of the usufruct to claim the payment of these debts from the assets of the estate. There are various approaches to this problem. The usufructuary may regard these payments in the same way as periodical charges on the property, and pay them out of the interest generated by the property. The owner, who inherits the property, may choose to inherit with the benefit of an inventory. Alternatively the owner may pay off the debts and then reclaim payment from the usufructuary.

The usufruct of the surviving parent presents an obstacle to the heirs, who must wait for the usufructuary to die before they can become full owners. The law provides a mechanism around this, whereby the heirs can offer the surviving spouse a *rente viagère* (annuity) instead of the usufruct.

(7) Limited usufruct

The Civil Code also provides for a more limited form of usufruct, *l'usage et habitation*.[77] This is established and extinguished in the same way as usufruct. The grantee has an obligation to treat the property

[75] If only adulterine children are left, then the surviving spouse is entitled to full ownership of a half of the estate (Art. 759 C. *Civ*.).

[76] This is referred to as the *assiette de l'usufruit*, and consists of existing property; *inter vivos* gifts which can be brought back into the estate for the purposes of calculation; property to which the deceased had a reversionary interest; legacies which have been rejected.

[77] See Arts. 625–636 C. *Civ*.

correctly and not to abuse the right. If such abuse occurs, the court may extinguish the right or convert it into a lesser right, for example an annual rent. If the grantee uses all the fruits of the property or occupies the entire building, then his position is virtually the same as a usufructuary and he must make the necessary reparations to the owner.[78]

Although these are classified as principal real rights, they are more limited in scope than usufruct. They are also distinguishable from servitudes.

While neither the law nor academic writing specifically limits these rights to immovables, they do not appear to arise in the case of movables. The holder of the right of use only has the right to exercise those rights which directly correspond to his personal and family needs.[79] Similarly, the person who has the right of residence has no more than that. In this sense these rights have a strictly personal character.[80]

Unlike a usufruct, they cannot be sold or alienated in any way to a third party, nor can they be claimed by creditors. Because of these limitations it is clear that such rights are not strictly speaking patrimonial rights in as much as they have no commercial value.[81] The property subject to such rights is however burdened by them and so any third party purchasing a house subject to such a grant or reservation—for example by the vendor in favour of himself over part of the property—takes subject to it.

(C) QUASI-USUFRUCT

Things which are consumable have no use other than their consumption.[82] The question, therefore, arises whether such things can be subject to the enjoyment of another. The solution seems to be that where the thing is one of a class, which is replaceable in kind, then there can be a usufruct over it, even though this conflicts in principle with the

---

[78] See Art. 635 C. *Civ*. In this respect, special laws apply in the case of woods and forests.

[79] This is applicable even if at the time of the grant the grantee was not married (Art. 632 C. *Civ*.). However, for the purposes of this Article, it is unclear whether a *concubin* (unmarried cohabitee) is included within the concept of family—a decision of 1956 in Besançon held not but this decision is probably no longer good law.

[80] Personal non-usage by the grantee will not, however, amount to a renunciation of the right.

[81] Certain rights of usage may, however, have some commercial value in themselves even though they cannot be alienated, for example the right to use a forest. Where the right is commercial in this sense, it may be acquired by prescription over a period of 30 years, whereas usage which is not commercial in nature cannot be acquired by prescription.

[82] Whether the object of the usufruct is deemed to be consumable or not is not simply a matter of its nature but depends on how it is regarded between the parties. It can therefore be consumable by agreement as much as by nature.

usufructuary's duty to conserve the thing. This implies that the usufructuary is assuming the owner's power of *abusus*, however the obligation to make restitution of the thing remains. In this context the owner is not disadvantaged and the usufructuary only becomes temporarily owner, during which time the *nu-propriétaire* is the usufructuary's creditor. This situation, which is provided for by the Code (Article 587) is called *quasi-usufruct*.

TOPIC THREE
MULTIPLICITY OF OWNERS: CO-OWNERSHIP AND MULTIPLE OWNERSHIP

Not only is it possible to have a number of inherents over property, it is also possible to have a number of owners. However, accommodating a plurality of owners within the framework of French property law creates a number of challenges, not least because of the concept of ownership.[83] A fundamental conceptual problem with a multiplicity of owners is the incompatibility between the rights of ownership over the whole and the rights of ownership over a part.[84] Moreover, ever since the French Revolution, the law has been reluctant to uphold arrangements whereby property is tied up for a long period,[85] or the absolute power of the owner to dispose of the property is fettered in any way. Nevertheless, French law does provide certain structures for situations where there is more than one owner of the same property, although initially the Code only envisaged short-term arrangements—five years under Article 815 C. *Civ.*—or temporary situations, such as pending the devolution of a deceased estate.[86]

Gradually the courts had to develop certain formulae to deal with the problems created by holding, on the one hand, that each co-owner had unrestricted rights over his or her share, and on the other, that the co-owned property could not be seized by creditors, or affected by the action of the owners without unanimous consent.[87] Notwithstanding the importance of this judicial law-making, co-ownership effectively lacked any legal status until an Act of December 31, 1976, subsequently amended by an Act of June 10, 1978,[88] although some statutory

---

[83] Roman law recognised the concept of *consortium*, which was communally owned property, but this was essentially indivisible. Similar concepts were to be found in Germanic and ancient French law. Subsequently the idea of a number of rights held by different individuals over the same property or thing existed, but each of these had separate *dominium*, the notion of a part or share was inconsistent with that of ownership.

[84] One solution has been to suggest that there is a distinction between the right over a thing and the thing itself; *l'indivision* relates to the right rather than the thing: see, *e.g.* Weill and Terré, *Droit Civil: Les Biens* (Dalloz, 3rd ed., 1985) p. 479.

[85] Lack of enthusiasm for this institution is evident from the wording of Art. 815 C. *Civ.* "*Nul ne peut être contraint à demeurer dans l'indivision et le partage peut être toujours provoqué*".

[86] Provision for *l'indivision successorale* was made in an Act of July 12, 1909, which favoured it for the preservation of family property.

[87] There is a huge amount of academic comment on this concept particularly dating from the early part of this century, and many divergent theories. For an indication of the *doctrine*: see F.L. Zénati, *Les Biens* (P.U.F. 1st ed., 1988) pp. 277–278.

[88] These Acts resulted from many years of legal pressure from the National Congress of

intervention had occurred in the case of agricultural holdings in order to prevent their uneconomical and socially disruptive fragmentation.[89] The 1976 Act confirmed much of the judicial development that had taken place and provided the procedural mechanisms for resolving disputes and solving crises. Gradually co-ownership has emerged as a positive legal structure which has a number of economic and social advantages, not least in the context of residential apartments—*la copropriété des immeubles bâtis*.

The two terms *indivision* and *copropriété* are in a primary sense synonymous. Both indicate the rights that a number of people have over one or several objects. However, whereas *copropriété* represents a form of ownership resulting from a plurality of title holders over a definite object, *indivision* is the creation of law which includes elements which are indivisible and those which are separate.[90] The distinction is more apparent than real however, and it appears that the different terms are usually largely to indicate different circumstances of multiple ownership. Thus, it is more common to find the term *copropriété* being used in situations where the law makes specific provision for co-owners, for example co-ownership of a building divided into flats. *Indivision* is used to apply to those situations of co-ownership where the co-ownership can be terminated by *partage* even if this is postponed to a distant date.[91]

(A) *L'Indivision*

In its very terms—*l'indivision* or *copropriété*—French law reflects the anomalies presented by a plurality of owners of the same thing. The object of the ownership remains undivided, but the institution of co-ownership is also presented as undivided—the co-owners share the same rights of ownership, which they exercise concurrently. At the same time the individual rights of each co-owner are not diminished. Although the possibility of division is there, it is to a certain extent

---

Notaries; the Law Reform Commission; and the Society for Legislative Studies: see A. Weill *et al.* (n. 83, above) p. 484, nn. 15–17.

[89] See the *décret-loi* of June 17, 1938 and the Act of December 19, 1961.

[90] An alternative distinction, which is criticised by A. Weill, F. Terré and P. Simler, *Droit Civil: Les Biens* (Dalloz, 3rd. ed., 1985) p. 480, is that *indivision* is imposed rather than chosen, and *copropriété* is voluntary. This distinction may be applicable in the case of *indivision* which arises by operation of law, *e.g.* among heirs, but *copropriété* can also arise in this way, *e.g.* between neighbours—*mitoyenneté*.

[91] The term *copropriété* is applied in the case of physical things, whereas *indivision* may be applied to all forms of property, including the co-ownership of rights such as usufruct.

hampered by the rights of non-division of the other owners, and the indivisible nature of the thing itself. Therefore, while each co-owner has full rights of ownership which may be exercised against third parties, as regards each other, these rights may be more restricted—for example because they require the consent of the other co-owners, or they have rights of pre-emption.[92] A distinction can be made between rights which can be exercised without disrupting the harmony of the co-ownership—for example the right of one party to revindicate the property confirms the strength of the co-ownership—and others which threaten this harmony. In part the problem is resolved in the context of *l'indivision* by the fact that co-ownership is regarded as being temporary or provisional, either because it can be terminated at the will of the parties or because the purpose for which it exists is of a temporary nature.[93] Indeed under the provisions of the Civil Code, no one can be constrained to remain in a co-ownership arrangement.[94] Each co-owner always has the right to demand the dissolution of the co-ownership. This right—*partage*—is fundamental to notions of property ownership and public order.[95]

Consequently co-ownership can be regarded as a rather precarious arrangement. This aspect has been modified somewhat by the Act of December 31, 1976 relating to the structures for co-ownership. It is also possible for a judge who is called on to resolve contentious co-ownership issues to modify the immediate effect of termination if circumstances permit.

There are three types of co-ownership in French law: ordinary co-ownership; ownership *en tontine*; and ownership *en indivision*. The reforms introduced by the Act of 1976, created two legal regimes. One, the *régime legal de l'indivision*, applied to all forms of co-ownership, whatever it origins and could not be excluded, the other, *organisation conventionnelle de l'indivision*, applied only to co-ownership entered into by agreement.[96]

[92] Conceptually this presents a conflict because what is owned individually cannot be owned in common—the two notions are contradictory.

[93] This is facilitated by the principle that even during the period of co-ownership, each co-owner has a notional *lot*—share—over which he or she exercises exclusive rights. When division is agreed, effectively each co-owner is renouncing any right to exercise rights of ownership over any portion other than his own. The effect of this is necessarily suspended during the co-ownership but comes into effect immediately the co-ownership ends.

[94] See Art. 815-1 C. *Civ*.

[95] In practice this is subject to some modification, *e.g.* walls between neighbours cannot be divided even if co-owned, although one co-owner may renounce his right or abandon it. Similarly, co-ownership of communal facilities in residential buildings, *e.g.* halls and stairways, cannot be divided.

[96] See Arts. 815–815(8) and Arts. 1873(1)–1873(18) C. *Civ*. respectively.

Ordinary co-ownership

Ordinary co-ownership arises automatically in certain circumstances. The most usual example is after the death of someone, when the heirs to the estate become co-owners of the inheritance until such time as it is divided among them.[97] Similarly upon divorce, or where one spouse has died, where there has been a community of property regime the spouses remain co-owners until division—*l'indivision post-communautaire*.[98] Even in the case of spouses married under a separation of property regime, *l'indivision* may arise where one spouse cannot establish separate ownership of the property.[99] It also applies when two or more persons buy a house together, or inherit a legacy together, or are the joint recipients of a gift, or where a number of persons—for example a club or association—acquire property.

This form of co-ownership is always of a temporary nature, for a longer or shorter time depending on the circumstances. It is regarded as being economically unsatisfactory and an abnormal state of affairs, which must be ended as soon as possible by the restoration of individual ownership—although in fact such *indivision* may last for some time and indeed in certain circumstances may be maintained by a court order.[1]

Ownership *en tontine*

Ownership *en tontine* is one of two forms of co-ownership of property where such co-ownership arises intentionally rather than automatically. Ownership *en tontine* is similar to the English law concept of joint tenants. There is effectively no division into shares. Thus, when one co-owner dies, his or her share passes to the other co-owner, by-passing the ordinary rules of succession, because the property is deemed not to fall into the deceased's estate (similar to the rule of survivorship in English law). The device is useful for couples who are not married because it means that the survivor—who would not have any rights of succession in law to the reserved share—is provided for. During the period of joint-ownership both co-owners have the right to use the

---

[97] This is referred to as *l'ouverture d'une succession*.

[98] This also happens in the case of judicial separation, or where dissolution of the community is ordered by a court, *e.g.* because the administering spouse is mis-managing the fund.

[99] See Art. 1542 C. *Civ.* and Art. 1538 C. *Civ.*

[1] This is the case with agricultural small-holdings, property employed for professional purposes, or articles used for earning a living, and originates from an Act of December 19, 1961. Similarly under the provisions of Art. 815(2) C. *Civ.* a court may order a delay of two years.

property and may not exclude each other from any part of it. Neither party can dispose of his or her share without the consent of the other. There is no limit to the number of co-owners.

Ownership *en tontine* is not provided for in the Code, but has been developed through case law.

Ownership *en indivision conventionnelle*

Prior to 1976 ownership *en indivision conventionnelle* was largely regulated by the rules relating to succession—for example Article 815 C. *Civ*. This is because with this form of co-ownership each co-owner's share passes into their estates on death. Because each co-owner owned a divided share, the co-ownership arrangement could always be terminated, even if there was an agreement to the contrary. The 1976 Act[2] enlarged Article 815 through the drafting of Article 1873 which now deals extensively with co-ownership *en indivision conventionnelle*.[3]

Two forms of co-ownership *en indivision* are now provided for: that which is governed by the ordinary law, that is *indivision ordinaire*, and that arising by express agreement of the parties, in which case the effects of such co-ownership may be chosen by the parties.

Under Article 1873, the co-owners can agree in writing on the division of shares and that the co-ownership arrangement will continue for a maximum initial period of five years, renewable thereafter for maximum periods of five years at a time. While the agreement is in force, only the most profound disagreement or rupture between the parties will persuade the court that the arrangement should be set aside. Co-owners may also agree to an indefinite period for the co-ownership. In this case the arrangement may be terminated at any time by notice, except where the right to give notice is abused or used in bad faith.

An agreement for a fixed period automatically becomes for an indeterminate time—subject to notice—on the death of a co-owner, or where the share of a co-owner becomes vested in someone other than one of the original co-owners, or a company becomes a co-owner.

Indivision ordinaire

Where there is no agreement, then the co-ownership is governed by Article 815 C. *Civ*. Also if the agreement for a fixed period of time is not renewed at the end of that time, then the co-ownership arrangement will

---

[2] Act of December 31, 1976.

[3] The location of this Article in that part of the Code dealing with the organisation and functioning of companies, places this institution at the cross-roads of property law and

become one of *indivision ordinaire*. During the period of co-ownership, if one co-owner wishes to dispose of his or her share, then a month's notice of intention to sell must be given to the other co-owners, who have the right of pre-emption in respect of that share and may therefore offer to buy it.

(B) RIGHTS AND POWERS OF CO-OWNERSHIP

Although in theory co-owners have full rights of ownership, in practice their rights of disposition and of exclusiveness are curtailed. In a normal situation the owner of property has exclusive and absolute rights over his property and may do with it whatever he wishes. In co-ownership one co-owner cannot ignore the wishes of the others. No single co-owner can exclude another from any part of the property, or from the exercise of any right relating to that property.[4] Co-owners do, however, have the right of exclusivity against third parties and, similarly to any ordinary owner, may take protective measures to exclude third parties.

Each co-owner has the benefit of using the property, but this is exercised in a collective manner and so the exercise of this right by one co-owner must not reduce or interfere with the same right of another co-owner.[5] Above all the co-owners must respect the integrity of the undivided property—rather like a usufructary—and remember that he or she is not simply benefiting from their own property but that of another.

Where the co-owned property is productive in some way, then all the co-owners are entitled to a share of the profits in proportion to their nominal shares—*quote-part*.[6] If the profits have resulted from the particular labour or efforts of one of the co-owners, this does not enhance his share, but he may claim some form of remuneration or indemity from the others.

---

contract law, indicating the legal perception that this is a commercial structure, suitable for moral persons as much as physical ones, and directed at meeting economic and social needs.

[4] Exceptionally a court may order that one co-owner has an exclusive power, *e.g.* where a violent spouse is ordered to leave the co-owned matrimonial home; or parties to a divorce may agree that one remains in occupation of the home and the other leaves it, although a compensatory sum may be demanded in return.

[5] Inevitably this balance may be difficult to maintain, although it may be modified or elaborated by agreement or, in the case of dispute, by the intervention of a court. Any imbalance may be redressed by the payment of a compensatory sum.

[6] Because the object of co-ownership remains physically undivided, the notion of co-ownership rights relates to a nominal, rather than actual, share, and even on the termination of the co-ownership this generally relates to a share of the value rather than a portion of the actual property.

Any acts of alienation by a co-owner can only be exercised over his own share, no disposition of the whole can take place without the consent of the others.[7] If there are difficulties in obtaining the unanimous consent of all the co-owners—either because of absence or obstinacy[8]—and the welfare of the common interest is imperilled as a result, a court may authorise the act.

The law only proscribes those acts which relate to the whole property. Personal obligations, such as debt, relate to the value of the undivided share in the individual's patrimony. Therefore, if one of the co-owners secures a debt against his share of the co-owned property this does not bind the whole property. On the other hand, if all the co-owners have consented to, for example a mortgage, over the whole property, then the creditor will have the right to seek satisfaction against any or all of the property.[9]

As far as the administration of the co-owned property is concerned, the requirement of consent each time would be unrealistic, so each co-owner may act alone in matters relating to the preservation of the communal property and take whatever measures seem necessary in emergency situations. If expenses are incurred in doing this, the co-owner who initiated the measures can seek compensation from the other co-owners. In situations which are not deemed to be emergencies, one co-owner may administer the property, either by agreement or implied mandate or implied agency, gratuitously, or for a fee.[10] In extreme cases a judge may order certain measures to be taken, such as prohibiting the disposal of movables, ordering the recovery of debts, etc.

Each co-owner may, without prejudicing the rights of the other co-owners, exercise rights of disposition over his or her own share. In this respect the exercise of the power and the object of that exercise need to

---

[7] The requirement for unanimity extends to cover not only acts such as sale, but any act which transfers, abolishes or creates real rights.

[8] Where a co-owner is particularly difficult this could be regarded as an "abuse of right".

[9] Even the right of a personal creditor to exercise rights over the indebted co-owner's share can create problems. It is undesirable that an unknown third party may seek to exercise the rights of an indebted co-owner and so the creditor must wait until the relevant share materialises. This could be detrimental to the creditor, *e.g.* if there is a long delay, and so execution of the debt may be ordered by the court, through an order of sale. To resist this, the remaining co-owners may satisfy the creditor and then seek reimbursement through a redistribution of shares.

[10] Where the administration and management of the property is not according to an agreement and there are disputes, a court may intervene and appoint one of the co-owners to act in this capacity, at the same time levying a *caution*, or deposit of insurance moneys. In such a case the administrator may have more extensive powers than usual—similar to those of a spouse who administers the community fund.

be distinguished. The alienation of one co-owner's share to a third party does not alter the material composition of the co-owned property, but simply makes the new co-owner a concurrent owner.[11]

Because the right of disposition by one co-owner may be prejudicial to the others, these latter will have a right of pre-emption, subject to the price and terms stipulated by the co-owner wishing to dispose of his share. This option prevents a third party stranger from coming into the co-owned property. This right of pre-emption may be exercised by one or all of the co-owners.[12]

A similar right exists when the share of a co-owner has been disposed of by a court order. This is a right of *substitution* whereby the other co-owners may apply, after the event, to replace the co-owner. In both cases certain formalities and time-limits have to be observed, primarily to avoid any claims of prejudice or abuse of right.[13]

(C) PERPETUAL CO-OWNERSHIP

Perpetual co-ownership only arises in connection with shared facilities relating to property, for example a courtyard, a playground, wells, rights of way, partitioning walls between flats or gardens, etc. As such it is perpetual and passes from one co-owner to another. It is particularly important in the case of jointly owned supporting structures between neighbouring properties—*copropriétés de voisinage*. The law in this area has been primarily developed through the courts, particularly as the usual consequences of *l'indivision*—with the possibility of *partage*—are unsuitable for this permanent state of affairs. Nor is the law relating to servitudes exactly applicable as there is no dominant and servient tenement, and the creation and acquisition of servitudes is governed by different rules.[14]

---

[11] As a result, if third party purchasers mistakenly think that they are acquiring the rights of absolute owner over a thing and then discover that they are only acquiring the rights of a co-owner, they may have the contract set aside (Art. 1599 C. *Civ.*).

[12] The same right of pre-emption applies in the case of usufruct over the co-owned property.

[13] *E.g.* in the case of *substitution*, if the formalities are not complied with, the beneficiaries of the co-owner may challenge the exercise of these rights and get the transaction annulled.

[14] Although some neighbouring co-ownership rights may be acquired by prescription, *e.g.* where a neighbour builds sheds against a boundary wall, this wall becomes co-owned if the sheds remain there for more than 30 years without interruption or dispute.

(D) CONDOMINIUM CO-OWNERSHIP

Although modern living conditions and construction techniques have been instrumental in requiring a legal structure to accommodate the property interests of flat owners, the concept of division of one building among several owners was found in Roman law and in the Middle Ages, particularly in the case of fortified towns.[15]

Initially there was virtually no legal provision for the ownership of buildings divided into flats. The only form of co-ownership of a building envisaged in the Code was where the building was divided into different levels on floors, each being owned by a differnt owner. In such a case Article 664 C. *Civ*. made provision for the apportioning of liability for repairs to the roof and external walls, the floors and ceilings and the staircases. Legal developments to cope with the changing complexity of communal occupation of buildings had to come about either by judicial enlargement of the provisions of this Article, or increasingly through agreements between the occupant-owners of the different flats.[16]

The first statute to provide for co-ownership in this context was an Act of June 28, 1938. This abolished Article 644 and gave legal status to co-ownership of flats. The new law made provision for the formation of a company or corporate structure to own the building, and introduced a regime of *copropriété*. The advantages of the former, which particularly related to construction companies, were that it was a legal person, perpetual and already recognised in law. The object of these companies was to obtain or construct, and enjoy residential property. Today this form of co-ownership—whereby each flat owner has exclusive and absolute ownership of part of the building and shares other communal parts—is provided for under an Act of July 10, 1965, subsequently amended by Acts of 1971[17] and 1982.[18]

The law regulates the relationship between the owners of each floor or flat—depending on how the building is divided—particularly the rights of owners to shared parts of the building, for example staircases, lifts, parking areas, etc. The law determines which parts of a building are deemed to be common and which are exclusive; how liability for maintenance and costs or repairs are to be apportioned; and how the

[15] Restrictions on building and living space within the walled town or city necessarily meant shared facilities and mutually owned support walls, open spaces, etc.
[16] These became known as *règlements de copropriété*, they were, however, entirely contractual and there were doubts as to whether they were enforceable against third parties, *e.g.* a successor in title to the property.
[17] Act of July 16, 1971.
[18] Quilliot Act of June 22, 1982, relating to the obligations between tenants and co-owners.

management of common parts is to be administered. Where the co-owners act together and have common interests, they acquire the legal personality of a *syndicat*.[19] This *syndicat* is responsible for taking decisions concerning the property as a whole. Thus, a co-owner will be a member of this syndicate but also an individual owner.

(E) TIME-SHARING

France was the innovator of the concept of time-shares. The idea originated in 1965 as a result of demands for holiday accommodation in the French Alps. Promoters of the industry suggested that it was cheaper to buy a share in the property than to rent or pay for a holiday. Time-shares appeared to meet a need for cheap affordable holiday accommodation at a time when hotel costs were rising and fewer people could afford to buy a flat in the Alps or at the coast. The leisure market was expanding but traditional forms of property holding were too expensive. Time-sharing was a concept that could be applied to flats and villas and even boats. It was attractive to both French nationals and foreigners.

France has also been in the forefront of adopting new legal measures to deal with some of these issues raised by time-sharing, being only second to Portugal in implementing specific legislation. In 1986,[20] legislation was passed creating legal structures for the time-share industry.

Prior to the legislation, time-sharing, which had grown considerably in France during the last twenty-five years, was referred to by a number of terms most of which involved the word "*propriété*" and which was therefore misleading because this implied ownership of property, which in fact a time-share did not confer. For example the terms "*multipropriété*", "*copropriété saisonnière*", "*propriété spatio-temporelle*" and "*propriété à temps partageé*" were all used. Lawyers and consumer organisations were concerned both about the marketing aspects of the time-share industry and about consumer confusion about what it was they were acquiring.

Prior to the 1986 Act, because the trust concept is unknown in French law, the only way of creating a legal framework for time-sharing was the use of companies. This use of companies dates back to 1925 when "Companies of Ownership" were established. The objective of such companies was to construct buildings for division in to flats. These

---

[19] This legal creation is distinct from that of a company—*société*—and does not fall under the definition given in Art. 1832 C. *Civ*.—and is not the owner of the property, but is responsible for the administration of the property—and may hold a small fund to defray running expenses—and can be held liable for any damage caused to third parties.

[20] Act of January 6, 1986.

companies were the forerunners of the "Building Companies" created under the Act of June 28, 1938 amended by Title II of Act 579 of July 5, 1971 which provided for the creation of "Enjoyment Companies". These latter companies were created in order to offer the exclusive right of enjoyment to each partner of the company to a fraction of the building. In the case of financial difficulty and subsequent liquidation, each partner of the company would be allotted an individual right in the property as regards his fraction of the building. However, these legal structures did not really cater for time-sharing which is concerned with the division of the right of enjoyment of one flat among a number of people according to periods of time.

The effect of the Act

The aim of the new Act was to clarify the legal relationship between promoters, builders and purchasers, to establish specific rules applicable to the companies chosen and to guarantee better protection of shareholders.

Under the Act *sociétés d'attribution d'immeubles en jouissance à temps partagé* now have special legal status. The Act adopts the company model, whereby buildings intended for time-share occupancy are owned by a company, and individuals wishing to purchase a time-share buy shares in the company, the ownership of shares conferring a right of occupancy of a particular apartment for a particular period of time. The body of time-sharers with an interest in a particular building control the management of the block and bear the cost of service contracts for management, etc.

The type of company incorporated to own the actual building may be a commercial company such as a *société anonyme* or *société à responsibilité limitée*—equivalent to a limited liability company in English law—or a non-commercial company such as a *société civile*—the equivalent of which does not really exist in English law. Normally this type of company has unlimited liability but when used for time-sharing the Act provides that its liability will be limited.

Because the time-share structure relates to company law, the time-share purchaser is entitled to inspect the company documents, for example Articles of Association and the company Memorandum, as well as documents relating to the division of the building; arrangements for management; accounts of the previous year; indication of service charges; building specifications; and inventory of furnishings and fittings. If the time-share block is not yet completed, then there are also safeguards to ensure its completion, including guarantees in the event of non-completion. Similarly there has to be an annual general meeting and the company is controlled by a board of directors or an executive committee which may be removed by the shareholders.

A time-sharer may let his time-share to others, but remains personally liable for any defaults. Service costs are determined in proportion to the size of the share-holding which in turn may be determined by the occupancy period, for example a time-share in high season requires more shares than in low season. Local taxes are paid by the company that owns the building and then appportioned to the time-share holders.

The share acquired is regarded as personal not real property and cannot, therefore, be used as security to raise money in France. As personalty, a time-share is not subject to the French rules of succession where the owner is domiciled elsewhere, but may be subject to French death duties as these are not dependent on domicile but source of origin. In practice death duties are unlikely to be payable because of the relatively low value of the time-share and short period of occupancy.

If the company owning the property goes into liquidation, the shareholders have a right to divide up whatever is left of the sale price, after the debts of the company have been met, among themselves in proportion to their shares.

The right of enjoyment must be exercised in conformity with the company's Articles and Memorandum and any other agreed regulations.

Shareholders participate in the losses and liabilities of the company to the extent of their shares. They also contribute to the capital necessary for the construction, completion or alteration of the building in proportion to their shares.

Impact of the Act

The provisions of the Act do not apply universally. Some existing time-share schemes have switched to the Act some have not. The legislation only applies to whole buildings which are dedicated to time-sharing and not to buildings which are only partly used for time-sharing. It is also not clear if the Act applies to non-French flat owners who sell time-shares in their property, or to non-French companies holding time-share properties.

The power of the time-share holders to exercise a say in the management of the property and to participate in annual general meetings, etc., may be defeated by the fact that many time-sharers may reside elsewhere and not be able to attend such meetings. Poor attendance among co-owners of property owned *en copropriété* at such meetings resulting in bad management suggests that the problem may be aggravated in the case of non-French time-share owners. The consequence may be that proxy agents arise, costing the time-sharer more in expenses.

Alternatives

Because there is some uncertainty over the operation of the Act, two other forms of shared ownership have arisen. The first is *nouvelle propriété*, whereby a purchaser is the full owner of a flat purchased for holiday use, but in return for a rebate of 26–30 per cent of the real price, the promoter of the scheme is permitted to rent out the flat for a period of 9–11 years (depending on the size of the rebate), while the purchaser is only allowed to use the property during this period for six weeks in the year. The second is *prépropriété* where the rebate is greater—40–50 per cent—but the purchaser only buys the possession of the property, while the promoter retains legal title to the property and management for a period of 12 years. After this time the purchaser becomes full owner. In the interim the purchaser may only exercise the right to possession for a limited period each year.

TOPIC FOUR
THE SALE AND CONVEYANCE OF LAND

The French concept of property and real rights means that the alienation and acquisition of immovable property is primarily governed by the law of contract.

French law knows no doctrine of estates—a feudal concept which was eradicated by the 1798 Revolution.[21] The owner of land is, therefore, absolute owner in the sense that he owns the actual soil of the land.

Under Article 1138 C. *Civ.* ownership of immovables may pass simply as a result of the contract between the vendor and purchaser—although the vendor cannot pass on any better title than the one he has, so that if he is only a usufructary, he can only pass on this. In principle there is no requirement for conveyance or registration. This potentially creates a precarious situation for transferees, particularly if there are a number of successive transactions. As a result the passing of title to immovable property has been regulated by law so that both registration and publicity is necessary.[22] As a consequence of this, in France all freehold land is registered in the *cadastre*—Land Registry—each *parcelle* or plot of land separately noted, along with its use, for example, agricultural or residential. As the Land Register is a public record, the onus is on the individual to check it and to update it. The State offers no guarantee that it is accurate. The publication of the transaction by registration has no effect on the contracting parties themselves, but operates to resolve disputes between successive transferees of the same transferor and to provide a full picture of the most important—that is real rights—which affect the property. In this topic the focus is on residential rather than commercial property, although this is not such a great distinction as might at first appear, because in commercial transactions French law distinguishes between the sale of the premises of the business and the sale of the business itself, and the former is not essentially different from the sale of any immovable property.[23]

---

[21] The feudal system brought to England by William the Conqueror was, in any case, never applicable to the whole of France.

[22] See, *e.g.* the early legislation of March 23, 1855, November 30, 1935 and of January 4, 1955. As a result preference in the case of conflicting claims is given to the first registered owner.

[23] The premises of a business fall into the corporeal elements of the assets of a commercial enterprise. The sale of a business will also include the sale of its incorporeal assets and other corporal assets such as machinery, which will have to be categorised before it can be determined whether they form part of the premises or other assets of the business.

(A) PRELIMINARY STEPS

In towns and the more urban areas the sale of land will be negotiated through estate agents,[24] but in more rural areas it is quite likely that the sale of land will be undertaken by a local *notaire*,[25] who, for example, may be administering a deceased estate.[26] Where an estate agent is used,[27] he must have a clear mandate setting out the agreed terms and commission.[28] The estate agent may draw up the preliminary draft contract but the final contract of sale will be drawn by a *notaire*. The latter, whether involved from the outset, or subsequently, has the task of determining the intention of the parties, explaining the legal and fiscal implications of the transaction, advising on the value of the property in order to assist the parties to come to terms on the transaction, and warning the parties about the various taxes which they will be liable for as a result of the transaction.[29]

Notaires draw up the draft contract, carry out the searches, draw up the final conveyancing document, witness its signature and collect and distribute the deposit[30] and final purchase price. If both parties have their own *notiare* the fee for the transaction is split, but it is quite possible for the same *notaire* to act for both vendor and purchaser and to apportion the fee between them. If there is a dispute as to the choice of *notaire* then this must be determined either by agreement or by the location of the property, in the absence of which there is a tradition that the buyer's *notaire* is to be preferred.

In French law a contract for sale is treated as a sale once there is agreement as to price and subject-matter.[31] Consequently the agree-

---

[24] Under an Act No. 70.9 of January 2, 1970 all estate agents have to be licenced annually by the *préfet* of the *départment*, and according to a *décret* of July 20, 1972 estate agents must display details of their licence, name and registered office.

[25] On the *notaire*, see Dadomo and Farran *The French Legal System* (2nd ed., 1996) pp. 126 *et seq*.

[26] This can have advantages because the local *notaire* may well be acquainted with the property, the vendor and any controversy or competing rights affecting the property. As he acts in the best interest of the law—and can act for both parties to the transaction—his knowledge may be invaluable.

[27] This is increasingly the case and accounts for probably 50 per cent of all transactions.

[28] Commission is between 4 and 8 per cent. Reputable estate agents are registered with the national association of *Agents Immobiliers* (FNAIM), and besides having professional permits, will have insurance indemnity and financial guarantees. All terms and conditions must be in writing and for a fixed term.

[29] E.g. costs and incidental expenses of the sale are payable by the buyer: see Art. 1593 C. *Civ*.

[30] The *notaire* acts as stake-holder of any deposit—or alternatively the estate agent may do this. Both are bonded so the moneys are protected.

[31] See Art. 1589 C. *Civ*.

ment to purchase is binding and there is no equivalent to the two-stages of English law conveyancing of exchange of contract and subsequent conveyance.[32] The agreement is supported by payment of the deposit to the stake-holder. Until the deposit is lodged the contract is incomplete.

The majority of searches and inquiries are undertaken after this stage, although it is advisable for the purchaser to make some checks before this. In particular the purchaser might wish to establish if there are any planning controls on the property,[33] any rights of pre-emption,[34] easements, restrictions and boundaries,[35] and the state of the property.[36] Most information can be found in the local town hall—*mairie*—and the local land registry—*bureau des hypothèques*.[37]

(B) THE AGREEMENT

The preliminary agreement can be one of two types and take one of two forms.

Compromis de vente

Compromis de vente is a bilateral agreement to sell and buy, which commits both parties. It includes certain suspensive conditions which may even include the payment of the price. If these are not met, the

---

[32] One result of this is that in French law "gazumping"—whereby a subsequent, usually higher, offer is made and accepted by the vendor thereby ousting the purchaser who has been accepted initially—is not known in France.

[33] Planning (*urbanisme*) is the responsibility of the local authority and is determined by the local *plan d'occupation des sols*—which include local structure plans and the designation of land—and various *schémas*. There are major planning schemes, local ones (*schémas directeurs*) and small-scale ones (*schémas de secteur*). The local planning office will confirm the planning status of a building or plot. A *certificat d'urbanisme* is necessary if there has been construction, extension, demolition or change of use and takes about two months to acquire. If the certificate reveals unacceptable restrictions, then the purchaser may wish to withdraw from the contract. Sometimes, because of the delay in obtaining this, a let out clause is incorporated into the sale agreement.

[34] *E.g.* by co-owners, creditors, sitting tenants or local authorities. In particular the purchaser should check if the French Land Commission (SAFER) has any claim. With property over a certain size, the Commission has to give prior approval to the sale and may pre-empt sales by purchasing the land itself—*e.g.* to consolidate agricultural holdings in order to rationalise local agriculture.

[35] An abbreviated certificate stating whether there are any restrictions on planning or use, or local authority compulsory purchase proposals, is available in the form of a *note de renseignements d'urbanisme*. Where a property borders a public highway an *arrêté d'alignement* will indicate any road widening schemes.

[36] It is more unusual to find surveyors being used than in England, unless the boundary lines have to be re-drawn following sub-division.

[37] A register of all mortgages and other charges is kept. Mortgages are usually for a shorter

contract can be cancelled, providing that the obstacles have not been of the parties own making.

Promesse de vente/d'achat

Promesse de vente/d'achat is a unilateral agreement, either to sell or to buy, whereby the vendor (or buyer) agrees to sell (or to buy) the property for a determined price, the agreement being valid for a certain period and subject to certain conditions. This gives the buyer (or seller) time to reflect on the transaction, and to make searches, etc. The buyer must deposit a sum—usually around 10 per cent—as a guarantee and will lose this if he withdraws, unless there is an agreement to the contrary. Exercise of the option at the end of the time period converts the *promesse de vente* into a *vente parfaite*.

This form of contract may take two forms:

- *Sous seing privé*, which is an agreement made under seal, in triplicate—one copy each for the buyer, seller and registry—which must be stamped and registered at the tax office within ten days of being made in order to be valid. This form is also used in the case of the *compromis de vente*; or
- *act authentique* which is a notarial act, drawn up by the *notaire*, who deals with the stamping requirements within one month of the act being drawn up.

The agreement, whichever form it takes, will contain similar information. This includes: the identity of the parties; the proper identification of the property; declaration by the vendor that it is sold with vacant possession and free from encumbrances; agreement by the respective parties to buy and to sell at a given price; the amount of the deposit and the name of the stakeholder; the terms on which the deposit is made[38]; any let out clauses—*clauses suspensives*[39]; the time limit, where applicable (usually 60–90 days); any relevant matrimonial property regime; the date and place for completion.

---

period than in England, *i.e.* 5–15 years, and rarely for the full price—usually for not more than 80 per cent.

[38] *E.g.* that the buyer will lose his deposit if he withdraws or that the vendor will have to refund the deposit plus an indemnity equal to its value if he is the one who withdraws.

[39] These are open to the parties to agree, but usually include provisions such as: the sale is subject to availability of a mortgage (Act of July 13, 1979—not applicable in the case of purely commercial properties); the approval of SAFER (see n. 34, above), where applicable; the issue of a satisfactory *certificat d'urbanisme* by the local planning authority if this has not been obtained previously.

(C) BETWEEN AGREEMENT AND TRANSFER

In the interim period between agreement and transfer the *notaire* draws up the draft conveyance—*projet de l'acte de vente*—for consideration by the purchaser and vendor. This will contain more detailed information concerning the parties and the subject-matter of the sale. The plot will be indicated by its number and an extract of the plan, its root of title—*origine de propriété*,[40] and there will be an abstract of title of the vendor. Any easements or restrictive covenants must be stated, and guarantees given to the purchaser against eviction or hidden defects.[41] The final documents will confirm the planning status of the property and indicate the date at which the buyer will take possession.[42]

If there is a dispute or uncertainty regarding the boundaries, then these will need to be re-drawn at this stage by a land surveyor who will prepare a new plan for the land registry.[43]

Any outstanding searches or inquiries are made by the *notaire* who also verifies the vendor's identity and right to sell; obtains copies of all the applicable land registry documents; notifies those who may have a right of pre-emption of the vendor's intention to sell[44]; and contacts the *conservation des hypothèques* which issues a document called the *état hors formalité*, showing the possible existence of mortgages or securities on the property.[45]

(D) TRANSFER

The final act, *acte authentique de vente*, which takes place in the office of the *notaire*, has formal and financial consequences.[46] Obligations are imposed on both sides. The vendor must guarantee the subject-matter of the sale and deliver it to the purchaser—at least symbolically. The purchaser must deposit the oustanding moneys with the *notaire*, who

[40] This must date back 30 years where relevant.

[41] Any exemption clause in a contract which excludes or limits liability for hidden defects is void in the case of sales between individuals (Act of January 10, 1978). The existence of these guarantees obviates the need for surveyors, etc.

[42] This will rarely be before transfer because of the significance of possession in establishing rights over property in French law: see above.

[43] The *géomètre* must be paid prior to completion. This is not an unusual requirement where large estates are being broken up.

[44] *E.g.* sitting tenants may have a right of first refusal when a landlord intends to sell (Act of December 31, 1975 as amended on January 4, 1980 and June 22, 1982, and *décret* No. 77-742 of June 30, 1977). Similarly co-owners (see Art. 815 C. *Civ.*).

[45] This includes checking to see whether the vendor himself is not bankrupt or using the property as collateral for a loan.

[46] Certain terms are compulsory and non-compliance with the formalities can result in the contract being declared void and restitution ordered.

retains any money required for taxes payable by the vendor, and sees to the payment of these.[47] The purchaser must pay the fee of the *notaire*, and if a separate estate agent has been used, then any commission agreed under the original mandate must be paid—usually by the purchaser. It is usually the purchaser who must pay the registration fee,[48] which varies according to the age and use of the property,[49] and any costs incurred by the *notaire*.[50] Once the *acte de vente* is signed the purchaser becomes the legal owner of the property. If one or other party to the transaction is not available to sign, then this may be done by proxy through the use of a power of attorney—often by the clerk of the *notaire*.[51]

Although the purchaser has become owner at this point, a copy of the conveyance has to be stamped at the Land Registry and returned to the *notaire* who keeps the original and gives the purchaer and the vendor a copy.[52] The sale is also registered at the *bureau des hypothèques*. When all the taxes have been calculated and paid through the office of the *notaire*, any surplus will be reimbursed to the purchaser.

---

[47] The tax implications on the transfer of land are quite complicated. Companies and individuals pay the same taxes but calculated according to a different formula. The main categories of tax applicable are: registration tax; value-added tax; capital tax; and local tax. These latter include: *taxe foncière/impôt foncier* which is a general rate payable by the owner and levied by the local *commune*, based on the notional letting value of the property; *taxe d'habitation* payable by the occupier which is variable depending on the general amenities of the property and its nominal letting value and is determined by the *région* on a basis of 5 or 15 per cent of the value; and *taxe de publicité foncière* which is only payable if there are no building works proposed for the next four years, and varies in amount depending on whether the current building is habitable or not.

[48] This may, however, be apportioned between the purchaser and the vendor if there is an agreement—either written or oral—to this effect. However, this will not be the case where there is a unilateral promise to buy or to sell, subject to suspensive conditions.

[49] There is no registration fee payable on buildings of less than five years old.

[50] See Art. 1593 C. *Civ*. Costs amount to about 10–16 per cent of the price and are calculated as an estimate, any surplus being returned once all the taxes, etc., have been settled.

[51] Like the *notaire* there is no conflict of interest here and the clerk could act for either party.

[52] This process may take a couple of months. Keeping one copy of all transactions can create serious storage problems for busy *notaires* over a period of time, and there are some proposals to create a national electronic database.

Part Two
Public Law

Chapter Three
Constitutional Law

French Constitutional History

It is undoubtedly an understatement to say that some knowledge of France's constitutional development is essential for a good understanding of today's French Constitution. Studying French constitutional history is fascinatingly rich and disturbing at the same time. Since the French Revolution of 1789, which put an end to the monarchical *Ancien Régime* and set the ideological, social and constitutional foundations of modern France, France is the only country in the world which has experienced 15 constitutions[1]—plus six which were fully drafted but never enacted[2]—and 19 *de facto* or interim governments.[3] In total 40

[1] These are:
- the Constitution of September 3, 1791;
- the Constitution of June 24, 1793 (year one of the Revolutionary calendar);
- the Constitution of 5 *Fructidor An III* (August 22, 1795);
- the Constitution of *22 Frimaire An VIII* (December 13, 1799);
- the *Sénatus-consulte organique* of *16 Thermidor An X* August 4, 1802);
- the *Sénatus-consulte organique* of *28 Floréal An XII* (May 18, 1804);
- the Constitutional Charter of June 4, 1814;
- the Constitutions of the Empire (Supplementary Act) of April 22, 1815;
- the Constitutional Charter of August 14, 1830;
- the Constitution of November 4, 1848;
- the Constitution of January 14, 1852 and amendments;
- the *Sénatus-consulte* establishing the Constitution of the Empire of May 21, 1870;
- the Constitutional Acts of February 25, 1875 (on the organisation of the Government), of February 24, 1875 (on the establishment of the Senate), and of July 16, 1875 (on the relationship between Government institutions);
- the Constitution of October 27, 1946;
- the Constitution of October 4, 1958.

[2] For example the draft Constitution following the granting of full powers to Maréchal Pétain by the French Parliament on July 10, 1940; and the draft Constitution adopted on April 19, 1946 but rejected by referendum on May 5, 1946.

[3] These are:
- the Cabinet of the *Assemblée Nationale* period (June 17, 1789–June 20, 1791);
- the second Cabinet of the *Assemblée Nationale* period (June 20–September 14, 1791);
- the Cabinet of the *Assemblée Législative* period (August 10–September 20, 1792);
- the Cabinet of the *Convention Nationale* period (September 21, 1792–October 26, 1795);
- the provisional Government (April 9–June 4, 1814);

systems of government were tested or designed during the last two centuries.

From the other side of the Channel, this rich constitutional history could certainly be viewed as a sign of instability, chaos and the product of incoherent successive historical events among a people lacking political maturity. However, this constitutional instability is more apparent than real. First, many statesmen have served successive governments, thus bringing with them their political experience from previous regimes. Secondly, some institutions such as the *Conseil d'Etat* and other major public institutions have survived the major political upheavals. Thirdly, some coherent and logical evolution of the French system of government towards democracy can be perceived in this constitutional diversity: although many French have shown constant dissatisfaction with all these imperfect forms of government, they were doubtlessly inspired by the quest for an ideal form of democracy.[4]

- the Napoleon's Hundred Days Dictatorship (March 20–June 1, 1815);
- the Napoleon's Hundred Days Dictatorship (March 20–June 1, 1815);
- the *Commission municipale* and the Duke of Orléans' Cabinet (July 29–August 9, 1830);
- the provisional Government of 1848 (February 24–May 4, 1848);
- the Cabinets of the *Assembly Constituante* period (May 4–December 20, 1848);
- the dictatorship of Prince President Louis-Napoleon Bonaparte (December 2, 1851–March 29, 1852);
- the Cabinet of the *Défense Nationale* period (September 3, 1870–February 13, 1871);
- the Thiers Cabinet (February 17, 1871–May 24, 1873);
- Maréchal Pétain's dictatorship (July 11, 1940–April 18, 1942);
- the dual leadership of Maréchal Pétain and Pierre Laval (April 18, 1942–August 20, 1944);
- the Secretary-General's interim leadership (August 20–25, 1944);
- the Cabinet of the *Libération Nationale* period (August 25, 1944–November 9, 1945);
- the transition Government under the Act of November 2, 1945 (November 9, 1945–December 24, 1946);
- the transition Government under the Acts of June 2 and 3, 1958 (June 4, 1958–February 5, 1959).

[4] A number of theories have been put forward by leading constitutional lawyers of this century. Our purpose is not to discuss the validity of each of these theories, nor is there the space here. This has been fully done by J. Cadart (see *Institutions Politiques et Droit Constitutionnel* (Economica, Paris, 3rd ed., 1990) 2d. vol., pp. 847–853) and D.G. Lavroff (see *Le Droit Constitutionnel de la Ve République* (Dalloz, Paris, 1995) pp. 21–23). Therefore we will more modestly present them in a summarised way. At the beginning of this century, A. Hauriou explained in his *Précis de Droit Constitutionnel* (re-published by C.N.R.S. in 1967) that French post-revolutionary political history developed through a series of cycles, each being divided up into three stages:
- a revolutionary one, which was characterised by a *régime d'assemblée*, *i.e.* a system of government dominated by parliament;
- an authoritarian one, in which dominance of the Parliament gave way to dominance of the executive power; and

Six major stages may be distinguished in this long quest for democracy:

- 1789–1814: the introduction of the democratic principle in the French Constitution;
- 1814–1848: the birth of French parliamentary democracy;
- 1848–1870: the introduction of the principle of universal suffrage;
- 1870–1940: the parliamentary democracy of the Third Republic;
- 1940–1944: the Vichy Regime and the "national Revolution";
- 1944–1958: the search for a new political balance.

These different stages will be examined briefly.

(A) THE REVOLUTION AND THE EMPIRE PERIOD

Starting with a political, social, economic and financial crisis and finishing with military and political defeat, the Revolution and the Empire period is one of concentrated constitutional and political instability. Based on the principles of the Declaration of Man and the Citizen of 1789, the Constitution of 1791 established a regime of limited monarchy which was soon to be replaced in 1793 by a Republic, based on the dominance of a single chamber Parliament, the *assemblée*. However, the 1793 Constitution never came into force. In order to resist external and internal anti-revolutionary forces, a *Comité de Salut Public* was set up and, under the dictatorship of Robespierre, a period of Terror was to leave its scars. Following the execution of Robespierre, the *Convention* drafted the 1795 Constitution with the purpose of stopping the dominance of the Assembly and to restoring the authority of the executive power. Owing to its imperfections, its four years of application were riddled with *coups d'état*, the last of which brought Bonaparte to power on *18 Brumaire an VIII* (November 9, 1799) and with him

---

- a period of constitutional balance which would degenerate into a period of parliamentary dominance.

The first cycle ran from 1789 to 1848 (Revolution, First Empire, Parliamentary monarchies) and the second one from 1848 to 1870 (Revolution, Second Empire, third Republic).

M. Deslandres rejected the idea of cycles and advocated that of phases:

- a phase of political instability (1789–1814);
- one of semi-instability (1814–1870); and
- one of stability since 1870.

In the mid-twentieth century, G Vedel, far from searching for a logical development, preferred the idea of democratic waves for that of cycles. In his *Manuel Elementaire de Droit Constitutionnel* (1949), Vedel explained that, although the French failed three times to establish a democratic government, some irreversible *acquis démocratique* was gained from each constitutional experience.

imperialism until 1814. During that period, the quest for democracy proved to be much more than difficult and all democratic hopes were nearly lost under the Napoleonic dictatorship. Following Napoleon's defeat, democracy was given a second chance.

(B) THE FIRST STEPS OF PARLIAMENTARY DEMOCRACY

Between 1814 and 1848, the monarchy was re-established and the basic elements of a parliamentary democracy introduced.

Under the Constitutional Charter of 1814—which was imposed by Louis XVIII as a condition of his acceptance of the throne—no attempt was made to restore the pre-Revolution regime. On the contrary, influenced by the English Constitution, Louis XVIII advocated limited monarchy and maintained civil liberties. A two-chamber Parliament, to which the King's ministers gradually conceded to be answerable, shared the legislative power with the King. The Charter thus established a balance between monarchy and liberalism.

Charles X attempted to reverse this process but was forced to abdicate after the Revolution of July 1830. The 1830 Constitutional Charter, a new version of the 1814 one, was adopted by the Chambers and imposed on King Louis-Philippe, thus emphasising the idea that the monarchy was no longer based on divine right but on a covenant between the King and his people. The King was no longer the King of France but the King of the French. The principle of national sovereignty—a legacy of the Revolution—was also proclaimed. Institutionally, the King kept his former powers except for that of amending Acts of Parliament and of preventing their implementation; the Parliament's powers were increased and answerability of ministers to Parliament was definitely endorsed.

Though the parliamentary system found its real foundations in the 1830 Charter, its institutions were much more liberal than democratic. Based on a limited democracy and undermined by political corruption, the monarchy was swept away by the Revolution of February 1848.

(C) THE INTRODUCTION OF UNIVERSAL SUFFRAGE

The period from 1848 to 1875 witnessed a heterogeneous range of forms of government. The second Republic (established by the Constitution of November 4, 1848) was based on the principles of the people's sovereign right and of separation of powers—the single headed executive, embodied by a President of the Republic, and the single chamber Parliament being on an equal footing. Following the coup of December 2,

1851, master-minded by Prince Louis-Napoleon, the Republic was artificially maintained until the Constitution of January 14, 1852 was adopted. The Second Empire, unashamedly modelled on the institutions of the Napoleonic regime, was born. Napoleon III ran this new authoritarian government due to subservient institutions and a great sense of demagogy. From 1860 this regime moved towards more political and social liberalism. This highlighted its fundamental contradictions: dictatorial in its principle, it sustained economic progress; the people were led to believe that they were taking part in the decision-making process through their parliamentary representatives but were in reality manipulated by way of plebiscites. This regime was given the *coup de grâce* by the military defeat by Bismarck's Prussia at Sedan on September 1, 1870. After the fall of the Empire, a new period of parliamentary dominance was to start until a new Constitution establishing the Third Republic was adopted in 1875.

As mentioned earlier, this constitutional period was rather hectic. However, behind this heterogeneity, there was a common feature: the introduction of universal suffrage. Even during the Napoleonic dictatorship, the right to vote for all (except women of course!) was definitively upheld, though the democratic process was often used in order to assure the authority of the Emperor.

(D) THE VICISSITUDES OF THE THIRD REPUBLIC

Established by three Constitutional Acts of 1875, the Third Republic was the longest Constitution (65 years) France has experienced since the Revolution. Though the constitutional framework proved to be reliable, the form of government evolved under the pressure of changing political forces and the working of the original legal processes.

The 1875 Constitution was the result of a compromise between the monarchists and the republicans. The former accepted the creation of a Republic provided that it would be a conservative one. This resulted in the creation of a parliamentary democracy with simple institutions, the role of which was to maintain a moderate government.

The institutional balance was based on an executive power headed by a President of the Republic—politically unanswerable—and served by a cabinet of ministers—collectively answerable to a Parliament, made up of a *Chambre des députés* and a *Sénat*. This was a well-balanced parliamentary system as both powers had equal means of influence on each other. Unfortunately, in practice this led to the weakening of the Executive to the benefit of Parliament. Soon the President of the Republic was reduced to a mere figure-head to the benefit of an emerging head of Cabinet, and the Cabinet became the plaything of a constantly hung Parliament. This led to Cabinet instability[5] and to parliamentary inertia. Cabinets could not govern in the long run. Parliament did not have the means to run the country. This resulted in the practice of delegated legislation, whereby Parliament authorised the Government to legislate by means of *décret-lois*. This practice highlighted the absurdity of the system.

The military defeat by Hitler's army in 1940 put an end to the Third Republic and favoured the return of Maréchal Pétain.

(E) THE DARK YEARS OF VICHY

For four years, France was not run by a Government which was legitimately and constitutionally accepted. The Vichy Government was constitutional but had no legitimacy while the Government based in London, then Algiers, was legitimate but not constitutional.[6] However, during those darkest years of France's history, the French were run under a political system of government which, whether imposed on them by the German invaders or by French collaborators, is part of the French constitutional past and, as such, cannot be ignored. Headed by Maréchal Pétain, who was given full powers by Parliament on July 10, 1940, the Vichy regime was named after the city of Vichy where the new Government was based.

---

[5] The table below shows the magnitude of this institutional instability.

Presidents of the Republic	Term of office	Number of Cabinets
Jules Grévy	1879–1886	nine
Jules Grévy	1886–1887	eight
Sadi Carnot	1887–1894	ten
Casimir Périer	1894–1895	one
Félix Faure	1895–1899	five
Emile Loubet	1899–1906	four
Armand Fallières	1906–1913	nine
Raymond Poincaré	1913–1920	twelve
Paul Deschanel	1920	one
Alexandre Millerand	1920–1924	five
Gaston Doumergue	1924–1931	fifteen
Paul Doumer	1931–1932	three
Albert Lebrun	1933–1939	fifteen
Albert Lebrun	1939–1940	three

[6] Under the *Ordonnance* of August 9, 1944 on the re-establishment of republican legitimacy, the Third Republic was never abolished and the Vichy Government, which was deemed never to have had constitutional existence, was regarded as a *de facto* government.

The constitutional framework of Pétain's regime was rather rudimentary as it consisted of 11 short Constitutional Acts enacted by Pétain himself. The dictatorial nature of the Vichy regime was rapidly revealed as Pétain appointed himself Head of State in the first Constitutional Act and organised his succession in favour of Pierre Laval and then Admiral Darlan. Executive and legislative powers were concentrated in the hands of the Head of State. After April 18, 1942, when Pierre Laval was appointed Head of Government, the regime appeared to be based on a distribution of powers between Pétain and Laval but remained a dictatorship in the hands of the latter statesman. The people round Pétain were disciples of nationalist Charles Maurras and the Action Française Movement and admirers of the Spanish and Portuguese dictatorships under Franco and Salazar. Their first aim was to abolish the Republican regime and wipe out the inheritance of the Revolution in favour of the "French State".

In accordance with the Constitutional Act of July 10, 1940, a draft Constitution was completed and signed by Pétain on January 30, 1944. It aimed to guarantee the rights of "Labour, Family and Homeland" and established a hybrid system between a parliamentary democracy and a presidential regime. However this draft constitution was never promulgated because Pétain had his hands tied by the German occupants and Laval.[7] This Vichy regime collapsed under the Liberation of France and the question of the constitutional institutions was raised again.

(F) THE DIFFICULT SEARCH FOR A NEW POLITICAL AND INSTITUTIONAL BALANCE

A few months before the Liberation of France, the *ordonnance* of April 21, 1944 stipulated that the French people alone would decide about the country's future institutions and that a constituent assembly would be convened. More importantly, that of August 9, 1944 re-established a Republican form of French Government.[8]

Interim institutions were set up not only to run the country but also to draft a new republican constitution. In the circumstances of the time, the launch of the Fourth Republic in 1946 proved to be a laborious and complex process. There was even a false start with the first draft Constitution of April 19, 1946 being rejected by the French in a

---

[7] The text of this draft Constitution can be found in *Les Constitutions de la France depuis 1789* (GF-Flammarion, Paris).

[8] Art. 1 provided that the Republic had always been the only constitutional form of the Government of France and that all constitutional acts and laws passed under the Vichy regime were null and void.

referendum. After the French voted—with no great enthusiasm—in favour of the new draft, the new Constitution was promulgated on October 27, 1946.

The result of a compromise, the 1946 Constitution laid the foundation of a parliamentary democracy in which the two-chamber Parliament[9] had the prime role and a President of the Republic and the Cabinet, headed by a *President du Conseil*, shared the Executive power.[10] The Fourth Republic was designed to eradicate the defects of the Third. As noted above, one of those defects was Cabinet instability. In this respect, the 1946 Constitution established a complex mechanism guaranteeing stability which linked the power of dissolution to the frequency of Cabinet crises. The threat of dissolution could only be used after the first 18 months of Parliament's office and provided that two open Cabinet crises erupted within another 18-month period. Cabinet instability rapidly reappeared.[11] In general constitutional mechanisms proved to be inadequate and, despite some attempted reforms, the Fourth Republic soon foundered in disrepute. The Algerian War gave the last blow to this short-lived Republic.

In 1958 a new Constitution was drafted and passed: the Fifth Republic was born.

---

[9] In order to symbolically stress the difference between the Fourth and the Third Republics, the two houses were called *Assemblée Nationale* and *Conseil de la République* as opposed to *Chambres des députés* and *Sénat*. The *Conseil de la République* had more limited powers than the lower house and was confined to being a "*chambre de réflexion*" on the model of the House of Lords.

[10] Politically unanswerable, the President of the Republic enjoyed all the prerogatives of a Head of State but no real powers, as all his acts had to be counter-signed by the Head of the Cabinet who was the real head of the Executive.

[11] The average life span of a cabinet was 6 months as the table below shows:

Presidents of the Republic	Term of office	Number of Cabinets
Vincent Auriol	1947–1953	sixteen
René Coty	1953–1959	eight

THE FIFTH REPUBLIC

(A) FROM THE FOURTH TO THE FIFTH REPUBLIC

General de Gaulle criticised the 1946 Constitution from the very day it came into force and, logically, made constitutional reform a pre-requisite for his coming into power in May 1958.[12] However, the transition from the Fourth to the Fifth Republic was technically problematic. The latter had to be seen as originating from the former. This implied that the 1946 Constitution be amended and the amendment procedure be changed. By way of exception to Article 90 of the 1946 Constitution, Parliament passed an Act which authorised de Gaulle to initiate the drafting of a new Constitution.[13]

(B) THE SOURCES OF INSPIRATION OF THE 1958 CONSTITUTION

The Constitution of 1958 was the brainchild of General de Gaulle who drew his constitutional ideas from the works of Michel Debré, his Minister of Justice and chair of the working group on the new institutions.

One cannot understand the political development of the Fifth Republic without paying attention to the key ideas which inspired it. These were both varied and contradictory, and contributed to make the Fifth Republic an ambiguous and mixed regime from its very beginning. The draftsmen designed a constitution which marked a new start in French constitutional history by restoring the idea of a strong State while drawing from the liberal and parliamentarian republic tradition.

In his speech at Bayeux on June 16, 1946, de Gaulle expressed the idea of a powerful State independent from any internal considerations—notably the imbroglios of political parties which caused the collapse of the Third and Fourth Republics—and external interests. Independence would be guaranteed by re-establishing the balance of powers in favour of a stable Executive headed by a powerful Head of State and by redefining and rationalising the relationships between the Executive and the Legislature. The President of the Republic would be the guardian of the

---

[12] General de Gaulle was called into power to solve the political crisis of May 13, 1958 caused by insurrections in Algeria.

[13] This reform technique was similar to that formerly used in 1940. Nevertheless, in order to avoid any misuse of powers, as with Pétain, this delegation of constituent powers was limited by conditions regarding the form of the new government—a parliamentary democracy, based on universal suffrage and actual separation of powers—and the method of establishing it, prior to submitting the draft Constitution to the French by way of referendum, a Constitutional Committee and the *Conseil d'Etat* had to be consulted.

Constitution, national independence and territorial integrity, and an arbitrator ensuring the regular functioning of the public authorities and the continuity of the State.

Although criticised, the Fourth Republic was also a source of inspiration for the draftsmen of the new Constitution. First, the incorporation into the 1958 Constitution of the Preamble of the 1946 Constitution and of the Declaration of Man and the Citizen of 1789 is a direct legacy of the Fourth Republic. Secondly, drawing from the experience of the Fourth Republic, some constitutional institutions and mechanisms were improved (for example the *Conseil Constitutionnel* is a successfully improved version of the *Comité Constitutionnel*; the legislative powers of Parliament were limited under Article 34 and a new procedure of Cabinet answerability was created under Article 49, etc.). Finally, the parliamentary form of the new system of Government was a direct condition laid down in the Act of June 3, 1958. This was also the original wish of the draftsmen.[14]

(C) THE DRAFTING AND PASSING OF THE 1958 CONSTITUTION

The constitution was drafted in three stages:

- In June 1958, a first draft was drawn up by a working group chaired by Michel Debré and composed of members of the *Conseil d'Etat* and law professors, and examined by an inter-ministerial committee headed by General de Gaulle. The new draft was then approved in Cabinet and published at the end of July 1958;
- in accordance with the Act of June 3, 1958, the *Comité Consultatif Constitutionnel*—two-thirds of its members came from Parliament—was then consulted. Its recommendations were purely technical and did not put into question the general spirit of the draft;
- after the *Conseil d'Etat* was consulted on the amended draft, this was adopted in Cabinet on September 3, 1958.[15]

The draft constitution was then ratified by way of a referendum on September 28, 1958[16] and the new Constitution was promulgated on October 4, 1958.

---

[14] See the speech of M. Debré of August 27, 1958 delivered to the *Conseil d'Etat*: "*Pas de régime conventionnel, pas de régime présidentiel, la voie devant nous est étroite, c'est celle du régime parlementaire*".

[15] The whole procedure was not in line with the French republican tradition as this was not an elected Constituent Assembly and the opinion of this committee was not binding on the Government.

[16] Although the campaign was rather dull, the turn-out rate was very high (84.9 per cent of

(D) THE NEW CONSTITUTIONAL FRAMEWORK

Not surprisingly the new Constitution was the result of a compromise which did not fully meet the expectations of de Gaulle and Debré. It was also criticised for being vague and muddled, thus leaving room for liberal interpretation. However, after 38 years of existence, today it seems that the three main challenges have been met: constitutional stability (five Presidents of the Republic), Cabinet stability, and a satisfactory balance of powers.

voters). The yes was overwhelmingly clear: 17,668,790 in favour (79.2 per cent of the votes cast) and 4,624511 against (20.8 per cent).

TOPIC ONE
THE INSTITUTIONAL AND POLITICAL BALANCE UNDER THE 1958 CONSTITUTION

(A) THE BALANCE OF POWERS WITHIN THE EXECUTIVE

Under the 1958 Constitution the authority and the role of the Executive, which had been diminished under the two previous regimes, were restored. This is particularly reflected in the Executive being dealt with in the Constitution (Titles II and III) before Parliament (Title IV). Not only was the presidential power enhanced but also the role of the Cabinet re-defined and re-asserted.

Although the duality of the Executive is not specific to the Fifth Republic as was seen earlier, the balance of powers within the Executive and the way it operates is. The relation between the President of the Republic and the Cabinet, headed by a Prime Minister, is not only the product of the constitutional arrangement but, more importantly, of political majorities in Parliament.

The distribution of powers within the Executive

The enhancement of the role and position of the President of the Republic is an essential feature of the present Constitution. The draftsmen of the 1958 Constitution had deliberately given the predominant role to the President and, with it, increased powers.

On its part, the Government and the Prime Minister have, according to Article 20 of the Constitution, extended powers in order to "determine and conduct national policy".

Since the President of the Republic is politically unanswerable, under Article 19, some presidential acts of the President of the Republic cannot be legally effective if not counter-signed by the Prime Minister or the relevant minister so as to transfer answerability to the Government. This is the normal mechanism in a parliamentary democracy. Therefore, the principle is that of power-sharing between the two branches of the Executive.[17] Counter-signature certainly restricts the powers of the

---

[17] This includes:
- the appointment of members of Government on the proposal of the Prime Minister (Art. 8(1));
- the promulgation of Acts of Parliament whereby the President officially makes it applicable within 15 days after the passing of the Act—a process similar to the royal assent under the English Constitution (Art. 10(1));
- the request that Parliament reconsider an Act within 15 days after its adoption (Art. 10(2));
- the signature of *ordonnances* and *décrets* decided upon in Cabinet (Art. 13(1));

President. Nonetheless, apart from Article 15, under which action must be taken within 15 days, in all other cases the President's action is not subject to any time-limit. In practice, this has given him a power similar to a right of veto: where the President refuses to act, counter-signature is ineffective. He may then be able to block Government action by refusing to sign *ordonnances*[18] and *décrets*, to open an extra-ordinary parliamentary session,[19] or to suspend the constitutional amendment process,[20] etc. Combined with his role of guardian of the Constitution, this gives him real discretionary powers.

A more significant step towards a re-enhancement of the role of the President was taken by vesting him with *pouvoirs propres*. This basically means that the President may take action for which counter-signature is not required and which cannot entail the answerability of the Government. The concept of presidential *pouvoirs propres* is an innovation of the 1958 Constitution and is in sharp contrast with that of parliamentary democracy. Without these specific powers, however, the President would not have the means to fulfil his role as guardian of the Constitution and guarantor of national independence. This innovation reflected the new conception of the role of Head of State.

One should not over-estimate these *pouvoirs propres*[21] which overall

---

- the signature of *ordonnances* and *décrets* decided upon in Cabinet (Art. 13(1));
- the appointment to the highest civil and military State offices (Art. 13(2));
- the accrediting of ambassadors and envoys extraordinary (Art. 14);
- the granting of pardon (Art. 17);
- the opening of extraordinary parliamentary sessions (Art. 30);
- the negotiation and ratification of international treaties (Art. 52); and
- the proposal of constitutional amendments (Art. 89).

[18] During the cohabitation period of 1986–1988, President Mitterrand refused to sign under Art. 13 *ordonnances*, thus preventing Chirac's Government from passing legislation in lieu of Parliament.

[19] In 1960, General de Gaule simply refused to do so despite a request by the majority in Parliament. When, in 1987, Chirac requested Mitterrand to open an extraordinary session, the President made it clear that he alone could decide the best time at which to do so.

[20] Under Art. 89, the President has the power to choose, at a time which pleases him, to submit the amendment proposal to either the two Houses of Parliament meeting together in a Congress, or to referendum. The President holds a suspensive veto.

[21] Art. 19 lays down those acts which are exempted from counter-signature:
- the right to appoint the Prime Minister (Art. 8(1));
- the right to call a referendum (Art. 11);
- the right to dissolve the lower House of Parliament (Art. 12);
- the power to issue emergency laws (Art. 16);
- the right to send written messages to Parliament (Art. 18);
- the right to appoint the President and two other members of the Constitutional Court (Art. 61); and
- the right to submit Acts of Parliament and international treaties to the Constitutional Court (Arts. 61, 54).

are not very important except for two: the power to issue emergency laws, and the right to dissolve the National Assembly. Because the former power is subject to strict conditions under Article 16, the right of dissolution is the most effective power at the disposal of the President who may use it first as a threat against Parliament, then to settle a disagreement between the Government and the majority in Parliament by calling for general elections.

By enlarging his traditional powers or by creating new ones, the draftsmen have made the President of the Republic the "*clef de voûte des institutions*", that is, the keystone of the institutions. The role of the Government was not ignored however. It is not surprising that the Prime Minister and the Government occupy the second place in the Constitution of the Fifth Republic: the Government is an important piece in the present constitutional mechanism and the Prime Minister, unlike the previous *Presidents du Conseil* under the Third and Fourth Republics, has become, through his new status and powers, an effective Head of Government.

Under Article 21 of the Constitution, the function of the Prime Minister is to lead the Government and, more generally, under Article 20, to determine and conduct national policy.[22] In determining the national policy, the Prime Minister outlines the Government's programme and general policy[23] and implements specific policies.[24] In order to enable the Prime Minister to implement government policies, the Constitution has vested in him a *pouvoir réglementaire*, *i.e.* an Executive rule-making power. This enables the Government not only to take any necessary measures—in the form of a *décret*—with the view to implementing Acts of Parliament,[25] but also to legislate, under Article 37, on

[22] The French version, Art. 21 refers to "*action du gouvernement*" which would suggest that determination of policies is the work of the Government, not only the Prime Minister. However, it is questionable whether, in practice, this principle has been fully complied with.

[23] In this respect, under Art. 49(1) of the Constitution, the Prime Minister shall pledge the responsibility of the Government before the lower House of Parliament in respect of its programme or a statement of its general policy. This provision clearly put the Prime Minister under the obligation to have the Government's programme approved by the National Assembly and, as a result, get its confidence at the very beginning of its term of office. However, since 1958, government practice has been inconsistent, choosing either to comply with the Constitution or to request approval of its general policy only, or no approval at all.

[24] This can be done by means of *projets de lois*, *i.e.* government bills (Art. 39) and amendments to proposed legislation (Art. 44) as well as by directly legislating through *ordonnances* (Art. 38) and *règlements autonomes* (Art. 37).

[25] This is usually referred to as *pouvoir réglementaire d'application* or *supplétif*.

any matters which do not fall within the competence of Parliament as defined under Article 34.[26] In this task the Prime Minister is assisted by a government and, more importantly, by a civil and military administration of which he is the head. With the exception of *décrets simples* which the Prime Minister enacts and signs himself, *décrets* that are adopted in Cabinet must bear the signature of the President of the Republic (Article 13). It, therefore, cannot be assumed that this rule-making power is exercised by the Prime Minister alone.

Although constitutional and political collaboration between the President of the Republic and the Government is within the logic of a parliamentary democracy, the 1958 Constitution undoubtedly turned the President into the dominant branch of the Executive by vesting him with unfettered powers and the right to interfere with governmental matters. In practice, this constitutional re-inforcement of the role of the President of the Republic has turned into political supremacy.

The political supremacy of the President of the Republic

As seen above, the President of the Republic was meant to be the keystone of French parliamentary democracy. The draftsmen of the Constitution never envisaged that the President would be the leader of a parliamentary majority. In the original version of the Constitution, the President was no longer elected by members of Parliament, as was the case under the previous two Republics, but by a body of Grand Electors composed of Members of Parliament and local councillors. Being free from any allegiance to Parliament and political parties, the President of the Republic could then play his natural role of constitutional arbiter. As an "*arbitre*", the President is not a judge in a dispute between different political forces. Because this is a superior authority, placed above political parties, the President, as the guardian of the Constitution, ensures the proper functioning of the public power and the continuity of the State, and is the guarantor of national independence and territorial integrity.

Following the constitutional amendment of 1962 providing that the President of the Republic be elected by direct general suffrage, presidential elections have become the focus of French political life. Once they have elected their President, French voters invariably send to Parliament a majority supporting his policy. Inevitably, since 1965, the year of the first presidential election, the President of the Republic has become the head of a parliamentary majority, thus turning the French

[26] This new power, known as *pouvoir réglementaire autonome*, was a novelty under the 1958 Constitution: see Dadomo and Farran, *The French Legal System* (Sweet & Maxwell, 2nd ed., 1996) p. 33.

system of government into a Presidential Government. Parliamentary support is vital to presidential policies. Without it, the President of the Republic has no means to carry out his policy. It is not surprising then that all Presidents of the Republic have always urged the French to vote, in general elections, for supporters of their policies. A President of the Republic supported by Parliament is the commonest pattern. However, this pattern was broken in 1986 and 1993 by two-year periods of "*cohabitation*" between a socialist President and a right-wing government.

Where the President of the Republic and Parliament—notably the lower chamber—belong to the same political family, the centre of power is at the *Elysée* Palace. Policies are determined under the impetus and power of the President. The Prime Minister, who is directly appointed by the President, appears to be the President's chief of staff whose role is limited to carrying out presidential decisions. There is no Government's policy but a President's policy which the Government carries out. The President determines national policies in different ways. The most important political decisions are usually made by a "*conseil restreint*" (inner Cabinet) headed by the President and including the Prime Minister, the relevant ministers and the President's advisors. The President's political decisions are also made public by way of press conferences or interviews or public speeches. Regular letters to the Prime Minister containing instructions as to the policy to follow is another means, particularly favoured by President Giscard d'Estaing.

This pattern is only possible when the President and the Prime Minister are in complete agreement. Where this agreement no longer exists, the Prime Minister has no other alternative but to resign.[27] In practice, the Prime Minister has indeed become politically answerable to the President.

In the exceptional cases of *cohabitation*, those ties between the Head of Government and the Head of State disappear. The centre of power shifts from the *Elysée* Palace to *Matignon* and the Prime Minister is only answerable to Parliament. The Prime Minister and the Government regain control over the determination and conduct of national policy. The role of the President is not, however, reduced to that of a figurehead: under the two periods of *cohabitation*, President Mitterand was successful in re-asserting his role as guardian of the Constitution, in maintaining his powers in the domain of defence and foreign policy[28] and, at times, by obstructing the action of the Government.

[27] Chirac's resignation in 1976 under Giscard's Presidency was the most striking example of discord between a President and his Prime Minister.

[28] It is constitutionally difficult for the President and the Prime Minister to determine different defence and foreign policies. The President may not ratify treaties without the

In 1986, for the first time since the establishment of the Fifth Republic, the Constitution was applied in accordance with its terms and its parliamentary nature was revealed.

If political *cohabitation* was satisfactory in principle, it carried the risk of instability since it was based on a vulnerable agreement between the two heads of the Executive, especially when they knew that they would contest each other in presidential elections.[29]

De Gaulle's only conception of his role as a Head of State was that of a pre-eminent and active one to whom the Prime Minister was to be answerable and subordinate. For him the dual Executive model was not viable. Direct elections and a stable majority in Parliament contributed to his pre-eminence. In a period of *cohabitation* the President's supremacy is not disputed but the relationship between the two heads of the Executive adheres more closely to the letter of the Constitution.

(B) THE BALANCE OF POWERS BETWEEN THE EXECUTIVE AND THE LEGISLATURE

The major flaws of the Third and Fourth Republics were primarily remedied under the 1958 Constitution by a re-inforcement of the powers of the two branches of the Executive. Parliament was mainly held responsible for the deviations and malfunctioning of the constitutional arrangements of the former two Republics and for wide-spread anti-parliamentarianism. However, as parliamentary democracy was the only possible form of government of the Fifth Republic under the provisions of the Constitutional Act of June 3, 1958, the draftsmen of the 1958 Constitution had no other alternative but to limit the supremacy of Parliament. The fact that Parliament only ranks in fourth place in the Constitution may suggest that it has been reduced to a mere *chambre d'enregistrement*, that is a rubber-stamping institution with limited powers and controlled by the Government. One should not, however, jump too easily to such conclusions.[30] If, in many respects, Parliament has

agreement of the Prime Minister, but is, under Art. 5 of the Constitution, the guarantor of respect for international treaties and agreements to which France is party.

[29] On the cohabitation period, see notably P. Pascallon, *Plaidoyer pour la Constitution de la Vème République* (1986); M. Duverger, *Bréviaire de la Cohabitation* (1986); F. Luchaire and G. Conac, *Le Droit Constitutionnel de la Cohabitation. Bilan Juridique d'une Expérience Politique 23 Mars 1986–8 Mai 1988* (Economica, Paris, 1989); J. Gicquel, *De la Cohabitation*: [1989] 49 Pouvoirs 69.

[30] As J.P. Camby and P. Servent rightly observe, "this is probably the most wide-spread idea, but, like any pre-conceived idea, this is the most inaccurate one."; see *Le travail parlementaire sous la cinquième République* (Monstchrétien, Clefs Politiques, Paris, 2nd ed., 1994) p. 9.

indeed been strait-jacketed, it still remains an important institution of the Fifth Republic.

Parliament has gradually been politically and technically "domesticated". Under the previous two Republics Parliament failed to remember that it was representative of the Nation and was mandated by the People, and acted instead as if it was the sovereign power. The draftsmen of the 1958 Constitution aimed at putting Parliament back in its real place, that of the representative of the Nation. This was achieved by establishing, under Article 24 of the Constitution, a two-chamber system (*bicaméralisme*)[31] characterised by inequality between the two houses[32]; by transferring, under Article 59, control over the regularity of general elections to the Constitutional Court[33]; by subjecting, under Article 61, the Rules of Procedure of both Houses of Parliament to the control of constitutionality; by carefully regulating the number and length of parliamentary sessions; and by laying down, under Article 23, the principle that the duties of a member of Cabinet were incompatible with the exercise of any parliamentary office.[34]

Technically, the "domestication" of Parliament was referred to as "*rationalisation parlementaire*" and was aimed at preventing unnecessary obstruction of government action. Both supervisory and legislative powers of Parliament have been "rationalised". A few significant examples will illustrate how Parliament has been strait-jacketed.

Under Article 49(1) of the Constitution "... the Prime Minister may seek a vote of confidence from the National Assembly for the Government's programme or, as the case may be, a statement of general

---

[31] Art. 24 reads:
"Parliament consists of the National Assembly and the Senate. The members of the National Assembly shall be elected by direct suffrage. The Senate shall be elected by indirect suffrage. The representation of the territorial subdivisions of the Republic shall be ensured in the Senate."

[32] This is reflected in the minor legislative and supervisory role of the Senate. Senate may not approve the composition nor the policy of the Cabinet (Art. 49(4) of the Constitution provides solely that "the Prime Minister may seek the Senate's approval for a statement of general policy."). The Senate may not censure the Government either. Its legislative role is also diminished as the National Assembly always has the last word when passing an Act of Parliament.

[33] This power traditionally belonged to Parliament; see notably Art. 10 of the Act of July 16, 1875 and Art. 8 of the 1946 Constitution.

[34] This is a clear contrast with the British Constitution where one cannot be a member of Cabinet without being elected as a Member of Parliament. The principle of incompatibility of offices is founded in the Constitutions of 1791, 1848, 1851, 1875 and 1946. The draftmen of 1958 sought to ensure cabinet stability by limiting the powers of Parliament and its members. Confusion of cabinet and parliamentary offices was thought to facilitate instability as dismissed ministers could carry on their political career in Parliament. Cabinet crises had limited impact on members of the Cabinet.

policy". This provision enables the Government to check that it has the confidence of the Lower House. The vote of confidence is sought on general policy and not on a particular and specific issue. In this respect, this procedure more resembles a procedure of approval of the Government by Parliament than a procedure of control. However, this is far from being the case as the Prime Minister is under no obligation to seek the confidence of Parliament except during a period of *cohabitation*.[35] Under its second paragraph, Article 49 grants the Lower House the power to dismiss the Cabinet by a vote of censure passed by an overall majority of its members. Effective as it may be, the procedure for a motion of censure is set out under very strict and precise terms. Above all, if a motion of censure is rejected, another motion may not be proposed by the same signatories during the same session. In practice, the number of proposed motions cannot exceed four per session.[36] Article 49(3) enables the Cabinet to make a vote on a single provision or act an issue of confidence in the National Assembly, in which case the provision considered will be regarded as having been passed, unless a motion of censure is tabled and endorsed under the terms of paragraph two. This procedure of parliamentary control is closely related to the legislative process, as this enables the Government to exert pressure on Parliament to pass a bill whilst taking the risk of being thrown out of office.[37]

Similarly, in order to prevent Parliament from obstructing the work of the Government by failing to pass bills or by amending them in such a way as to render them inapplicable, legislative procedure was also "rationalised". Rationalisation has consisted in a restriction of the power to amend Government bills. In this respect, not only has the number of standing committees in each House of Parliament been limited to six (Article 43),[38] but also their powers have been encroached. Unlike their predecessors under the Third and Fourth Republics, committees may no

[35] In accordance with tradition and a parliamentary reading of the Constitution, a vote of confidence may be sought by the Prime Minister soon after the Cabinet is in office, as was the case between 1959 and 1988, and more recently, on April 8, 1993 and on May 23, 1995. It may also be sought under other circumstances as on January 16, 1991 during the Gulf War and on November 25, 1992 during the GATT negotiations.

[36] In effect, a proposed motion is admissible if it is signed by at least one-tenth (58) of the members of the National Assembly. As the opposition has logically less than five-tenths of the seats, only a maximum of four motions may be tabled. At present, the opposition having saved only 91 seats in the 1993 General Elections, only one motion of censure may be proposed in each session.

[37] The set of provisions under Art. 49 have proved to be very efficient in ensuring Government stability since only one Government, that of G. Pompidou, was thrown out of office on October 2, 1962 following the passing, under Art. 49(2), of a motion of censure.

[38] Under the previous two Republics, there was no fixed number of committees.

longer amend bills tabled before Parliament but simply draft a report and an opinion on them. As a result, a Government bill is not altered when presented to the full assembly. The power of amendment of members of Parliament has also been limited in scope,[39] effect[40] and the consideration of amendments.[41]

Rationalisation has also included giving the Government control of the legislative debate. Under Article 48 of the Constitution, the agenda of the two Houses shall include discussion of Government and private members' bills in an order and priority determined by the Government. Besides, using the procedure of Article 49(3), the Government may put pressure on Parliament to pass proposed legislation. Furthermore, under Article 44(3), the Government may request that the House concerned votes on all or part of a bill under discussion, including only those amendments proposed or accepted by the Government (the procedure of the so-called *vote bloqué*).

However "strait-jacketed" Parliament may appear to be, this remains the fundamental institution representing the Nation as a whole, as unequivocally provided for under Article 3(1) of the Constitution, which states that "(n)ational sovereignty belongs to the people, which shall exercise it through its representatives ... ". Furthermore, this remains the institution which passes legislation. In this respect it might be argued, as was the case in the early commentaries on the Constitution, that the legislative role of Parliament has been reduced as a result of the new distinction between *lois* and *règlements*. However, this view is far from reflecting the reality. Albeit the domain of legislation is limited, Parliament legislates on the most important social issues,[42] secondary

---

[39] Art. 41 clearly limits the right to propose amendments to matters which fall within the competence of Parliament as defined under Art. 34. However, it is fair to add that this provision is hardly used nowadays: between 1959 and 1980, Art. 41 has been used 37 times against amendments from the Lower House and 51 times against amendments from the Senate. Remarkably enough, the Government has not invoked Art. 41 since 1979. More remarkably, the *Conseil Constitutionnel* has ruled on this fundamental issue of the competence of Parliament eleven times only.

[40] Art. 40 prohibits amendments that would result in reducing public revenue or in creating or increasing public expenditure. This is an obligation which renders all amendments having such effect inadmissible (see C.C. decision 78–94, June 14, 1978). In practice, all amendments and private members' bills are filtered by Parliament (see Art. 98(4) of the Rules of Procedure of the Lower House and Art. 46 of the Rules of Procedure of the Senate).

[41] Art. 44(2) gives the Government the right to oppose, after the debate has begun, the discussion of any amendment that has not previously been submitted to the committee.

[42] This includes civil rights and liberties; nationality; status and legal capacity of persons; matrimonial regimes; succession; the definition of criminal offences and punishments; changes in the court structure and status of judges; assessment; rates and mode of collection of taxes; the issue of currency; nationalisation and privatisation of companies;

matters being left for the Government to deal with under Article 37. Article 34 has also been widely interpreted by the Constitutional Court and the *Conseil d'Etat*.[43] Furthermore, the list under Article 34 is not exhaustive since, under its last paragraph "(t)he provisions of this article may be further specified and complemented by way of *loi organique*".

Since 1958, an Act of Parliament is no longer the supreme expression of law with unlimited scope of application. This has to give way to the Constitution and international law, notably European Union law. However, despite these constitutional developments, the Parliament of the Fifth Republic still plays a fundamental role.

(C) THE NATURE OF THE FIFTH REPUBLIC'S POLITICAL SYSTEM

In the light of what has been discussed above, the question of the nature of the Fifth Republic's political system is inevitable but difficult to answer. If there is consensus regarding the British system of government as a typical parliamentary democracy or the American Constitution as a presidential democracy, there is none when it comes to classifying the French political system. The classification of the Fifth Republic has concerned commentators since its origins but is far from having been satisfactorily answered.

One way of analysing the nature of the Fifth Republic is to focus on the nature of the relationship of the different branches of power. In this respect different readings are possible. The findings of a literal reading of the provisions of the Constitution of 1958 are that it established a parliamentary democracy based on the principles of collaboration of powers and of answerability of the Government to Parliament. A distinction was even made by commentators between a "monist"[44] and a "dualist"[45] parliamentary democracy. If it can be inferred from the

---

the general organisation of National Defence; local government; education; ownership; liability in civil and commercial law; employment; trade-union; and social security law.

[43] See Topic Three on the Constitutional Court, below.

[44] A "monist" parliamentary democracy is a political system whereby, although the President of the Republic has extended powers, the Government is the main source of power as it is answerable solely to Parliament. This reading of the Constitution may be inferred from Art. 20, 49 and 12 of the Constitution. Its only drawback lies in the fact that it ignores the constitutional powers of the President of the Republic which, under the 1958 Constitution, are far more important than they should normally be in a typical "monist" parliamentary regime.

[45] In "dualist" parliamentarism, which developed during the 1830 monarchy (see Introduction, above), the Government is equally answerable to Parliament and to the Head of State. It is possible to argue that under Art. 5 of the 1958 Constitution, the President of the Republic has an arbitration role which puts him in a position of political competition with the Government. However, no form of political answerability of the

provisions of the Constitution and from the opinions of de Gaulle and Debré, two of its major inspiring forces, that the Fifth Republic's political system is a parliamentary democracy, and that both "monist" or "dualist" readings are possible, depending on political circumstances and the will of the political actors.[46]

Such a literal reading of the Constitution is rather limited. For that reason it is necessary to take into account the political circumstances within which power is exercised. However, here again, many opinions are possible according to which feature(s) is/are regarded as essential.

The institutionalisation of the referendum in French democracy may be regarded as the essential characteristic of the Fifth Republic. In effect, the referendum under the French Constitution is a means for the people to exercise their sovereign rights and for the President of the Republic to establish a close relationship of confidence with the citizens and to play his role of arbitrator. More than just the institution itself, it is the use of it which is significant and has led commentators, such as G. Burdeau[47] and M. Prélot,[48] to define the French political regime as a "plebiscitary democracy", a "plebiscitary monocracy" or even an "authoritarian and referendum Republic". Another reading of the Constitution is that the French regime combined into a mixed form of government both presidential and parliamentary democracies. According to M. Duverger, the Fifth Republic is a semi-presidential democracy.[49]

Both readings are certainly interesting but fail to take into account other significant elements of the French Constitution and give a rather seductive but incomplete picture of the Fifth Republic. First, if referendum is a significant institution under the 1958 Constitution, it may not be the only criterion for classification, notably because this has not played a major role between 1969 and 1992. Secondly, as G. Vedel observed, if a semi-presidential democracy were to exist in France, this would be less a synthesis of parliamentary and presidential democracies than an alternation of presidential and parliamentary cycles.[50]

Government to the President is actually provided for in the text of the Constitution itself. Furthermore, as Professors V. Constantinesco and U. Hübner put it, such a reading of the Constitution ignores the fact, under Art. 11, that the President of the Republic can call referenda (see *Einführung in das französiche Recht* (Verlag C.H. Beck, 3rd ed., 1994) pp. 45, 46).

[46] See D.G. Lavroff, *Le Droit Constitutionnel de la Ve République* (Dalloz, 1995) pp. 818–819, and J. Cadart, *Institutions Politiques et Droit Constitutionnel* (Economica, 3rd ed., 1990) vol. 1 pp. 1394–1398.

[47] See *Droit Constitutionnel et Institutions Politiques* (L.G.D.J., 21st ed., 1988) p. 636.

[48] See *Précis d'Institutions Politiques et Droit Constitutionnel* (Dalloz, 1972) pp. 603 *et seq*.

[49] In *Echec au Roi* (Albin Michel, Paris, 1978).

[50] See *Synthèse ou parenthèse*, February 19–20, 1978: [1978] Le Monde.

A third and original way of understanding the nature of the Fifth Republic's regime is offered by D.G. Lavroff.[51] According to Lavroff, the two major features of the Fifth Republic's system of government lie in the direct election of the President of the Republic and a parliamentary majority which either supports the President's action or not. Where the President is supported by a sufficient and disciplined majority in Parliament, the Fifth Republic is a presidential Republic. Where this pattern is not reproduced, as was the case during the two periods of political *cohabitation*, the Fifth Republic changes in nature and turns, along the lines of the Constitution, into a parliamentary democracy with a powerful Head of State.

This reading of the 1958 Constitution is certainly the most accurate one as, by combining the previous two readings, it provides a perfect understanding of the nature of the Fifth Republic, which takes into account the practical development and adaptation of the Fifth Republic's institutional framework and its originality[52] while avoiding too rigid a categorisation.

---

[51] See *op. cit.*, above, pp. 821 *et seq.*

[52] See also P. Avril who states that "... we now know the theoretical model of the regime that we are experiencing, which does not resemble the English regime nor the American regime but fits within our own constitutional development and, in this context, is self-sufficient" in *Une revanche du droit constitutionnel?* [1989] 49 Pouvoirs 5 at 13.

TOPIC TWO
DECENTRALISATION IN FRANCE

(A) THE PROCESS OF DECENTRALISATION IN FRANCE

In 1979 the Conservatives, under the leadership of Margaret Thatcher, came to power in the United Kingdom. In 1981, the Socialists, led by François Mitterand, came to power in France. It would be a truism to state that the policies of the British and French Governments have diverged in many respects. This is notably true of their policy on local government. However, for both Thatcher and Mitterrand, local government was a key issue of their general policy: for Thatcher, it was essential to control local spending centrally; for Mitterrand, it was time to put an end to the French tradition of centralised power[53] which had become "the most backward mode of organisation, decision and implementation".[54] Echoing General de Gaulle's speech of March 24, 1968, President Mitterrand declared on July 15, 1981 that "France needed a strong and centralised power to make herself. Today she needs a decentralised power to keep herself". Decentralisation had indeed been "*la grande affaire du septennat*", that is, one of the major institutional reforms instigated by the French Left Wing which, far from being put into question by the Right Wing—despite its early imperfections—had received general consensus.

Of all the reforms undertaken under the Mitterrand administration, that of decentralisation had immediate, profound and irreversible effect.[55] The Socialists wanted to mark a clear and swift change from the previous law. Less than a year after his coming into office at Beauvau Square, Gaston Defferre, the Secretary for Home Affairs and Decentralisation, asked the President of the Republic to promulgate the Act of March 2, 1982 on the Rights and Freedoms of Local Authorities,[56] which was in itself a sort of "constitution" for local authorities and a "code" of decentralisation. How was it possible to engage in such an immense task in such a short period of time and succeed where others had failed before?

---

[53] This tradition has not been adhered to by all the political regimes since 1789. However, all moves towards decentralisation had resulted in a mere internal re-structuring of the centralised State while respecting its unitary and indivisible form. See J.-M. Ohnet, *Histoire de la Décentralisation Française* (Librairie Générale Française, Paris, 1996) and P. Bodineau and M. Verpeaux, *Histoire de la Décentralisation* (P.U.F., Coll. Que-sais-je?, Paris, No. 2741, 1993).

[54] M. Crozier, *La Société Bloquée* (Editions du Seuil, Paris, 1970).

[55] See J.M. Colombani and H. Portelli, *Le Double Septennat de François Mitterrand*) (Grasset, Paris, 1995) p. 67.

[56] *Loi 82–213 "Droits et libertés des communes, des départements et des régions"*.

In 1985, in an interview with American sociologist Vivien Schmidt, Gaston Defferre was to explain that he reversed the logic of the decentralisation process.[57] The logical process would have been to transfer powers to local authorities together with budget allocations prior to transferring new powers. Instead, Defferre chose to grant new powers to local authorities straight away. As he put it "I knew that, once the local authorities had the power, they would ask for the rest; and this is exactly what happened". With this strategy, Defferre made the whole process politically irreversible and opened the way for a long-term dynamic transformation of the institutional structure of the State and the underlying thinking behind this. The 1982 Act was to be supplemented by a number of other Acts, notably those of January 7, 1983; July 22, 1983; January 25, 1985 and January 5, 1988.

(B) THE LEGAL FRAMEWORK

The foundation of decentralisation: the Act of March 2, 1982[58]

With its 108 sections, the Act of 1982[59] established the major principles which were to turn upside down the long-accepted "tutelage" of local authorities by the central government through the *préfets*, its local representatives. The objective of the legislator was clearly to free local authorities from political and administrative central supervision, the so-called "*tutelle administrative*". Article 1(1) of the Act unequivocally stated that

> "*Communes*, *départements* and *régions* are independently administered by elected councils."

Prior to this Act, *préfets* could exercise their control not only over the councils' decisions but also over councillors themselves. Control by the *préfets* could take the form of the power to annul decisions made by local councils, to give prior approval to a number of local decisions, notably in budgetary and financial matters, and even to dismiss mayors, their deputies or councils. Although, with time, this control had become increasingly less rigid, this was considered to be an unbearable pressure by

[57] Interview of May 23, 1985, subsequently published in *Pouvoirs Locaux* of March 1992. See also V. Schmidt, *Democratizing France* (Cambridge University Press, 1989).

[58] For a commentary of this Act, see the special issue of *Actualité Juridique de Droit Administratif* of May 1982.

[59] This was regarded as unconstitutional by the Constitutional Court with respect to the supervisory powers of *préfets* only. See decision of February 25, 1982: [1982] Rec. Lebon 38, [1982] A.J.D.A. 294.

local councillors, notably urban ones, who aspired to make and implement decisions free from any political and administrative interference. The 1982 Act put an end to this legal anachronism by abolishing *tutelle administrative*, thus granting full executive power to elected councils (see Title One, Chapter 1 of the Act). Decisions and acts of local authorities became self-executory (Articles 2, 23 and 59 of the Act) and subject to judicial supervision (Articles 3, 46). The Act of July 22, 1982, made it a legal requirement that local authorities simply inform—and no longer submit to—*préfets* of their decisions. *Préfets* may no longer prevent the implementation of a local authority's decision but may challenge it before the local administrative court or, in a budget-related matter, a regional court of auditors.[60]

Beside the abolition of *tutelle administrative* and the transfer of executive powers to local authorities, the strengthening of the economic role of *communes* was also a significant aspect of the reform. Under Article 5 of the 1982 Act, cities and towns have powers of economic and social intervention by means of direct or indirect aids to businesses and through co-operation with other local authorities.[61] These powers may be exercised with a view to boosting local economic development, protecting the economic and social interests of local people and guaranteeing public services in rural areas. The acknowledgement by the Government that local authorities were major and essential economic actors was justified by the extent of the economic crisis of the time and the need to tackle unemployment.[62] The latter issue seemed to be the main concern of the Socialist Government, as the provisions of Article 5(2) might suggest. In effect, this power of intervention is allowed where the "protection of the economic and social interests of the local people requires so". However, the economic and social powers of municipal authorities are not unlimited. They must be exercised in compliance with European Community law (notably the rules on state aid laid down in Articles 92 to 94 of the Treaty of Rome); the so-called general principles of law[63] (mainly the principles of equality of citizens before the law, and of free commerce and enterprise); the objectives of the five-year

---

[60] On the regional court of auditors, see Dadomo and Farran, *The French Legal System* (Sweet & Maxwell, 2nd ed., 1996) p. 103.

[61] Art. 5(III) expressly excluded financial participation of a municipal authority in any commercial enterprise or profitable organisation which is not running municipal public services or activities in the interests of the community.

[62] Those provisions, however, were some of the most controversial ones and gave rise to bitter debates in Parliament.

[63] See Dadomo and Farran *op., cit.*, p. 27.

economic social and cultural plan (the so-called *Plan*) and town and country planning rules.[64]

Finally, the 1982 Act gave new life to two major territorial sub-divisions of the French State: *départements* and *régions*. Before 1982 the status of *départements* was rather ambiguous. Although *conseils généraux*, *département* councils were directly elected, executive powers were in the hands of *préfets*, solely answerable to central government. The 1982 Act effected a complete transfer of decision-making powers from the State's representatives to the presidents of *conseillers généraux* whilst abolishing *tutelle administrative*.[65] Above all the Act of 1982 was a turning point for *régions*.[66] On April 15, 1982, the 26 French regions became directly elected *collectivités territoriales*[67] with full executive powers vested in *présidents de régions*. However, these were to lose their former status of *établissements publics* after March 16, 1986, the date of the first direct regional elections.[68]

Distribution of powers: the 1983 and 1988 Acts

The Act of 1982 laid down the foundations for the new powers of local authorities and the institutional framework of the decentralisation process, but was only the first stage of that process. This was to be followed by other Acts which clearly distributed the powers between the various local authorities and central government. The principle of distribution of powers at national and local levels was set out in the Act of January 7, 1983.[69] However, owing to the complexity of the whole process, this Act covered four areas only, namely general planning, town planning, housing and professional training. Another Act of July 22, 1983 was passed to deal with transfer of power in the fields of education, health and social policy, the environment, cultural policy and ports and waterways.[70]

---

[64] For a useful commentary of those provisions, see J. Moreau, *La Commune et la Loi du 2 Mars 1982* [1982] A.J.D.A. 307 and 329.

[65] See J.-F. Auby, *La Nouvelle Organisation Départementale*, [1982] A.J.D.A. 331.

[66] See P. Sadran, *La Région en Devenir* [1982] A.J.D.A. 339.

[67] Under French administrative law, a *collectivité locale* or *territoriale* is a grouping within a territorial sub-division of national territory, which has been granted legal personality by central government and has the right to be administered independently by elected councils.

[68] Prior to those elections, under the Act of 1972, regional councils consisted of Members of Parliament and local councillors elected by *conseillers généraux* and cities' councillors.

[69] Regarding this Act, see J.-P. Lebreton, *La Loi du 7 Janvier 1983 Relative à la Répartition des Compétences entre les Communes, les Départements et l'Etat* [1983] I J.C.P. 3107.

[70] On this second Act, see J.-M. Pontier, *La Deuxième Loi Relative à la Répartition des Compétences entre l'Etat et les Collectivités Locales* [1983] A.J.D.A. 466; and A. Delcamp, *La Loi Complémentaire de Décentralisation* [1984] A.J.D.A. 88.

Before 1983, a simple distinction was made between national and local affairs, and local authorities were in charge of local affairs. Since 1983, although this distinction remains, local authorities deal with affairs that "fall within their jurisdiction" (Article 1 of the 1983 Act), that is those affairs which Parliament would consider as being better dealt with at local level rather than national level. Article 1 clearly set out the principle of subsididarity. At each level, local authorities were granted separate and exclusive powers (principle of *compétences exclusives*) and Article 2 of the first 1983 Act prohibited supervision by a higher local authority over a lower one. For example, the council of a *région* may not approve or disapprove of action taken by the council of a *département* or of a *commune* on matters which fall within their respective jurisdictions. However, in practice, where a *commune* relies on subsidies from a *région* or a *département*, some form of supervision is inevitably re-established.

Powers have been transferred from central government to local government according to a fairly simple principle: *communes* are in charge of land, town and country planning and local amenities; *départements* are responsible for housing, transport (notably school transport), road maintenance, junior secondary education,[71] rural development, the environment, cultural affairs and social and health policies; *régions* are given more prospective tasks such as programming and initiating economic action, town and country development, professional training. However simple this principle of distribution of local powers seems to be, there are various practical difficulties. First, a local authority may not always have exclusive competence. For instance, although regions are in charge of planning regional development, a group of *communes* may set out their own economic, social and cultural development programme[72] (Article 29 of the first 1983 Act). Similarly, although *communes* are responsible for town and country planning, protection of special sites remains a matter for central government. Secondly, competence may be shared in certain areas such as education or management of ports.[73] Thirdly, in order to avoid contradicting and conflicting local policies, local authorities have either opted for single or multi-level consultations or acted within frameworks set out by a higher local authority or even central government.

---

[71] Primary education (up to the age of 10) is a matter for *communes* while senior education (age 14 plus) is dealt with at regional level.

[72] The French term used is "*charte*". However, this has no specific legal meaning.

[73] Central government is responsible for national maritime ports; *régions* for river ports (of no national interest); *départements* for fishing and trade ports; and *communes* for pleasure harbours.

(C) ASSESSMENT OF THE PROCESS OF DECENTRALISATION

As Pierre Rosanvallon put it, the 1982 Reform on decentralisation was based on two simple ideas: modernising the running of public affairs by bringing decision-making and power closer to the citizens; remedying the imperfections of parliamentary democracy and striking a balance between public authorities and individual freedoms.[74] Rather than a legal concept, the idea of decentralisation was a political key-word which was associated with the ideas of modernisation, further democratisation and the protection of individual freedoms.

For more than 30 years there have been many attempts towards decentralisation. Some were successful, others failed. The reform of the 1980s was a decisive stage in this process and, in the mid-1990s, can be regarded as globally positive while incomplete.[75]

The transfer of executive powers from *préfets* to elected *département* and *région* councillors, the transfer of competence from central government to all three levels of local government and the abolition of *tutelle administrative* have not led to the serious problems feared at the time by certain politicians. On the contrary, within the first ten years, devolution has led to better control over local expenditure and a qualitative improvement of local public amenities.[76] However, from the early 1990s local authorities were faced with the consequences of economic recession, notably a rise in unemployment and homelessness, and an erosion of their revenues.[77] Financial difficulties faced by many cities and other local authorities have highlighted the need for a complete and coherent reform of local taxation. This is a complex undertaking and is still at the initial stage of a proposal.[78]

---

[74] See *Le Processus de Décentralisation in Décentralisation: Bilan et Perspectives* [1992] A.J.D.A. (special issue).

[75] See G. Gilbert and A. Delcamp (eds.), *La Décentralisation, Dix Ans Après* (L.G.D.J., Paris, 1993) and *Décentralisation, Bilan et Perspectives* [1992] A.J.D.A. (special issue).

[76] In *départements* notably, councils have shown their ability to run social services at lower costs. Also operating costs of secondary schools are better controlled by local authorities than they were by central government and cities' and towns' public services have been rationalised and are more effectively run. Local authorities have also used their new freedoms to increase investments in amenities. Investment in education by *départements* and *régions* is a striking example of the will of local authorities to improve the quality of amenities. See D. Hoeffel, *Le point de vue d'un élu* in [1992] A.J.D.A. *op. cit.*, p. 35 and J.-M Ohnet *op. cit.*, pp. 264 *et seq*.

[77] See J.-M. Ohnet, *op. cit.*, pp. 266 *et seq*.

[78] Notably the basis of *taxe professionnelle* (business tax), of *taxe d'habitation* (council or residence tax) and *taxe fonciere non bâtie* (tax on undeveloped land) have been regarded as inequitable but not all these questions of local taxation have been resolved. For instance, the Juppé Government has recently renounced a comprehensive reform of the business tax (see Le Monde, June 5, 1996).

One of the cornerstones of the 1982 Act was the abolition of supervision of central government over local affairs. To what extent has this been a reality? One of the first consequences of the transfer of government power to local authorities has been a drastic reduction of personnel in government services: around a third of personnel from *préfectures*; two-thirds from *Directions Départementales d'Assistance Sociale* (social services); and a tenth from *Directions Départementales de l'Equipement* (services for public amenities). *Préfets* have lost their executive powers within a *département* and control over its budget and their role is now confined to government affairs. However, formal abolition of *tutelle administrative* did not mean that interference from *préfets* in local decision-making processes completely disappeared. This is notably the case with small rural towns or parishes which face practical difficulties in running their affairs independently. Mayors themselves have contributed to maintaining a strong presence of the state at local level. For instance, with respect to the legality of mayoral decisions, *préfets* agreed not to automatically challenge the legality of a mayor's decision within the required two-month limit, with the view to reaching an agreement on unlawful decisions. This practice of prior negotiations between *préfets* and mayors has weakened the mechanism of control by administrative courts over the action of local authorities[79] and re-enforced the State representatives' advisory role to *communes*. Technical *tutelle* has not fully disappeared either and, in many cases, government decentralised administrative services, such as those mentioned above, maintained some role as technical and legal advisors. Furthermore, local authorities do not hesitate to "borrow" personnel from those services to staff their own services. All these factors have contributed to maintaining strong government services at local level.

Last but not least, the reform of the 1980s failed to improve local democracy. One of its key-ideas was to bring power closer to the citizens and improve the transparency of local decision-making processes. Though local citizens were better represented and were closer to local power, they were in no way associated with decision-making. The multiplicity of local decision-makers, the complexity of public policies

---

[79] Guy Braibant, the President of the Report and Research Division of the *Conseil d'Etat*, observed that the overall number of local decisions being challenged in court was very small and varied from one *département* to another. He further noted that in 1989, out of 731, 711 local planning decisions only 272 were referred to court by *préfets*: see M. Crozier and S. Trosa (eds.), *La Décentralisation, Réforme de l'Etat* (Pouvoirs Locaux, Paris, 1992) p. 155. Although this is regarded by some as a sign that local authorities stick to the rules on decentralisation (see D. Hoeffel, *op. cit.*, p. 35), others feel that this is evidence of an alarming weakness of the reform on decentralisation (see J. Moreau, *Bilan Jurisprudentiel du Contrôle Administratif de Légalité* [1992] A.J.D.A. *op. cit.*, p. 55.

and of taxation and financial sources did not help the development of local democracy either. In fact, the process of decentralisation was above all based on the sole logic of giving power back to local councillors ("*donner le pouvoir aux élus*" as G. Defferre used to say).[80]

In the early 1990s, the Senate made a number of proposals with the aim of boosting the process of decentralisation. In the light of the first ten years' experience, it appeared necessary to clarify the distribution of competence between central and local government, notably in the area of social aid and professional training. Transfer of new powers to local authorities was also insisted upon, in particular in the field of higher education where it was felt by local politicians that the State failed to face up to its responsibilities and, as a result, forced *régions*, *départements* and *communes* to take on an increasing role in the funding of universities. It has, therefore, been argued that *régions* should be given powers to build, maintain and fund universities. Also, environmental protection could be more efficient, if the powers of central and local government were more clearly defined.

The process of decentralisation might also improve if the relationship between the different local authorities on the one hand, and between central and local government on the other, were better defined. For instance, co-operation between towns and cities is an essential element of decentralisation in a country where there are around 36,000 *communes*. At the same time, the relationship between *régions* and *départements* must be based on a better, more coherent and more efficient distribution of competence and better co-ordination of their respective action.[81] Furthermore, and more importantly, more light needs to be shed on the relationship between central government and local authorities. *Déconcentration*, that is internal decentralisation of central government services, is the necessary corollary of the process of decentralisation in order to tackle the new problems and difficulties which face the external services of central government. Within the first ten years, central government did not take into account the full consequences of the process of decentralisation. Central government failed to devolve sufficient decision-making powers to its own external services. The roles of those services had to be more clearly defined.

The Act of February 6, 1992 on the Territorial Administration of the Republic attempted to provide some remedies. Its first Article stipulated

---

[80] See J.-M Ohnet *op. cit.*, pp. 228 *et seq*. See also C. Grémion, *Quelles Méthodes pour Evaluer la Décentralisation*, in [1992] A.J.D.A. *op. cit.*, p. 115. More generally, on local democracy in France, one may also refer to *La Démocratie Locale* [1995] 73 Pouvoirs.

[81] The opposition between these two tiers of local government has always been the subject of political debate.

that the territorial administration of the Republic falls within the competence of *collectivités territoriales*—that is the local authorities—and of *services déconcentrés de l'Etat*—the external services of central government. Local authorities and external services of the government were put on an equal footing and it is these which became the foundation of the Republic, no longer central government services. Under this Act, more powers were devolved from the central to external services of the Government. *Préfets* were put in charge of most government tasks at local level while central services remained competent to undertake decision-making, co-ordination and regulation. The Act of 1992 has decentralised central government services to its extreme in order to facilitate their relationship with local authorities. It also tried to encourage co-operation between local authorities. To this end it contained a number of provisions on co-operation between *régions* and *communes*. With respect to the latter, the Act added new forms of association between towns and cities to those already existing[82]: *communautés de communes* and *communautés de villes*.

Under these two objectives, the Act of 1992 aimed to co-ordinate the action and policies of central government services throughout the country and those of the various local authorities, and to guarantee some general coherence of their respective action.

The Act also aimed to improve local democracy by providing better information to citizens and local councillors—notably by means of local consultative committees composed of councillors and local associations' representatives, and regional economic and social committees. Referenda may also be organised in towns and cities but these have no legal binding effect.[83]

---

[82] These are: *syndicats intercommunaux* which may carry out single or several tasks; *districts urbains* and *communautés urbaines*, designed to provide more efficient public services.

[83] For a commentary on this Act, see notably M. Bourjol, *La Réforme de l'Administration Territoriale, Commentaire de la Loi d'Orientation du 6 Février 1992* [1992] A.J.D.A. *op. cit.*, p. 140.

TOPIC THREE
CONSEIL CONSTITUTIONNEL AND JUDICIAL REVIEW OF CONSTITUTIONALITY

(A) THE *RAISON D'ETRE* OF JUDICIAL REVIEW OF CONSTITUTIONALITY

The purpose of judicial review of constitutionality is to ensure that any action by a public authority which is not in compliance with the Constitution is declared unconstitutional and deprived of its legal force.

In most democracies it has been long accepted that acts of government should be subjected to judicial review of constitutionality in as much as these must not only comply with Acts of Parliament which they implement but also with the Constitution, which is the fundamental law. In common law countries, judicial review of government action is exercised by ordinary courts. In France this power is vested in the administrative courts headed by the *Conseil d'Etat*.

However, and above all, judicial review of constitutionality should apply to Acts of Parliament. Except in a few rare countries, like England, which do not have a codified Constitution and where, by nature, an Act of Parliament may change constitutional rules, judicial review of constitutionality of legislation is no longer the subject of controversy.[84] Although, for a long time, this was regarded as a peculiarity of the American constitutional system, this has gradually been introduced into European democracies, notably after the Second World War. Nowadays, judicial review of constitutionality of legislation is viewed as a mechanism which is necessary to correct possible abuses by Parliament.

(B) JUDICIAL REVIEW OF CONSTITUTIONALITY IN FRANCE

Over 200 years after the Revolution and the drafting of the first Constitution, judicial review of constitutionality only became an undisputed reality 37 years ago. For nearly two centuries French constitutional law was dominated by the doctrine of Rousseau according to which the law was the expression of the general will. The general will

---

[84] However, politicians find it difficult sometimes to accept the decisions of constitutional courts when these interfere with their actions. For instance, in France, L. Jospin regretted that the *Conseil constitutionnel* prevented the promulgation of the 1982 Act on Nationalisations which was "at the heart of a policy set out by a legitimately elected President and assembly". More recently, in 1993, after the *Conseil* declared some of the provisions of the Immigration Act unconstitutional, C. Pasqua, the Home Affairs Secretary, openly criticised the Court for ruling by way of interpretation, rather than a mere application of provisions, with a view to "preventing the Government from implementing its policy".

was meant to reflect the general interest common to all citizens. The citizens—or at least the majority of them—being always right, and, therefore, any law as the expression of that majority being by nature always good law, judicial review of constitutionality of legislation would be deemed undemocratic. This myth was made an absolute principle enshrined in Article 6 of the Declaration of Man and the Citizen.[85] However, according to Montesquieu, another philosopher who exercised great influence over the Revolutionaries, the people are better at electing their representatives than at running their own affairs. Following this view, the original idea of Rousseau was re-interpreted in favour of Parliament: the general will would exist only once it had been expressed by the people's representatives. Therefore, in the French republican tradition, not only would the *loi* be made sacred but also the institution responsible for its creation, Parliament. Logically, any attempt to set up a constitutional mechanism of review of Parliament's action was inconceivable.[86]

Under the Third Republic, this opposition to judicial review of constitutionality persisted. L. Duguit, a leading constitutionalist of the time, noted that the logical consequence of parliamentary and representative democracy is that the will of Parliament is that of the Nation itself and may not be limited by a superior authority.[87] Consequently, Parliament could unlimitedly legislate in any area, including that of fundamental freedoms. As in the British Constitution, Parliament was fully trusted as the protector of rights and freedoms.

As explained in the introduction to this Chapter, the Third and the Fourth Republics were victims of dominant but impotent Parliaments. A Constitutional Court, the *Comité constitutionnel*, had certainly been created under the 1946 Constitution, but this had only limited powers, namely that of protecting the powers of the *Conseil de la République*, the second chamber of Parliament, which had been considerably reduced. Furthermore, this Court could not invalidate unconstitutional Acts of Parliament but simply prevent their promulgation until the Constitution was amended.[88]

---

[85] This provides that:

"(t)he law is the expression of the general will. All citizens have the right to take part in its creation, either personally or through their representatives (. . .)"

[86] Sieyes' idea of a "*jury constitutionnaire*", a body composed of members of political assemblies, was rejected in 1795 by the *Convention*. This body was regarded by Count Antoine Clair Thibaudeau as a "monstrous power" which would be "everything within the State" and a "master which would chain up" public authorities.

[87] See *Traité de Droit Constitutionnel* (De Boccard, Paris, vol. 1, 3rd ed., 1927).

[88] See Articles 91–93. This was a clear indication that the draftsmen of the 1946 Constitution regarded it as merely technically superior to an Act of Parliament.

Under the 1958 Constitution, Parliament is controlled: the legislative procedure is detailed in the Constitution; the number of standing committees is limited; organic laws and the rules of procedure of both chambers are to be submitted to the *Conseil constitutionnel*, etc. So is the application of the Constitution: under Article 61, Acts of Parliament may be referred to the *Conseil constitutionnel* as to their adoption and their provisions. The *Conseil constitutionnel* was created to guarantee the institutional balance established under the Constitution. Originally designed as a "*régulateur des pouvoirs publics*", notably to control Parliament—but not government[89]—the *Conseil constitutionnel* gradually established itself as the protector of individual freedoms by examining the compliance of Acts of Parliament not only with the provisions of the Constitution but also with principles of constitutional value drawn from the Preamble to the Constitution, the Declaration of Rights of Man and the Citizen, and from the so-called laws of the Republic.

(C) IS THE *CONSEIL CONSTITUTIONNEL* A COURT?

If nowadays no one would dispute that the *Conseil constitutionnel* is a court, its nature has long been a source of debate. Why was this constitutional body called *conseil* and not *comité* as its predecessor, or *cour*, as in other European countries? According to F. Luchaire, the term *conseil* was chosen for the degree of ambiguity it carried. While the word *comité* is usually used for inferior bodies, that of *cour* would have suggested too strongly that Parliament was placed under its control. *Conseil* had the advantage of designating either a political body—like the *Conseil de la République*—or a court—like the *Conseil d'Etat*.[90]

The composition and mode of appointment of the *Conseil*'s members was another source of ambiguity. At the time of its creation no solution seemed to be the ideal one. Had the *Conseil* consisted of judges only, many would have feared a *gouvernment des juges* or judicial activism. Had its members been appointed by Parliament, the *Conseil* would have become the subject of political bargaining. Therefore the draftsmen of the Constitution chose to leave the matter to the wisdom of the President of the Republic and the Presidents of the Houses of Parliament.

---

[89] This is what B. Chantebout calls the "original sin" of the *Conseil constitutionnel* in *Droit Constitutionnel et Science Politique* (Armand Colin, Paris, 12th ed., 1995) p. 619. The *Conseil* could not oppose any government's encroachments upon Parliament's competence, or transfers of powers from the Prime Minister to the President, etc. This led some to regard the *Conseil* a being dependent on the government. In 1978, F. Mitterrand called it a "Napoleon III style institution" which had to be got rid off.

[90] See *Le Conseil Constitutionnel* (Economica, Paris, 1980) p. 21.

Because of the political nature of the appointing authorities and because no specific technical qualifications and competencies were required—unlike many other European constitutional courts—the *Conseil* could be regarded as political by nature. It is true to say that, in its first years of existence, the *Conseil* consisted of political personalities, thus casting a shadow on its independent character. Nevertheless, this is no longer the case and, though political considerations cannot be excluded during appointment, most appointees were or are renowned jurists.[91] The technical competencies of the Members of the *Conseil constitutionnel* are therefore no longer a matter for debate.

The internal organisation of the *Conseil*, with a Secretary-General and various administrative services, is also typical of that of a court. However, the most relevant question is whether the *Conseil* performs a judicial activity. In this respect, it cannot be denied that the *Conseil* rules in law and not in equity, and that its decisions have *autorité de chose jugée*, that is *res judicata*, and are conclusive. This being the most important feature of a court, there is no doubt then that the *Conseil* is one. It can certainly be argued that the *Conseil* also acts as a consultative body.[92] Nevertheless, its judicial functions outweigh the advisory ones. However, this is also the case with the *Conseil d'Etat* and the *Cour des comptes*, whose judicial nature has never been questioned. Furthermore, Article 62(2) of the Constitution clearly stipulates that the decisions of the *Conseil* are not appealable and are binding on governmental, administrative and judicial authorities.

Nowadays, even though the opinion of politicians may vary, depending on whether the *Conseil* has ruled their way or not, that of the *doctrine* is unambiguous: the *Conseil constitutionnel* is a court.[93]

(D) THE ROLE AND CASE LAW OF THE *CONSEIL CONSTITUTIONNEL*

Over the past 38 years, the *Conseil constitutionnel* has, through its decisions, greatly contributed to the development of French law. The Constitution re-gained its value as the country's fundamental law that it

---

[91] R. Cassin, Professor of law and vice-President of the *Conseil d'Etat* (1960); J. Waline, Professor of law (1962); B. Chenot, Member of the *Conseil d'Etat*; F. Luchaire, Professor of law (1965); F. Goguel, former Secretary-General of the Senate (1971); Prof. Coste-Floret (1971); G. Vedel, Professor of law (1980); Prof. R. Badinter, *avocat* and former Minister of Justice (1986); J. Robert, Professor of law (1989); M. Rudloff, *avocat* and former senator (1989), etc. Other members who are not jurists, are respected political scientists (G. Abadie, Mrs N. Lenoir-Fréaud) or historians (M. Faure).

[92] On the jurisdiction of the *Conseil constitutionnel*; see Dadomo and Farran *op. cit.*, p. 111.

[93] See notably M. Waline in Preface to L. Favoreu and L. Philip's *Les Grandes Décisions du Conseil Constitutionnel* (Dalloz, Paris, 8th ed., 1995) XI; L. Favoreu and L. Philip, *Le*

had lost before 1958. The principle of *constitutionnalité* was re-affirmed, whereby public authorities—including Parliament as the *Conseil* reiterated in its decision of January 16, 1982[94]—are subject to a set of rules of constitutional value.[95]

The contribution of the *Conseil* can be examined particularly through its case law in two major areas: that of the respective legislative competence of Parliament and government, and that of civil liberties and fundamental freedoms.

Before 1958 and since the 1789 Revolution, Parliament had sole power to legislate by means of *lois* which the government could implement and complement by way of *règlements*. There was no specified areas within which Parliament could not legislate and *règlements* had to strictly comply with Acts of Parliament.[96] What French lawyers eloquently refer to as *hiérarchie des normes*, that is a hierarchy of sources of law, was therefore very simple: *lois* and *règlements* were the sole sources of law, the latter being inferior to the former. The draftsmen of the 1958 Constitution attempted to orchestrate a legal revolution. Under Articles 34 and 37, law is no longer the creation of Parliament only. Parliament may only legislate in those matters which are stipulated under Article 34, while government may enact *règlements* in all other matters. *Domaine de la loi* was limited and *domaine du règlement* was extended.

During the drafting of the Constitution, the provisions of Articles 34 and 37 were severely criticised by the two advisory bodies, the *Comité consultatif constitutionnel* and the *Conseil d'Etat*, on the ground that, in a democratic society, law may only be the expression of the people's will or that of their representatives. Nevertheless, although it was originally

---

Conseil Constitutionnel (P.U.F., Coll. Que-Sais-Je?, No. 1721); and F. Luchaire, *op. cit.*, pp. 41 *et seq.*, and *Le Conseil Constitutionnel est-il une Juridiction?*: [1979] R.D.P. 28.

[94] In this decision, the *Conseil* ruled out as unconstitutional some of the provisions of the Act on Nationalisation of 1982: Decision No. 81–132 DC: [1982] R.D.C.C. 18, and G.A.D.C. 444.

[95] This is known as *bloc de constitutionnalité* which was set out by the *Conseil*. This allowed the Constitutional Court to extend and tighten up its control over Parliament. This set of "norms" includes the 1958 Constitution, the Declaration of the Rights of Man and of the Citizen of 1789 (notably individual freedom, the right to property, equality, etc.), the Preamble to the Constitution of 1946 (which contains political, economic and social principles such as right to strike, right to health and right of asylum, etc.), the "fundamental principles recognised by the laws of the Republic" (*e.g.* freedom of association, freedom of education, natural justice, independence of administrative courts, etc.), and "principles of constitutional value" (*e.g.* the principle of non-interruption of public services).

[96] In order to guarantee that the government complied with Acts of Parliament, a mechanism of judicial supervision of the government's acts was devised: administrative courts, headed by the *Conseil d'Etat*, could declare any unlawful act null and void (administrative judicial review) and criminal courts were bound not to implement them.

designed to ensure that those constitutional provisions be strictly complied with, notably by Parliament, the *Conseil constitutionnel* has interpreted Article 34 in favour of Parliament, thus limiting the significance of the 1958 constitutional change and restoring the prestige of *lois*.

Article 34 distinguishes between matters in which Parliament may define *règles* and those in which it may lay down *principes fondamentaux*. The Constitutional Court could have easily limited the competence of Parliament by interpreting restrictively the notion of fundamental principles and the matters on which an Act of Parliament could determine the rules. This was not the case however. First, each matter listed under Article 34 has been interpreted in such a way as to give it the widest possible scope of application.[97] Secondly, the distinction made under Article 34 between rules and fundamental principles was removed.[98] Thirdly, Parliament is under the obligation to exercise its legislative powers to its fullest.[99] Finally, the Constitutional Court ruled that provisions of an Act of Parliament, which fall within *domaine réglementaire*, are not necessarily unconstitutional on the ground that they may eventually be amended by way of *décrets* under Article 37(2).

---

[97] The matters listed under Art. 34 are described in fairly ambiguous terms. For instance, it is provided that Parliament shall be competent to create "*nouveaux ordres de juridiction*" (new systems of courts) and "*catégories d'établissements publics*" (categories of public corporations). Strictly speaking there are only two systems of courts—ordinary and administrative courts—and two categories of *établissements publics*—administrative ones (*e.g.* the Post) and industrial and commercial ones (*e.g.* the Railways Company). Had the *Conseil* stuck to those narrow definitions, Parliament's competence would have been very limited. On the contrary, the court interpreted those two concepts much more broadly so as to give Parliament more leeway. See decision of November 29, 1959: [1959] R.D.C.C. 67, in which the court ruled that *R.A.T.P.* was a category of *établissements publics*; and decision 14–L of July 18, 1961: [1961] R.D.C.C. 38, in which newly created *tribunaux d'instance* with exclusive criminal jurisdiction were regarded as constituting an "*ordre de juridiction*" distinct from ordinary *tribunaux d'instance* (see commentary on this court interpretation in G.D.C.C., *op.cit.*, at 137).

[98] An analysis of the case law of the *Conseil* shows that the Constitutional Court—like the *Conseil d'Etat*—has chosen to ignore the literal approach to the provisions of Art. 34 so as to give Parliament the same extent of powers, whether it determines *règles* or *principes fondamentaux*. See notably commentary in G.D.C.C., *op. cit.*, at 68 *et. seq*.

[99] Since its decision of January 26, 1967: [1967] R.D.C.C. 19, the Constitutional Court has consistently ruled that, under Art. 34, Parliament may not enable the government to legislate by way of *règlements* on any matters which fall within its competence. In other words, the Court has sought to protect Parliament against any unnecessary delegation of powers. Any Act of Parliament containing insufficiently precise provisions, thus leaving it to government to determine the essential rules, would be regarded as unconstitutional on the ground of "*incompétence negative*" ("negative lack of competence"). This would notably be the case where Parliament deals with civil liberties and fundamental freedoms.

As a consequence of this decision it appears that *domaine de la loi* can be extended and may encroach on that of *réglement*, for a certain period of time at least.[1]

Overall the legal revolution instigated by the draftsmen of the Constitution has been reduced by the *Conseil constitutionnel* to merely a new technical divide between *lois* and *règlements*. Far from playing the role of a "canon aimed at Parliament" and "guard dog", the *Conseil* was concerned to re-inforce and protect the rights of Parliament.

The *Conseil* adopted a very liberal approach to Articles 34 and 37. The interpretation of its own role proved to be even more liberal. Departing from the draftsmen's original conception of *régulateur des pouvoirs publics*, the *Conseil* gradually established itself as a recognised protector of civil liberties.

The *Conseil constitutionnel* as a protector of civil liberties

It was not the intention of the draftsmen to guarantee the constitutional protection of civil liberties. The fact that, originally, only four political officials and no citizens could refer legislation to the *Conseil* was indicative that this was not its role. Furthermore, no civil liberty is expressly protected and guaranteed by the Constitution. The Preamble to the Constitution certainly refers to the Declaration of 1789 and to the Preamble to the 1946 Constitution.[2] However, it is drafted in fairly vague terms and is far from having the same constitutional force as those provisions which are enshrined in foreign Constitutions and which are clearly aimed at protecting specific rights and freedoms.[3]

---

[1] See decision of July 30, 1982: [1982] R.D.C.C. and G.D.C.C., *op.cit.*, at 517, which concerned the Act on Prices and Income Freezing. It is interesting to note that government welcomed and even encouraged such encroachment on the part of Parliament. In effect, Parliament, unlike the government, is not under the obligation imposed by the *Conseil d'Etat* to comply with general principles of law. It may therefore be in the interest of the government to let Parliament enact laws and to avoid facing possible judicial review. This was notably the case with the *lois de validation* whereby government measures, which were likely to be declared unlawful by the *Conseil d'Etat*, were subsequently validated (see decision of July 22, 1980: [1980] R.D.C.C. 46, and G.D.C.C., *op. cit.*, at 404, in which the *Conseil constitutionnel* regarded those Acts as being in compliance with the Constitution).

[2] The first paragraph of the Preamble to the 1958 Constitution reads:

> "The French People solemnly proclaim their attachment to Human Rights and to the principles of national sovereignty as defined in the Declaration of 1789, confirmed and complemented by the Preamble to the Constitution of 1946."

The first paragraph of the Preamble to the 1946 Constitution re-affirms the rights and freedoms enshrined in the Declaration of 1789 and the fundamental principles recognised by the laws of the Republic.

[3] As is the case, for instance, of the American Constitution, the German Fundamental

Despite this, it is on the basis of this rather vague Preamble that the *Conseil* developed its new role as protector of civil liberties. In its decision of July 16, 1971: [1971] R.D.C.C. 29, in which it examined a provision of an Act of June 30, 1971, aimed at restricting freedom of association, the *Conseil* referred to the Preamble as an integral part of the Constitution and observed that freedom of association was amongst those fundamental principles recognised by the laws of the Republic and solemnly re-affirmed in the Preamble. By including the Preamble in the *bloc de constitutionalité* and by elevating those fundamental principles recognised by the laws of the Republic to the rank of rules of constitutional value, the *Conseil* drastically changed the traditional belief that citizens' rights and freedoms could only be protected by Parliament. From then on, the *Conseil*'s new role was to ensure that Parliament complied with the constitutional provisions guaranteeing those rights and freedoms.

Since this cornerstone decision, the *Conseil* has drawn from the 1789 Declaration a considerable number of other rights and freedoms that needed to be guaranteed by way of judicial review of constitutionality. For instance, the principle that all citizens are equal in law (Article 6 of the Declaration) has been elevated by the *Conseil* to a general principle of constitutional value,[4] from which other principles can be drawn, such as *égalité d'accès aux emplois publics* (equal access to public office or employment); *égalité de traitement des fonctionnaires d'un même corps* (equal treatment of civil servants); *égalité devant les charges publiques et devant les impôts* (equal bearing of public burdens and taxation); *égalité des usagers devant le service public* (equal treatment of users of public services); *égalité devant la justice* (equality before the law)[5]; *egalité du suffrage* (equal right to vote),[6] etc.

Law or the Italian and Spanish Constitutions.

[4] See decision of December 27, 1973: [1973] R.D.C.C. 25, in which the *Conseil* ruled that "to create discrimination against citizens with respect to the possibility of bringing evidence against an automatic decision of taxation ... infringes the principle of equality before the law laid down in the Declaration of the Rights of Man of 1789 and solemnly re-affirmed in the Preamble to the Constitution". See also G.D.C.C., *op. cit.* at 277 *et. seq.*

[5] See the decision of July 23, 1975: [1975] R.D.C.C. 22 (citizens prosecuted for the same offences may not be tried by courts composed according to different rules); decision of July 27, 1982 (legal persons have the same right of reply as natural persons); decision of October 22, 1982 (victims of strike action may not be prevented from claiming damages in court), etc.

[6] See the decision of January 11, 1979 (a legislative provision providing that, at elections in businesses, employers had a number of votes proportionate to the number of employees, was deemed unconstitutional); decision of November 18, 1982 (a legislative amendment stipulating that, at local elections in towns of more than 3,500 inhabitants, lists of candidates could not include more than 75 per cent of persons of the same sex,

Similarly, from the principle of free communication of thoughts and opinions and the right to speak, write and publish freely (Article 11 of the Declaration), the *Conseil* has drawn the right of citizens to information,[7] and hence, that of the right to multiple sources of information in the written and audiovisual press—the so-called *pluralisme de la presse*.[8]

Equally, the *Conseil* used Article 4 of the Declaration of 1789 to guarantee freedom of trade and industry and free enterprise, and Article 17 to vest the right to property with constitutional status.[9]

Where the 1789 Declaration was not offering an adequate constitutional basis for the protection of fundamental freedoms and rights, the *Conseil* had no other alternative than to refer to fundamental principles recognised by the laws of the Republic. However, despite the fears of some, it resisted the temptation to over-use this rather vague formula. On the basis of those principles, the *Conseil* guaranteed, through its case laws, freedoms and rights such as freedom of association,[10] freedom of education,[11] the independence of university professors,[12] individual freedom,[13] protection of the rights of defence,[14] the independence of administrative courts and their exclusive jurisdiction to annul unlawful administrative acts,[15] the principle of ordinary courts as sole protectors of private property,[16] etc.

---

was unconstitutional); decision of August 8, 1985 (unequal representation of citizens between constituencies at elections in New Caledonia), etc.

[7] See decisions of March 17–18, 1964: [1964] R.D.C.C. 33 and of January 30, 1968: [1968] R.D.C.C. 23.

[8] See decision of October 10–11, 1984: [1984] R.D.C.C. 78; decision of July 29, 1986: [1986] 110; and decision of September 18, 1986; [1986] 141. In all these decisions, *pluralisme de la presse* is regarded as making free communication of thoughts and opinions an effective right, as guaranteeing a free choice of information without interference of private interests or of public authorities, and, overall, as a necessary pre-requisite for democracy.

[9] See the decisions on the Nationalisation Act of January 16, and February 11, 1982: [1982] R.D.C.C. 18.

[10] See the decision of July 16, 1971, *op. cit.*; and decision of October 10–11, 1984, (n. 8, above) on activities of political parties.

[11] See the decision of November 23, 1977: [1977] R.D.C.C. 42.

[12] See the decision of January 20, 1984: [1984] R.D.C.C. 30.

[13] See the decision of August 13, 1993: [1993] R.D.C.C. 224. This decision, which principally concerned the status and rights of immigrants, dealt with individual freedom, freedom of movement, freedom of marriage and the right to privacy: see commentary in G.D.C.C. *op. cit.* at 817.

[14] See the decision of December 2, 1976: [1976] R.D.C.C.

[15] See the decision of January 23, 1987: [1987] R.D.C.C. 8. See also Dadomo and Farran, *op. cit.*, p. 49.

[16] See the decision of July 26, 1989: [1989] R.D.C.C.

(E) IS THERE A RISK OF *GOUVERNEMENT DES JUGES*?

The accusation of judicial activism against constitutional judges is not novel. This was first made against the American Supreme Court when it declared unconstitutional a number of Acts of Congress aimed at implementing the "New Deal" policy of President F. Roosevelt. The criticism of a "government of judges" called into question the very legitimacy of judicial review of constitutionality of legislation as contrary to the will of the representatives of the people.

The European Court of Justice has also been the subject of similar criticism, notable amongst British politicians, for its integrationist interpretation of European laws. The *Conseil constitutionnel* has been no exception in this respect. The development of judicial review of constitutionality has taken such an unexpected turn that many French politicians have denounced the judicial activism of the *Conseil*.

If judicial activism or *gouvernement des juges* means that political decisions are taken by judges, not politicians, and that courts' decisions are not based on identifiable legal provisions, then the French *Conseil constitutionnel* has not been guilty of this. This does not necessarily imply, however, that sometimes the *Conseil* may not have been too liberal with the Constitution.

It is undeniable that the *Conseil* has contributed to the development and re-enforcement of the Rule of Law or *état de droit* in France. This has directly resulted from a quantitative increase in the number of rulings—following the 1974 constitutional amendment, enabling Members of Parliament, and consequently the Opposition, to challenge the constitutionality of Acts of Parliament—as well as a qualitative improvement in its decisions, its audacious interpretation of constitutional provisions and the creation of novel principles of law.

Since its important ruling of July 16, 1971, whereby it established itself as the protector of fundamental rights and freedoms, it is arguable that the *Conseil* has shown great circumspection, notably between 1981 and 1985, when none of the major reforms of the Socialist Government were prevented. However, this does not include instances where the *Conseil* might have created principles of constitutional value without firm reference to an existing constitutional provision. The ruling of August 13, 1993 may provide a good instance. The Government had made the fight against illegal immigration one of its foremost policies. On July 13, 1993, Parliament passed an Act on *Maîtrise de l'Immigration* aimed at clamping down immigration. Naturally, this was referred to the Constitutional Court by the Opposition. Of the 51 provisions of the Act, eight were declared unconstitutional and the "amended" Act was later promulgated on August 24, 1993. Not surprisingly, the *Conseil's* ruling caused a heated debate in the press and the wrath of the political establishment. This decision was certainly an important step in the case law of the *Conseil* as it established a constitutional status for foreign citizens and contributed to the development of fundamental rights and freedoms. Although this ruling was well received by the majority of the *doctrine*, some writers, like D.G. Lavroff,[17] believed that the *Conseil* has reached the limits of creative interpretation of the Constitution. He notably reproached the *Conseil* for drawing new constitutional principles from a very liberal reading of the laws of the Republic. For instance, the French Constitutional Court ruled for the first time that freedom of marriage has constitutional force on the basis of paragraph 10 of the Preamble to the 1946 Constitution,[18] and that this may not be subject to any pre-requisites. However, objects Lavroff, by making this freedom unconditional, the *Conseil* failed to acknowledge the fact that marriages of convenience may be a means for foreign citizens to obtain residence permits more easily. Also, the *Conseil* interpreted paragraph 4 of the Preamble to the 1946 Constitution,[19] as conferring upon the right of asylum not only full constitutional force but, more importantly, the highest protection. The *Conseil* not only declared that:

> "respect for the right of asylum, as a principle of constitutional value, generally implies that a foreign citizen who relies on this right, be entitled to remain (in France) for the time being until his/her application has been examined; . . . (paragraph 84)."

but also that:

> "being a fundamental right, the recognition of which determines the exercise by those concerned of freedoms and rights generally granted by the Constitution to foreign citizens residing in the territory, its conditions (of exercise) may only be set out by statute in order to make it more effective or reconcile it with other rules or principles of constitutional value. (paragraph 81)"

This marked a clear change in the position of the Constitutional Court which, until this decision, simply referred to statutes and international conventions implementing the right of asylum. In a way, this used to be regarded as a right of second rank. The ruling of 1993 came, therefore, as a surprise as this conferred immediate effect upon paragraph 4 of the Preamble and imposed positive obligations on the State.

---

[17] See *Le Droit Constitutionnel de la République* (Dallow, Paris, 1995) p. 216.

[18] This reads: "The Nation shall ensure to the individual and to the family the conditions necessary for their development."

[19] This reads: "Anyone persecuted by reason of his/her activities on behalf of freedom has a right to asylum in the territories of the Republic."

So far the *Conseil* has refrained from resorting to the so-called *appréciation de l'opportunité* of legislative provisions whereby the Court could interfere with Parliament's discretion and substitute its own judgment for that of Parliament. However, the Constitutional Court has borrowed from the *Conseil d'Etat* the doctrine of *erreur manifeste d'appréciation* (manifest error in the assessment of facts)—which could be assimilated to the Wednesbury principle of unreasonableness.[20] Furthermore, the *Conseil* has declared legislative provisions unconstitutional on the ground that they did not provide an *efficient* safeguard for constitutional principles, such as pluralism of information.[21] Finally, the *Conseil* tends to include in the very grounds of its rulings so-called *strictes réserves d'interprétation*, whereby it may indicate to Parliament how to reach its objectives without infringing the Constitution.[22]

These new methods of interpretation have certainly emphasised the tendency of the *Conseil constitutionnel* to verge on judicial activism. Nevertheless, as long as this Court does not interpret too liberally the task conferred upon it by the Constitution, the accusation of "*gouvernement des juges*" is nonsense. The *Conseil* has greatly contributed to safeguarding freedoms and rights which reflect the fundamental values and principles on which the French society is based. It is arguable that the Constitutional Court is not judge and King together, and that, ultimately, it is for the People to decide what is best for society.[23] However, the will of a sovereign People, which is at the heart of democracy, remains a fiction if compliance with the Constitution by the Government and Parliament is not ensured. In this respect, it is regrettable that Mitterrand's proposed amendment of Article 61 of the Constitution faced strong opposition from the Senate. This would have enabled citizens, in a case pending before an ordinary or administrative court, to refer to the *Conseil* Acts of Parliament deemed to infringe fundamental rights.[24] A *posteriori* judicial review of constitutionality would undoubtedly constitute progress for the Rule of Law.

---

[20] See the decision of August 8, 1985 on the new electoral system in New Caledonia: n. 6, above.

[21] See the decision of July 29, 1986 on press law and of September 18, 1986 on audiovisual law: n. 8, above.

[22] For instance, in its decision of June 25–26, 1986, the *Conseil* ruled that the Act enabling the Government to privatise parts of the public sector by way of *ordonnances* was not infringing the Constitution, provided that certain strict formal pre-requisites were met.

[23] See Lavroff *op. cit.*, p. 218.

[24] See the recommendation of the Vedel Committee in charge of reflecting on necessary constitutional reforms. For an opposite view, see Lavroff *op. cit.*, p. 208.

Chapter Four
Administrative Law

INTRODUCTION

(A) THE "*RAISON D'ETRE*" OF FRENCH ADMINISTRATIVE LAW

Administrative law is a special body of law which governs the actions of public authorities such as central or local governments, etc. However, this definition is not sufficient to explain the existence of administrative law. In other legal systems, and in particular systems of common law, the view is (or has been) that no specific law should apply to public authorities. This would result in treating the Administration as a body which has privileges and consequently would breach the principle of equality before the Rule of Law, thus jeopardizing individual rights.[1]

The question is whether subjecting the Administration to the Rule of Law is better guaranteed by a common or a special body of law. It is arguable that certain rules which are applicable to administrative action are irreducibly of a special nature as they deal with the very nature of administrative action, that is *puissance publique* or public authority. For instance expropriation, taxation, etc. are specific forms of expression of *puissance publique*, which should only be governed by special rules and principles. On the other hand, the principle of *légalité administrative* is also based on concepts, methods and even principles which have been borrowed from private law.

In France, the origins of administrative law are found in the principle of separation of administrative and judicial authorities laid down in the Revolution period,[2] and in the decision of *Blanco* of the *Tribunal des*

[1] As Wade and Bradley point out: "(t)he study of administrative law in Britain was for many years dominated by the comparison which Dicey drew between the system of administrative jurisdiction (*le contentieux administratif*) in France, . . . , and the common law in England." Dicey's conclusion that the latter gave the citizen better protection against arbitrary action by public authority than the French system led to the denial of administrative law in England. However, senior judges, like Lord Diplock, Lord Reid and Lord Denning M.R., have understood that their power to control the actions of public authorities is of constitutional significance and have contributed to the development of a "rational and comprehensive system of administrative law".

[2] See Dadomo and Farran *The French Legal System* (Sweet & Maxwell, 2nd ed., 1996) pp. 46–49.

conflits of February 8, 1873 (D 1873.3.17), which ruled that the Administration's power:

> "may not be governed by the principles laid down in the Civil Code . . . "

and that:

> "It [the Administration] has its own special rules which vary according to the needs of the service and the need to reconcile the rights of the State with private rights."

Although this cornerstone ruling applied to Government liability (see below, Topic Three), it could be equally applied to administrative action in general. In this decision, the *Tribunal des conflits* confirmed the historical and logical principle of *autonomie du droit administratif*. Administrative law is, by definition, a law which attempts to address the natural imbalance in the relationships between private individuals and the Administration and which rests on the opposition between private interests and the general interest. One must, however, not jump too hastily to the conclusion that this special body of law is more favourable to the Administration than private law. The Administration must act in compliance with procedural rules and fundamental principles of law.

(B) SCOPE OF APPLICATION OF ADMINISTRATIVE LAW

Administrative law could be defined as being that branch of public law which relates to the action and organisation of public administration, that is central and local government, *établissements publics* and *groupements d'intérêt public*. This includes administrative action (public services, administrative contracts, administrative liability), the civil service, public property, judicial supervision of administrative action (general organisation of administrative courts, jurisdiction, procedure, courses of action).[3]

However, specific action of public authorities may also be subject to private law when it does not have an administrative character. For instance, the administration of private property of public authorities is governed by private law. So are contracts which do not relate to the performance of a public service or public work and which do not contain clauses departing from the private law of contracts (see below, Topic One). The application of administrative law has also been excluded in favour of private law with respect to a special category of public

---

[3] On the organisation of administrative courts and judicial supervision of administrative action, see Dadomo and Farran, *op. cit.* pp. 89–107 and 221–243.

authorities, the so-called *établissements publics à caractère industriel et commercial* (see below, Topic Two).

(C) SOURCES OF ADMINISTRATIVE LAW

Unlike private law, French administrative law is predominantly judge-made law. Administrative courts, and the *Conseil d'Etat,* in particular, have laid down the fundamental principles of administrative law. However, the development of administrative law has been more recently influenced by written laws and regulations, notably in new areas of law which have not been so much influenced by case law, such as competition law, town planning law, employment law, external trade law, etc., or in areas regarding the role and organisation of the State which has been rapidly transformed in the past decade at great speed (for example decentralisation (see above, Chapter Three, Topic Two), nationalisations or privatisations, etc.).

General principles of law, which have been created by the administrative courts, also constitute a major source of administrative law. Examples of such principles are the *droits de la defense* (rights of defence or natural justice or due process); non-retrospective character of administrative measures; equality before the law; unjustified enrichment; etc.

Administrative authorities must also comply with constitutional rules and principles. Any administrative measure may be declared void and annulled by an administrative court on the ground that it infringes a constitutional provision or a principle laid down by the Constitutional Court.[4]

International treaties and Community law have equally become an essential part of administrative law. Article 26 of the 1946 Constitution and Article 55 of the 1958 Constitution stipulate that international treaties which are duly ratified are superior to Acts of Parliament. Therefore administrative courts regard these as a source of legality, the infringement of which by an administrative act entails annulment of the latter (see *Dame Kirkwood* (CE) May 30, 1952: [1952] Rec. Lebon 781).

[4] See *Sté Eky* (C.E.) February 12, 1960: [1960] Rec. Lebon 101. However, this is not a form of judicial review of constitutionality of legislation, since administrative courts or ordinary courts do not have the power to control the compatibility of an Act of Parliament with the Constitution. Administrative courts may only control the compatibility of administrative action with Acts of Parliament. However, they may declare void an administrative measure which does not comply with a constitutional rule, unless this act has been adopted on the basis of an Act of Parliament, which is itself unconstitutional but had been promulgated without being referred, under Art. 61 of the Constitution, to the Constitutional Court.

After long resistance against the principle of primacy of European Union law, the *Conseil d'Etat* has recognised the supremacy of the European treaties' provisions (see *Nicolo*, October 20, 1989: [1990] 1 C.M.L.R. 173) as well as that of European regulations (see *Boisdet*, September 24, 1990: [1991] 1 C.M.L.R. 3) and directives (see *Compagnie Alitalia*, February 3, 1989: [1989] A.J.D.A. 387 and SA *Rothmans International France et SA Philip Morris France*, February 28, 1992: [1993] C.M.L.R. 253).

All these sources of law, together with Acts of Parliament and regulations enacted by the Government under Article 37 of the Constitution, form this body of *légalité* which restrict the action of the Administration.

(D) READING AND UNDERSTANDING AN ADMINISTRATIVE COURT'S DECISION

Given the important role played in administrative law by the courts, it seems relevant to give some explanations about the structure of a court's decision and the way it has to be read and understood.

The decision is drafted in the form of a single sentence, the subject of which is at the beginning of the decision ("*Le Conseil d'Etat* ... ") and where the verb is just before the ruling ("*décide* ... "). Between the subject, which indicates what court has ruled, and the verb, which states its power to rule, there are a number of statements which give some indication about the object of the litigation, the arguments of the parties, the applicable legal provisions and the grounds of the judgment.

Each decision is made up of three main parts whose function and legal authority may vary.

1. The *visas* are a sort of summary of the dossier. They refer to the application of the plaintiff, the reply of the defendant and, sometimes, arguments put forward by third parties who may have an interest in the solution of the dispute. These are the *visas des conclusion des parties*. They also refer to the legal texts on the basis of which the judgment was passed. These are of particular relevance when the judgment is challenged in appeal, thus enabling the appeal judge to examine whether the law has been adequately applied by the court of first instance.

2. The *motivation* consisting of paragraphs starting with "*considérant que* ... " or "*attendu que* ... ", constitutes the grounds of the decision. These may also be the place where the court will express its views on a fundamental question which transcends the dispute itself.

3. The *dispositif* in which the court has the obligation to give a solution to the case. This has binding force, that is *res judicata* or *force de chose jugée*. It is usually divided into articles.

Copies of the decisions bear the indication: "*Cette décision sera publiée au Recueil Lebon*" (to be reported) or "*mentionnée dans les tables du Recueil Lebon*" (mentioned in the index of the reports). The publication in the reports is a sign that the decision is an important one.

The Division of the court which has passed the judgment is generally mentioned next to the name of the court. For instance, this could be *Section du contentieux* (Judicial Division) or *Assemblée* (Full Court), which indicates that the case was of the utmost importance and established major principles.[5]

A decision is usually published in legal journals together with the opinion of the *Commissaire du gouvernement* (who plays the same role as the Advocate-General in the European Court of Justice), which deserves particular attention since it places the case in its general context of the administrative case law and helps explain the background to the case.[6]

---

[5] As to the organisation of the *Conseil d'Etat* see Dadomo and Farran *op. cit.* pp. 88, 89.

[6] On the role of the *Commissaire du gouvernement*, see Dadomo and Farran *op. cit.* p. 90.

TOPIC ONE
ADMINISTRATIVE CONTRACTS

In their relationship with the citizens, administrative authorities may employ two different categories of action. Unlike in private law, *acte unilatéral*, in the form of a *décision exécutoire*, is the principal means of action of the Administration. However, contractual relationships between the Administration and private individuals are also common. These two means of administrative action have clear and distinct legal effects. Whilst unilateral action on the part of the Administration imposes unilateral obligations on the citizens, contractual relations produce effects between the parties to the contract only.[7]

The distinction between the two types of administrative action has practical implications. First, unlike unilateral action, except in special circumstances (see below), a contract made between the Administration and private parties may not be unilaterally amended or cancelled by the Administration. Secondly, a contract in administrative law may be challenged by way of *recours de pleine juridiction* only, not by way of *recours pour excès de pouvoir* (judicial review of administrative action).[8] Thirdly, liability resulting from the enforcement of a contract may not be challenged under the rules of non-contractual liability. Finally, save in certain cases, a contractual provision may not be amended by subsequent *règlements* or *lois*.

Although the notion and nature of contract is similar in administrative and private law, the legal regimes are different. Not every contract made by an administrative authority is a *contrat administratif*, governed by special rules of public law and determining which litigation falls within the jurisdiction of administrative courts. In practice, administrative authorities frequently pass *contrats de droit commun*, that is private law contracts, which are subject to the principles of the Civil Code and are dealt with by the ordinary courts.[9]

---

[7] As is the case in private law under the principle of the "relative effect" of a contract as formulated in Art. 1165 C. *Civ.* ("Conventions carry effects between the contracting parties only") applies.

[8] On the distinction between the two courses of action, see Dadomo and Farran, *op. cit.*, pp. 223, 224. *Recours pour excès de pouvoir* is directed at challenging unilateral action of the Administration which infringes "*règles de droit objectives*", *i.e.* rules which apply equally to identical situations (as opposed to "*règles de droit subjectives*", *i.e.* rules which derive from rights granted to individuals in specific contexts).

[9] This is notably the case where, for instance, an administrative body purchases land, sells parts of its private property, rents offices, etc. Resorting to ordinary contracts is also the rule in the administration of industrial and commercial public services (see below, Topic Two).

(A) THE CRITERIA OF ADMINISTRATIVE CONTRACTS

There is no formal criterion which enables one to immediately tell the difference between an administrative contract and a private law one. In a number of cases, however, this is decided by the law. For instance, all contracts relating to *marchés publics* (public procurement) and to the sale of State-owned immovable property are administrative contracts by virtue of the Act of 1800 (*loi du 28 pluviôse an VIII*). So are contracts concerning the use of public property (*décret-loi* of June 17, 1938) and agreements between social security authorities and the medical profession (Act of July 20, 1975).

Where the law is silent, it falls to the administrative courts to determine the criteria of administrative contracts. An administrative contract is defined by the combination of two complementary criteria, the nature of the parties and the object of the contract and a subsidiary criterion, the nature of the contract terms.

A contract is an administrative contract if at least one of the parties is a public authority, that is the State, a local authority or an *établissement public* (public corporation).[10] If both parties are public authorities, the administrative nature of the contract is presumed (see *U.A.P. v. Secrétaire d'Etat aux P. & T.* (T.C.) March 21, 1983: [1983] A.J.D.A. 356) unless its object makes it fall within the category of private law contracts.[11] By nature, contracts entered into by private individuals or legal persons are not administrative ones even though one of the parties administers a public service (see *Société Interprofessionnelle du lait et de ses dérivés* (T.C.) March 3, 1969: [1969] A.J.D.A. 307).[12]

The criterion of the quality of the parties to a contract is not sufficient

---

[10] Before S.N.C.F., the national railways company, was made an *établissement public* by the Act of December 31, 1982, all public procurement contracts into which it entered were private law contracts while similar ones passed by R.A.T.P., the Parisian transport company, were administrative ones because this was a public corporation.

[11] For instance, contracts relating to the private property of public authorities or to the commercial relations between public corporations (*e.g.* supply of electricity by E.D.F. to public authorities).

[12] However a number of exceptions to this rule can be found in the administrative case law. The *Tribunal des conflits* ruled that contracts passed by private law companies, administering motorways under concessions, were administrative ones on the ground that they were entered into on behalf of the State and that the construction of public highways was governed by public law (see *Société Entreprise Peyrot* (T.C.) July 8, 1963: [1963] Rec. Lebon 787). This ruling was subsequently applied to private companies who undertook public works under concessions on the basis of the doctrine of implied mandate, whereby those private companies were regarded as acting on behalf of the public authority which granted the concession (see *Société d'équipement de la région montpéllieraine*, (C.E.) May 30, 1975: [1975] Rec. Lebon 326 and *Commune d'Agde* (T.C.) July 7, 1975: [1975] Rec. Lebon 798).

in itself. To be regarded as an administrative contract, its object or purpose must be closely linked to *exécution d'un service public*, that is the administration of a public service. Although the notion of *service public* is not itself crystal clear (see below, Topic Two), the following three types of contracts can be deemed to fulfil this criterion: (1) contracts which confer upon the co-contracting parties the task of administering a public service—for instance, in the case of a concession[13]; (2) contracts which have as their object or effect to directly involve the co-contracting party(ies) in the running of a service[14]; (3) contracts which provide for the administration of a public service.[15]

Where a contract is not linked to the administration of a public service, it will still be deemed to be an administrative contract if it contains *clauses exorbitantes*, that is terms which derogate from private contract law principles. This is a decisive criterion. Any such term is said to be a *clause exorbitante* in the sense that this would not normally be found in a private law contract, or that it is specific to public law in its object or effect. Examples of such terms are those whereby a contract may be unilaterally modified or terminated by the administrative authority, or whereby powers of supervision and control are conferred upon the administration, or whereby privileges—for example levying dues—are granted to the other party.[16]

---

[13] See *Ministre de l'agriculture v. Consorts Grimouards* (C.E.) April 20, 1956: [1956] Rec. Lebon 168, which concerned a contract between the State forestry department and private individuals for the re-afforestation of private lands. See also *Epoux Bertin* (C.E.) April 20, 1956: [1956] Rec. Lebon 167, which concerned an oral contract between a public authority and the Bertins whereby the latter were to provide food to Soviet Union nationals awaiting repatriation (see also G.A.J.A. pp. 527 *et seq.*, for commentaries on both decisions).

[14] See *Vingtain & Affortit* (C.E.) June 4, 1954: [1954] Rec. Lebon 432 and *Lauthier* (C.E.) March 29, 1959: [1959] D. 281.

[15] For instance, in *Maison des Isolants de France* (C.E.) June 26, 1974: [1974] Rec. Lebon 365, a town entered into contract with a private company whereby the former promised financial incentives to the latter in consideration for creating a plant and jobs. Although the company was not involved in the running of a public service and its activities remained private, the contract was deemed to be an administrative contract on the ground that it was concluded in the general interest as an integral part of the public service of economic and town development.

[16] By way of exception, contracts concluded between consumers and bodies running *services publics industriels et commerciaux* (*e.g.* between consumers and the French Railway or the Electricity Board) are deemed to be private contracts even though they contain *clauses*

(B) THE FORMATION OF ADMINISTRATIVE CONTRACTS

The three main categories of administrative contracts are: *marchés*[17] *publics* (public procurements)[18]; *louages de services* (employment of a workforce); and *concessions de services publics* (concessions of public services).

Discretion of the administration as to the choice of its co-contracting party

Formation of contracts, other than public procurement ones, is not subject to specific obligatory rules. For public procurement contracts, the rules as to the choice of a co-contracting party and the form of contract are stricter and considerably limit the discretion of the Administration. These are compiled in a *Code des marchés publics.*[19] Any infringement of those rules entails nullity of the contract, which is *d'ordre public*, that is it must be automatically considered in a court challenge.

Three ways of concluding *marchés publics* are available to the Administration: *adjudication*, *appels d'offres*, and *marchés négociés.*[20] *Adjudication* (allocation of contract) is the traditional way of concluding a contract, whereby the administrative authority must allocate the contract to the most competitive bidder.[21] *Appel d'offre* (invitation of tenders) operates in the same way as *adjudication*, with the exception that the administrative authority is under no obligation to conclude the contract with the most competitive bidder and may take account of considerations other than price only, which have been pre-established. The technique of *marchés négociés* gives the Administration full discretion, as it may initiate informal negotiations under its own terms and, after competitive bidding, may allocate the contract to the bidder of its choice. However, this technique can only be used in a limited number

---

exorbitantes and any related litigation is dealt with by ordinary courts (see *Dame Bertrand* (T.C.) December 17, 1962: [1963] A.J. 105).

[17] Under French law, the term "*marché*" is synonymous with "*contrat*". However, if all *marchés* are contracts, not all contracts are *marchés*.

[18] These include *marchés de travaux publics* (public procurement contracts), *marchés de fourniture* (supply contracts), *marchés de service* (services contracts such as transport, maintenance, cleaning, etc.).

[19] These also include E.C. laws on public procurement.

[20] This is the terminology used in the Code of Public Procurements, but these contracts are also referred to as *contrats de gré à gré or par entente directe*.

[21] *Adjudication* is either *ouverte*, *i.e.* open to any potential bidder, or *restreinte*, *i.e.* limited to pre-selected bidders only.

of instances, such as contracts for research, experiments, surveys, contracts covered by secrecy (as in National Defence), etc.

Although, for a long time, *adjudication* was the traditional form of allocating contracts because this was financially more favourable to public authorities, nowadays, with the exception of *marchés négociés*, an administrative authority, be it a central government department or a local authority, is free to use either *adjudication* or *appel d'offre*. In reality, less than one per cent of public procurements are allocated by way of *adjudication*.

For all other contracts, notably those on concessions of public services, the Administration has full discretion in choosing the co-contracting party.[22] Nevertheless, the Administration is bound by general principles of law and must take account of the general interest when using its discretion.

The form of contracts

Although ordinary administrative contracts may be oral, public procurement contracts must be in writing in the form of a *cahier des charges*, which is a collection of general and specific documents on the rights and obligations of the contracting parties. The general documents consist of *cahiers des clauses administratives générales* (C.C.A.G.)—which determine provisions applicable to a whole category of public procurements—and of *cahiers des clauses techniques générales*—which determine the technical provisions applicable to obligations of the same nature. For each type of contract, the specific documents consist of *cahiers des clauses administratives particulières* and *cahiers des clauses techniques particulières*. C.C.A.G. are permanent documents adopted by way of *décrets* or *arrêtés*, but are not *règlements* themselves, and their binding force is the result of their incorporation into each individual contract.

(C) THE ENFORCEMENT OF ADMINISTRATIVE CONTRACTS

Introduction

Under Article 1134 C. *Civ.*, legally agreed conventions are binding on the parties. Contracts have therefore a binding force and may not be modified without the consent of all the parties, and parties are equally bound to each other.

It would be excessive to state that this principle does not apply to

---

[22] See *Compagnie luxembourgeoise de télédiffusion* (C.E.) April 16, 1986: [1986] Rec. Lebon 97.

administrative contracts but it applies only partially. When contracting, a public authority still exercises its public power prerogatives in return for financial advantages and guarantees granted to the co-contracting party. Such contractual relationship has no equivalent in private law.

Obligations and rights of the co-contracting party

Having been chosen by a public authority, the co-contracting party is under the obligation of performing its part of the contract personally. This means in particular that the co-contracting party may not sub-contract without prior approval by the public authority. However, sub-contracting was facilitated by a *décret* of 1975 provided the public authority does not object to it. The co-contracting party is also bound to perform its obligations fully and according to schedule, any delay carrying a penalty.

In return, the main right of the co-contracting party is a right to payment of the price as stipulated in the contract. Payment may be *forfaitaire*, that is paid in a lump sum for a number of obligations or *unitaire* for each separate obligation performed. It may be binding (*prix ferme*), variable (*prix ajustable*) or reviewable (*prix révisable*). In principle, payment is due after the performance of all the contracting party's obligations. However, lump sum advances or progress payments may be made.

Furthermore, under the doctrine of *imprévision*, the co-contracting party is entitled to compensation for any loss incurred as a result of exceptional and unforeseeable circumstances impairing the performance of the contract. *Imprévision* applies only if three conditions are met: (1) the parties to the contract could not reasonably foresee the occurrence of the events (for example a war,[23] a serious economic crisis or a natural disaster); (2) the parties had no influence on those events; and (3) the performance of the contract is disrupted.

The prerogatives of the public authority

The specific nature of administrative contracts is to be found above all in the prerogatives of the Administration. These are justified by the interest of public services. Some of them have their origin in the *clauses exorbitantes du droit commun*, in which case they are part of the contract

---

[23] In *Compagnie générale d'éclairage de Bordeaux* (C.E.) March 24, 1916: [1916] Rec. Lebon 125, the war caused the rise of the price of coal. As a result, companies which had a concession to provide street lighting could no longer do so for the price stipulated in their contract without facing bankruptcy.

itself. Others are the expression of the public power of the Administration and are not necessarily stipulated in the contract. In most cases, they give specific powers to the public authority but, sometimes, they may also impose specific obligations upon the co-contracting party.

First, the Administration has a power of control and supervision over the enforcement of the contract. In the case of public procurements, this power is even greater. The administrative authority can instruct the other party by way of *ordres de service*. For instance, the engineers of the *Ponts et chaussées* department (the Highways Authority) have free access to construction sites and may give orders to the constructor.

Secondly, the Administration has, under the supervision of an administrative court, a power of sanction against the other party who does not properly perform his obligations or ignores some of the contractual provisions. The administrative authority may impose pecuniary penalties, which are either stipulated in the contract and apply automatically when non-performance or improper performance occurs (*pénalités contractuelles*); or are calculated according to the damage caused (*dommages et intérêts*). Coercive sanctions are also available to the public authority, whereby it either performs the other party's obligations itself, or asks a third party to perform them, in both cases at the expenses of the original party ("*aux frais et risques du co-contractant*"). More drastically, the public authority has the power to terminate the contract without compensation by way of *résiliation aux torts*—in the case of public procurements—or by way of *déchéance*—in the case of concessions of public services.

Thirdly, independently of the above instance, the administrative authority has the power to rescind a contract in the interest of the public service, even in the absence of any wrong-doing on the part of the other party. The other party is then entitled only to damages.[24] Any contractual provision whereby the public authority would fetter this power is automatically deemed null and void on the ground that it is incompatible with the requirements of a public service.[25] This is an astonishing illustration of the departure, in the law of administrative contracts, from the classic principles that apply in private law contracts.

Fourthly, when a public service requires so, a contract may be unilaterally modified.[26] However, any amendment to the contract may

[24] See *Distillerie de Magnac-Laval* (C.E.) May 2, 1958: [1958] Rec. Lebon 246.
[25] See *Société Eurolat* (C.E.) May 6, 1985: [1985] Rec. Lebon 141.
[26] See *Union des transports publics urbains et régionaux* (C.E.) February 2, 1983: [1983] Rec. Lebon 33; and *Ministre délégué auprès du ministre de l'industrie et de la recherche v. Richard* (C.E.) May 6, 1985: [1985] Rec. Lebon 144.

not be such as to change the nature or the object of the contract[27] nor can the price be amended. In return, the co-contracting party is entitled to full damages, including loss of profit, and the cost of damage suffered (see *Huguet* (C.E.) March 18, 1925: [1925] Rec. Lebon 283). This power is, therefore, not one-sided but, once again, it illustrates the difference between the legal regimes applicable to ordinary and administrative contracts.

Last but not least, unlike the rule in private law, the co-contracting party may not rely on the administrative authority's failure to perform its own obligations (for example failing to pay the price) to stop performing its own obligations. The principle "*exceptio non adimplenti contractus*" finds no application in administrative contract law. The co-contracting party may then claim damages only. This is justified by the principle of *continuité du service public* (non-interruption of the public service). Only *force majeure* could exempt the co-contracting party from the performance of its obligations. However, this is construed very restrictively, notably financial *force majeure*.[28]

---

[27] If this were to be the case, the co-contracting party is then entitled to claim in court the rescission of the contract (see *Ravier* (C.E.) November 16, 1928: [1928] Rec. Lebon 1193).

[28] Where the contract is no longer economically viable, this may be terminated by order of an administrative court (see *Compagnie des tramways de Cherbourg* (C.E.) December 9, 1932: [1932] Rec. Lebon 1050).

TOPIC TWO
PUBLIC SERVICES

(A) THE *SERVICE PUBLIC*, FOUNDATION OF ADMINISTRATIVE LAW?

The concept of *service public* is one of the most important ones in French administrative law. It could even be regarded as typically French as its importance in French law seems to be much greater than in other legal systems, notably common law systems. In effect, the task of the Administration is essentially—but not exclusively—to run public services. For that purpose, it is vested with the necessary powers.

For a long time, the notion of public service had been the focus of the courts and the *doctrine*. This concept first appeared in the well-known *Blanco* decision of the *Tribunal des conflits* (February 8, 1873: [1873] S. 3.153), which concerned an accident in a state tobacco factory. The *Tribunal* notably observed that

> "... the liability of the State for any damage caused to private individuals by people employed in the *public service*, cannot be governed by the principles of the Civil Code ... " (emphasis added).[29]

and that state liability is to be governed by "special rules" and dealt with by an administrative court. In this decision, the *Tribunal des conflits* established a link between the notion of public service and the application of special rules of administrative law, and the jurisdiction of administrative courts. Later, in the decision of *Terrier* of 1903,[30] *Commissaire du gouvernement* Romieu observed that

> "whatever concerns the working of public services, either general or local ones, constitute an administrative activity."[31]

From this early case law, learned commentators deduced that the notion of *service public* was the *raison d'être* of administrative law and the sole relevant criterion for determining the jurisdiction of administrative courts.[32] The fundamental difference between private and public business matters lay in the fact that the latter was intended to serve the general interest through public services. As a result administrative law

---

[29] "... *la responsibilité, qui peut incomber à l'Etat pour les dommages causés aux particuliers par le fait des personnes qu'il emploie dans le service public, ne peut être ŕgie par les principes qui sont établis dans le Code civil* ... ".

[30] (C.E.) February 6, 1903: [1903] Rec. Lebon 94; See also G.A.J.A. p. 66.

[31] "*Tout ce qui concerne le fonctionnement des services, généraux ou locaux, constitue une opération administrative* ... ".

[32] This was the doctrine of the "*Ecole du service public*" to which Duguit, Jèze and Bonnard belonged.

could be defined as the law of public services. This doctrine, which regarded public services as the key-concept of administrative law, prevailed until the 1950s when it was then put into question in the light of divergences between the theory on public services and the practical applications of this concept by the courts.[33] The concept of *service public* became imprecise, illogical and unclear to the extent that some academic writers referred to a decline or crisis of the notion of public services.[34]

In effect, it soon appeared that the administration of public services was not the only purpose of the Administration and that the clear divide between public and private business was blurred by the concept of industrial and commercial public services—which, by their very nature and purpose, are governed by commercial and civil law rather than administrative law—or by the fact that public services may be run by private persons. In such circumstances it was no longer logical to regard public services as the fundamental principle of administrative law. However, this did not lead to the complete disappearance of the concept of *service public*. Far from it, in the mid-1950s, the *Conseil d'Etat* and part of the *doctrine* attempted to re-habilitate it. A series of decisions revived this notion by putting it at the heart of major concepts of administrative law on contracts,[35] public property[36] and public works.[37] The notion of public services also found new advocates with de Laubadère and Latournerie.[38] Nevertheless, in the 1980s, the notion of public service was to face the strongest criticism. For instance, D. Truchet explained

[33] Departures from this doctrine soon appeared in the case law of the *Conseil d'Etat*. For instance, in *Société des granits porphyroïdes des Vosges* (C.E.) July 31, 1912: [1912] Rec. Lebon 909, the court, following the opinion of *Commissaire du gouvernement* L. Blum, observed that a contract passed in the interest of a public service (here a contract between the city of Lille and a private company for the delivery of cobblestones) could be, in the absence of *clauses exorbitantes* (see above, Topic One) a contract under private law. Later on, in *Société commerciale de l'Ouest africain* (T.C.) January 22, 1921: [1921] Rec. Lebon 91 (better known as the "*Bac d'Eloka*" decision), the *Tribunal des conflits* ruled that some public services are industrial and commercial services which cannot be governed by administrative law. Finally, in the decisions *Etablissements Vézia* (C.E. Ass.) December 20, 1935: [1935] Rec. Lebon 1212, and *Caisse primaire "Aide et protection"* (C.E. Ass.) May 13, 1938: [1938] Rec. Lebon 417, the idea that public services may be administered by private persons was accepted. Extracts of those decisions and commentaries can also be found in G.A.J.A. pp. 144, 209, 293, 311.

[34] See V. Morange, *Le Déclin de la Notion Juridique de Service Public* [1947] D. 44; M. Waline, *Vissicitudes Récentes de la Notion de Service Public* [1948] Rev. Adm. 23; J.-L Corail, *La Crise de la Notion Juridique de Service Public* (L.G.D.J., Paris, 1954).

[35] See *Epoux Bertins* (1956) *op.cit.*

[36] See *Société Le Béton* (C.E. Sect.) October 19, 1956: [1956] Rec. Lebon 375.

[37] See *Consords Grimouards* (1956) *op. cit.*

[38] See respectively, *Revalorisation Récentes de la Notion de Service Public en Droit Administratif Français* [1961] A.J. 591; and *Sur un Lazar Juridique* (EDCE, Paris, 1960) p. 61.

that, in fact, there cannot be a clear definition of the concept of *service public* for the simple reason that there is no such concept. This is a mere label which does not reflect any reality but is used by administrative courts to protect their own jurisdiction.[39] Others, along the lines of the doctrine of free enterprise, regarded public services as a traditional instrument of the Welfare State restricting private initiatives and freedoms.[40]

Whether or not the concept of public services deserves to be the subject of passionate debate in favour or against, the fact is that this remains a fundamental concept of French administrative law without being its sole cornerstone. Although French administrative law does not revolve solely around the concept of public services, it could not exist without it.

(B) WHAT IS A *SERVICE PUBLIC*?

Service public could generally be defined as an activity pursued in the general (or public) interest, either by a public body or, under its authority, by a private person, and governed fully or partially by administrative law.

***Service public* and general interest**

Although the concept of general interest is rather vague, is variable in time and space and may be satisfied by private initiatives, it is the end which justifies a public service. The question is therefore: when should the general interest be satisfied by a public service? In principle, a public service is created where the intervention of an administrative authority is deemed essential to guarantee that social requirements are satisfied. It is for the public authority to assess the general interest—*reconnaissance de l'intérèt général*. State authorities have full discretion in this respect[41] whereas local authorities' assessment of the general interest is subject to judicial supervision.[42] The public authority may decide that the general

[39] See *Label de Service Public et Statut de Service Public* [1982] A.J.D.A. 427.

[40] See P. Delvolvé, *Services Publics et Libertés Publiques* [1985] R.F.D.A. 1985, who does not hesitate to see in the very notion of public services a threat to freedoms. Shifting the debate into the political arena, B. Barret-Kriegel even suggested that public services be simply abolished; see *L'Etat et la Démocratie* (La Documentation Française, Rapports Officiels, Paris, 1986).

[41] Except in the case of the creation of categories of *établissements publics* (which may be in charge of a public service), or of nationalisation (which may be used as a means of creating a public service), public services are created by way of *règlements* under Article 37 of the Constitution (save for the necessary funding to be voted by Parliament).

[42] A public service administered by a local authority may have been created by the State, in

interest concerned is to be satisfied by public intervention only, as in the case of public order (for example private militia are unlawful), or that private initiative may complement public intervention, as in the case of education.

Service public and public authority

If the general interest justifies the creation of a public service, this is not an absolute and sufficient condition for a service to be regarded as a public service. It is, indeed, necessary that the service is either directly administered by, or administered under the control of a public authority.

The most common situation is that of a *public authority* directly administering a public service, that is *en régie directe*, if the public authority concerned has general competence (for example the State or a *région*, a *département* or a *commune*)[43]; or through an *établissement public*, which is a public authority with limited competence.[44] Also, the public authority responsible for a public service may devolve its administration to private legal or natural persons, in which case a public service is said to be *en gestion privée*. The usual form of private administration is *concession de service public*, whereby a *concessionaire* administers a public service at his own expense and whose remuneration comes from payments of the price by the customers or users of the service concerned. *Concession de service public* being an administrative contract, the obligation of the *concessionnaire* are stipulated in a *cahier des charges*.[45]

Private administration of a public service may also be operated under contracts other than *concessions*, whereby the private person is directly remunerated by the public authority, as in the case of refuse collection; or

---

which case an Act of Parliament is necessary (*e.g.* the Act of January 7, 1983 transferring powers from Central Government to *régions* and *départements* in respect of secondary education, maritime ports, social assistance, etc.). Where a public service has been created by a local authority, the legality of such decisions may be questioned before an administrative court with respect to the authority's competence to create the public service concerned, the need of the local people for such a service, whether the creation of the public service concerned imposes new obligations on the people that are not created by law, and whether this infringes the freedom of commerce and industry.

[43] Examples of *service public en régie* are *Ponts et Chaussées* (Highways Authority) and *P.T.T.* (Post and Telecommunications)—until the Act of July 2, 1990 which created two separate *établissements publics industriels et commerciaux: La Poste* and *France Telecoms*. The term "*régie*" can be misleading as it may also be used in a different way to designate some *établissements publics*, *e.g. Régie autonome des transports parisiens (R.A.T.P.)*.

[44] Classic examples of public corporations—these have *personalité morale*—in charge of a public service are universities, State schools, public hospitals, *Caisse des dépôts*, *E.D.F.* (Electricity Board), *G.D.F.* (Gas Board), *S.N.C.F.* (Railways), etc.

[45] On the obligations of the *concessionnaire* and the powers of the public authority, see Topic One on contracts, above.

whereby the private person pays dues to the public authority and receive payments from customers (*fermage*).[46] Furthermore, the administration of a public service may be unilaterally conferred by a public authority to a private person. The latter, as administrator of a public service, will be granted *prérogatives de puissance publique*, that is powers of public authority. In the decision of *Caisse primaire "Aide et protection"* on the status of private social insurance institutions created under an 1898 Act, the *Conseil d'Etat* rules that these offered a public service even though they were private institutions.[47] Whether the institution administering a public service is governed by private or public law is therefore not relevant. What matters is the purpose and the nature of the service.[48]

A *service public* falls partially or fully under public law

Since 1921 (date of the "*Bac d'Eloka*" decision) there is no longer equivalence between public services and public law. *Service public* may be subjected to public and private law alike. While categories of public services—*services publics administratifs* and *services à gestion publique*—are exclusively governed by public law, others—*services publics à character industriels et commercial* and *services à gestion privée*—are governed by both private and public law.

Having already mentioned above the distinction between *services à gestion publique* and *services à gestion privée*, we will concentrate here on the distinction between *services administratifs* and *services industriels et commerciaux*.

The distinction between the two categories of public services was first drawn by the *Tribunal des conflits* in the "*Bac d'Eloka*" decision, which, to the surprise of most commentators, ruled that an accident, which occurred during the ferry-crossing of a lagoon administered by the colonial authority of the Ivory Coast—a public incorporated authority vested with general competence—fell within the jurisdiction of ordinary courts. The rationale behind this decision was that the colonial authority was running this transport service in the same way as a private business.

---

[46] This form of administration of a public service is often employed by *communes* for water distribution and drainage, public transport or car parking.

[47] Decision of May 13, 1938: [1938] Rec. Lebon 417 and G.A.J.A. p. 311.

[48] See also *Monpeurt* (C.E.) July 31, 1942: [1942] Rec. Lebon 239, in which the *Conseil d'Etat* ruled that *Comités d'organisation*, professional bodies in charge of distributing raw materials during the war, were in charge of a public service. Similarly, see *Bouguen* (C.E.) April 1943: [1943] Rec. Lebon 86: *ordres professionnels* (professional associations) were deemed to be *établissements publics*. Even associations can be said to be in charge of a public service as in the case of *Magnier* (C.E.) Janvier 13, 1961: [1961] Rec. Lebon 30, which concerned an association for the protection of culture.

How does one recognise industrial and commercial public services? This question—which relates to their criteria—is essential as any service which is not of an industrial and commercial character is an administrative public service. Where the nature of a service is not determined in a written legal provision, it is for the courts to do so.[49] In this respect, administrative courts have adopted a rather empirical approach, using not one single criterion but a series of characteristics. First the purpose of the service must be similar to that of industry and commerce, that is production, transformation and sale of products, or supply of services. Secondly, the financial resources of the service must be derived from the price paid for consideration of the service by *usagers*, that is customers.[50] Thirdly, the administration and organisation of the public service must be similar to those in the private sector. The service must be run under a mode of direction, working methods and staff relations, which are alien to those found in an administrative public service.[51]

A few examples will illustrate how these criteria have been applied. Toll bridges, *caisses de crédit municipal* (local pawnshops), public swimming pools, refuse collection services, local public funeral services, and even public ferry transport services,[52] have all been categorised as *services publics administratifs*. The national Electricity and Gas Boards (Act of April 8, 1946), the national Railways company, the Post and the Telecommunications company (since the 1990 reform),[53] *Agence France Presse* (Act of January 10, 1957), *Centre national d'études spatiales* (Act of December 19, 1961), coach and bus stations, the Mint, drainage services, all have been regarded as industrial and commercial public services.

Some public services may fall into both categories depending on their activities: for instance, the *Office national de la navigation* (the National

---

[49] However, the courts may re-define a public service wrongly described as "industrial and commercial" in a *règlement* (see *Société Distilleries bretonnes* (T.C.) June 24, 1968: [1968] Rec. Lebon 801: FORMA, an Agricultural Markets Guidance and Regulation Fund, originally defined as commercial and industrial under a *décret* was re-defined as an administrative service by the higher court).

[50] If its main source of income derives from a system of taxation, the service concerned will be deemed to be *administratif* (see *Préfet du Val d'Oise* (T.C.) May 28, 1979: [1979] Rec. Lebon 672).

[51] See *Union syndicale des industries aéronautiques* (C.E. Ass.) November 16, 1955: [1955] Rec. Lebon 434. There was no doubt that, before the 1990 reform, in the light of its mode of organisation the Post and Telecoms service was an administrative public service (see *Ursot* (T.C.) June 24, 1968: [1968] Rec. Lebon 798).

[52] See *Denoyer and Chorques* (C.E.) May 10, 1974: [1974] Rec. Lebon 274, concerning a ferry transport service between the island of Ré and the Mainland run by the *département* of Charente-Maritime. This may seem paradoxical in the light of the "*Bac d'Eloka*" decision.

[53] The fact that these boards and companies are monopolies has no influence on their categorisation as industrial and commercial services.

Bureau of Navigation) is an administrative service when it deals with the distribution of freight, but an industrial and commercial activity when it organises the trailing of barges. Port or airport authorities are administrative public services when they administer, maintain and police access to port or airport properties, and industrial and commercial services when using harbour or airport equipment and supplying services to users and passengers.

Owing to their nature, industrial and commercial services are governed by private law and any litigation relating to such services falls within the jurisdiction of ordinary courts. As a general principle, their personnel—except the management staff—are private employees covered by labour laws; their relationship with customers are of a civil and commercial nature; contracts with suppliers are private law contracts[54]; and their liability in tort is governed by private law principles (see below, Topic Three). However issues concerning the management personnel, public property used by the service, and public powers—such as powers of expropriation—that are granted to the service fall under public law.

Uncertainties regarding the definition of industrial and commercial public services and the mixed application to them of public and private law, have cast doubt over the justification of the existence of such category of public services. In many cases where the distinction was not crystal clear administrative courts have classified public services in the category of administrative services.[55] The concept of industrial and commercial public services seems to have declined in the case law of the courts and is even regarded by some legal writers as "one of the major errors of (French) administrative law" (P. Weil)—probably as a reaction to a prolific creation by Parliament and the Government of *établissements publics* which are of an industrial and commercial nature only by the title. However, Parliament has intended to give this concept a legal basis.[56]

(C) THE GENERAL PRINCIPLES OF PUBLIC SERVICES

Despite all the uncertainties which blur the notion of public services, a few general principles apply to all public services whatever their nature, characteristics or legal regime. These principles are intended to ensure

[54] Except in the case where the contract contains *clauses exorbitantes*, which make it an administrative contract (see above, Topic One).

[55] For instance, pawnshops were regarded as administrative services despite their financial activity; local theatres are administrative services on the ground that they pursue non-profitable cultural services; so are local public camping sites even though they are in competition with private camping sites.

[56] See Article L 323–1(1) of the *Codes des communes* which clearly stipulates that

that a public service always attains the objective for which it was created and serves the general interest. Identified for the first time by Berthélémy,[57] these are: *continuité*; *adaptation*; and *égalité*.

Continuité

Because its aim is to satisfy the general interest and it is seen as vital for the national and local communities, a public service may not be unnecessarily disrupted. This was made a "principle of constitutional force" by the *Conseil constitutionnel* (decision of July 25, 1979) and a "fundamental principle" by the *Conseil d'Etat* (*Dame Bonjean*, June 13, 1980).

Although the public cannot expect to have constant access to public services—except, for instance, telephone, electricity, police and emergency services—it is essential that they are accessible and available in such a way as to satisfactorily meet the demand of the public. Moreover, the public is entitled to expect that public services be carried out properly and punctually. For instance, the early closure of a post office (see *Anguet* (C.E.) February 3, 1911: [1911] Rec. Lebon 146), or the closure of a secondary school before the official end of term for a longer period than was necessary to organise *baccalauréat* examinations (see *Touchebeuf* (C.E.) February 13, 1987: [1987] Rec. Lebon 45) were declared unlawful.

Public services may only be disrupted in cases provided for by law or cases of *force majeure*. This has particular consequences on concessions of public services and on the right to strike of civil servants. Disruption of a public service by a *concessionnaire* is a serious fault which automatically entails the termination of the contract of concession. However, under the doctrine of *imprévision* (see above, Chapter Four, Topic One), if unforeseeable and irresistible events have disrupted the good performance of the contract of concession, the *concessionnaire* is entitled to *indemnité d'imprévision* (financial compensation) from the co-contracting public authority so as to enable him to carry out his tasks.[58]

The principle of *continuité* also implies that public services are not disrupted by strikes in the civil service. This was unequivocally established in the decision of *Winkell* (C.E.) August 9, 1909: [1909] Rec. Lebon 826. Any civil servant being on strike was seen as seriously infringing his fundamental duties. Following the recognition of the right

---

"*Communes* and *syndicats de communes* can directly administer services of an industrial and commercial character."

[57] See *Traité Elémentaire de Droit Administratif* (1901).

[58] This principle of compensation was established in the early decision of *Compagnie générale d'éclairage de Bordeaux*, *op. cit.* (exceptional and unexpected rise in the price of coal during World War I).

to strike for civil servants in the Preamble to the 1946 Constitution, the *Winkell* decision was no longer applicable and both principles had to be reconciled. The *Winkell* principle was overruled in the decision of *Dehaene* (C.E. Ass.) of July 7, 1950: [1950] Rec. Lebon 426, which subjected the right to strike to a "minimum service" limit. Furthermore, the Act of July 31, 1963 prohibited "*grèves tournantes*", that is a series of strikes affecting, on a rotating basis, the various components of a public service, and imposed the obligation on trade unions to inform the public authority of their intention to go on strike at least five days before—*préavis de grève*.

Adaptation

Under the principle of *adaptation*, the public authority must adapt a public service to circumstances and the changing requirements of the general interest.

For civil servants, this means that they may not rely on *droits acquis* and expect their status to be immutable. The contractual rights of those who entered into a contract with a public authority are limited by the power of the Administration to modify unilaterally the terms of contract, under judicial supervision and without upsetting the contractual financial balance.[59] For the public, this principle means that they are entitled to a public service which is carried out according to the law in force but may have to accept subsequent modifications, including its abolition.[60]

Egalité

Specific application of the general principle of equality before the law, *égalité devant les services publics* implies equal access to a public service and equal treatment of its users. More generally, a public service must be "*neutre*", that is unbiased towards the political or religious convictions of either its personnel or its users.

---

[59] See *Compagnie générale française des tramsways* (C.E.) March 21, 1910: [1910] Rec. Lebon 216, which concerned the power of a *préfet* to alter the terms of a concession of public transport by tramways by requiring the co-contracting company to extend the number of services in order to meet the increased public demand over the Summer. See also *Union des transports urbains et régionaux* (C.E.) February 2, 1983: [1983] Rec. Lebon 33.

[60] See *Vannier* (C.E.) January 27, 1961: [1961] Rec. Lebon 60, concerning a government decision to abolish the old television broadcasting standards which deprived owners of old sets of their television programmes.

TOPIC THREE
EXTRA-CONTRACTUAL LIABILITY OF PUBLIC AUTHORITIES

(A) GENERAL FEATURES OF EXTRA-CONTRACTUAL LIABILITY

In private law, liability is governed by Articles 1382 and 1384 of the Civil Code. These are very brief and general provisions. The whole body of civil liability is the result of more than 150 years of case law of the Court of Cassation and other inferior civil courts. The role played by the courts is even more important in public law since there is no general provision on the law of tort of public authorities. This was first developed in the decision *Blanco* (1873) which involved a little girl being run over by a trolley at a tobacco factory in Bordeaux. This was a fairly ordinary situation of tort, but what was remarkable was the decision of the *Tribunal des Conflits* which ruled that:

> "The liability (of public authorities) ... may not be governed by principles which are established in the Civil Code and which apply to relationships between private individuals. This liability is not general nor absolute; it has special rules which apply differently according to the needs of an administrative service and to the necessity to reconcile the rights of the State with private rights."[61]

This ruling is still valid today. However, if liability of public authorities is not *absolute*, it has developed in such a way as to include nearly all acts of sovereignty, that is treaties and statutes.

Technically, liability in public law is very close to that in private law despite some differences regarding the date from which damages should be calculated and the calculation of any interests. However, the fundamental difference between the two regimes of liability is in their respective legal basis. In private law, the basic idea is that the person held or presumed liable should make good the consequences of his fault (presumed or proved) or behaviour or action. In public law, the basic idea is that of "*charges publiques*" (public burden). The principle is that of *égalité des citoyens devant les charges publiques*, that is that each citizen should bear the same burden in the public interest. The liability of public authorities is based on the idea that their action or inaction—whether it

---

[61] *"La responsabilité (de la puissance publique) ... ne peut être régie par les principes qui sont établis dans le code civil pour les rapports de particulier à particulier. Cette responsabilité n'est ni générale, ni absolue; elle a ses règles spéciales, qui varient selon les besoins du service et la nécéssité de concilier les droits de l'Etat avec les droits privés."*

results from a fault or not—has placed the citizens in an abnormal situation of inequality.

The liability of public authorities may then be defined as reparation for a tort resulting from the infringement—be it the result or not of a wrong-doing—of the principle of equality in bearing public burdens.

(B) LIABILITY BASED ON FAULT

Liability of public authorities is usually based on fault. Administrative courts are competent to deal with this so long as there is a *faute de service*, that is a fault committed by a civil servant in the performance of his duties. This notion has been interpreted more and more extensively by the courts through the concept of *cumul des responsabilités*—joint liability of the Administration and of the civil servant.

In its opinion in the case *Laumonnier-Carol* (T.C.), May 5, 1877: [1877] Rec. Lebon 437), *Commissaire du gouvernement* Laferrièrre made the distinction between *faute personnelle*—which reveals man "under the influence of his weaknesses, passions and negligence"[62]—and *faute de service*—which arises "if the damaging action is impersonal, if it reveals that the civil servant is more or less likely to make an error".[63]

A *faute de service*, which will make the Administration liable, may be committed either anonymously or by one or more identifiable civil servants. There are multiple examples of *faute de service* and the degree of liability of a public authority may also vary from *faute simple* to *faute lourde*.

(1) Examples of *fautes de service*

When one or more civil servants commit a *faute de service*, they do so in the performance of their duties. In this case the Administration will be held liable in lieu of him or them. The fault may consist in a breach of a legal provision; various administrative actions; manifest error in the assessment of facts; cancellation of an administrative decision which had created rights for citizens; or refusal on the part of the Administration to take necessary action (for example a mayor who failed to take necessary measures to maintain public order as in *Dame Veuve Lefèvre* (C.E.), May 13, 1982: [1983] A.J.D.A. 476.

A *faute de service* may also be committed anonymously, in which case it is referred to as *faute du service*. By nature, it is more difficult to pinpoint

---

[62] "*l'homme avec ses faiblesses, ses passions, ses imprudencess*".

[63] "*si l'acte dommageable est impersonnel, s'il révèle un administrateur plus ou moins sujet à l'erreur*'.

and to prove it. Damage may be caused by maladministration or the bad organisation of a department (for example negligence, errors, loss of files, irregular implementation of decisions), or by constant delays (for example in the drafting of measures for the implementation of statutes), or by failure on the part of the Administration to take action.

(2) The degree of seriousness of a fault

Taking into account the complexity of certain administrative actions and circumstances, the administrative courts have distinguished between three degrees of seriousness of fault: (1) *faute simple* (non-serious fault); (2) *faute lourde* (serious fault); and (3) *faute d'une exceptionelle gravité* (fault of exceptional seriousness). This last degree of seriousness is no longer referred to, thus leaving a dual distinction.

Circumstances of time and place play a very important role in the assessment of a fault. In the case of epidemics, public calamities, wars, evidence of a *faute lourde* will be necessary for the Administration to be held responsible, whereas a *faute simple* would suffice in normal times. However, administrative judges pay particular attention to the nature of the administrative action causing the damage. Most of the time, the liability of the Administration is based on a *faute simple*. Nevertheless, in certain cases, a *faute lourde* is required on the ground of the complex and difficult nature of some administrative action. This is the case where the fire service,[64] the prison service,[65] the Inland Revenue[66] and, above all, the hospital services and the police are concerned. The latter two are particularly illustrative of the attitude of the courts.

Liability of hospital services

Traditionally a distinction was made between problems relating to the organisation and the working of a hospital service—in which case a *faute simple* was sufficient—and medical and surgical acts, for example the fact of leaving an operation instrument in the body of a patient—in which case liability could only be based on a *faute lourde* on the ground that, for obvious reasons, these acts are much more complex and difficult to perform. However this distinction was flawed as it was sometimes difficult to define the notion of *faute lourde*.

The administrative case law has shown some evolution: the *Conseil d'Etat* first restricted the scope of application of *faute lourde* and, at the

[64] See *Fédération Nationale des Coopératives de Consommation* (C.E.) April 15, 1983: [1983] Rec. Lebon 859.

[65] See *Garde des Sceaux, Ministre de la Justice v. Epoux J.* (C.E.) April 15, 1981: [1981] Rec. Lebon 859.

[66] See *Ville de Bastia* (C.E.) January 21, 1983: [1983] A.J.D.A. 375.

same time, extended that of *faute simple* relating to the organisation and working of the service. Subsequently *faute lourde* was determined according to the seriousness of its consequences and no longer according to the seriousness of the conduct or act which caused the harm. Later on, the *Conseil d'Etat* simply abandoned the notion of *faute lourde*. In the case *Epoux V.* ((C.E. Ass.) April 10, 1992: [1992] Rec. Lebon 171), it simply referred to "*faute de nature à engager la responsabilité de l'hopital*"[67] with respect to a medical fault.

However, the development of medical techniques has been the source of another question: should "therapeutic risks", inherent to new and complex treatments, be taken into consideration and should the principle of strict liability be applied in such a case? The *Conseil d'Etat* gave a positive answer to this fundamental question in M. *Bianchi* ((C.E. Ass.) April 9, 1993: [1993] A.J.D.A. 349 at 383). However, the principle of liability of public hospitals based on risk is subject to strict conditions: medical treatment must be necessary; the risk it entails must be known but exceptional; and the damage caused must be of an exceptional seriousness.

Liability of the police

Police liability has been established in the leading case *Tomaso-Grecco* (C.E.) February 10, 1905: [1905] Rec. Lebon 130). Basically, police liability is governed by the following rules. In principle, a police service is bound to make good only the damage caused by a *faute lourde* committed during police operations such as maintaining order. With respect to legal activities, a *faute simple* is sufficient to establish police liability; for example when a film release is prohibited, or when gambling games are prohibited (see *Société "Les films Marceaux"* (C.E. March 25, 1966: [1966] Rec. Lebon 240; *Ville de Paris v. Driancourt* (C.E.) January 26, 1973: [1973] Rec. Lebon 78).

Even if the distinction between *faute lourde* and *faute simple* is established, it is not applied too strictly by the courts. A *faute lourde* will be required in cases involving only regulation as well as police operations on the basis of the complexity and difficulty of the performance of the service. Every time a decision is difficult to take, a *faute lourde* will be required (see *Ville de Paris v. Marabout* (C.E.) October 10, 1972: [1972] Rec. Lebon 664; and *Dame Vve Thiémard* (C.E.) March 24, 1976: [1976] Rec. Lebon 177: in which, the *Conseil d'Etat* ruled that, although a decision was taken under an improper procedure, this could not lead to the award of damages because it was justified on the merits). Finally, strict liability is of importance in the regime of police liability. This is

[67] "A fault for which the hospital is likely to be held liable."

based on the notion of risk or that of *rupture de l'égalité devant les charges publiques*.

(3) Joint liability

Administrative courts have developed a case law whereby a combination of fault and liability offered better protection to the victim of harm. However, this new regime tended to overprotect civil servants and the relationship between the Administration and its civil servants had to be re-thought.

A citizen may be the victim of a damage originating from two distinct faults, a *faute personnelle* and a *faute de service*. The most famous example is that of the case *Anguet* (C.E. February 3, 1911: [1911] Rec. Lebon 146). In this case a customer of a post office had to leave through a rear exit which was reserved for staff because of the earlier closing of the office (this was a *faute de service*) but members of staff who saw him in this part of the office to which public had no access, treated him so roughly that they broke one of his legs (this was a *faute personnelle*). The *Conseil d'Etat* ruled that the prejudice as a whole had to be made good on the ground of *cumul de fautes*.

The administrative court was even more daring by holding the Administration liable on the ground of *cumul des responsabilités* as in the case of *Lemonnier* (C.E.) July 26, 1918: [1918] Rec. Lebon 718). The *Conseil* ruled that a harm resulting from the *faute personnelle* of a civil servant had to be made good by the administrative authority, as it would be in the case of a *faute de service*, if the operation of the administrative service made the fault of the civil servant possible or, as the *Commissaire du Gouvernement* Léon Blum put it in his opinion, when the administrative service has "conditioned" the commission of the fault. As he further said:

> "The fault may be disconnected from the service but the service may not be disconnected from the fault"[68]

This case was concerned with spectators in a municipal fair who were injured by shots from a shooting stand due to the mayor of the town failing to take the necessary safety measures. It suffices that the fault is in some way connected with an administrative service for the victim to be awarded damages on the ground of *cumul des responsabilités*.

For a long time, the *Conseil* continuously rejected the possibility of the Administration suing the responsible civil servant by means of *action récursoire* (see *Poursines* (C.E.) March 28, 1924: [1926] 3 S. 17).

[68] "*La faute se détache peut-être du service, mais le service ne se détache pas de la faute.*"

However, the supreme administrative court reversed its case law, which was too favourable to the civil servant. On July 28, 1951, it made two important judgments: in *Laruelle*—a case which involved a *cumul de responsabilité*—it recognised the right of the administrative authority to sue by means of *action récursoire* the liable member of its service. The civil servant concerned had caused a road accident while driving a public service car for his private use, and the public authority concerned had been found guilty of a *faute de ourice* for failing to take the appropriate measures to control the use of its cars by its servants. The Administration must make good any damage caused by one of its servants following a *faute personnelle*, but the administrative service itself then becomes a victim as it has to bear the consequences of its employee's fault and has obligations to make good the damage. In *Delville* where a driver of a Government Department involved in a car accident was sued by his victim before the ordinary courts, the *Conseil* allowed a civil servant to sue the Administration after he had been ordered to make good the damage in full, although this resulted from both a *faute de service* (the lorry he was driving had faulty brakes) and a *faute personnelle* (his drink-driving), that is a *cumul de fautes*. The principle is that the Administration should pay part of the damages in proportion to the seriousness of each of the faults. Today, Article 11 of the Act of July 13, 1983 provides that the administrative service concerned must bear the cost of damages when the *faute personnelle* of one of its members cannot be separated from the performance of his duties.

(C) STRICT LIABILITY

The recognition of strict liability in administrative law is certainly one of the most remarkable aspects in the development of the French law of government tort.

Strict liability is not specific to public law as the Court of Cassation has developed its case law on an interpretation of Articles 1384 *et seq.*—which concern liability on account of things (for example a pet, a car, etc.) or persons (for example children, employees) which, or who, are under one's control—whereby the owner of the thing, the parent or the employer is presumed liable.

Under public law, however, strict liability is originally associated with the notion of risk. Some activities are dangerous and may cause harm even in the absence of fault. The *Conseil* ruled that such harm had to be made good. At the end of the nineteenth century, *Commissaire du gouvernement* Romieu wrote in his opinion on a case which related to an accident which happened to a state employee, that the "State must protect its employees against risk resulting from works it has commissioned".[69]

The law of liability based on risk developed further. However, the Administration is bound to pay damages only when the risk involved exceeds an acceptable limit, that is the burden of the general interest that the citizens are expected to bear. Therefore two conditions must be met in order for an administrative authority to be held liable on the ground of risk: (1) the damage must be exceptional (as the French put it there must be a *charge anormale*); and (2) it must be specific to the victim (*préjudice spécial*). In other words there must be *rupture de l'égalité devant les charges publiques*.

Strict liability is *d'ordre public*. This means that the victim may invoke it at any time during the proceedings and the judge must automatically decide on the matter.

Of course, strict liability is very favourable to the victim since the victim need not prove evidence of a fault.

(1) Strict liability based on risk

Public works

Special rules on liability apply to damage caused by public works or *travaux publics*. These were laid down at a time when public authorities could not be held liable. The Act of *28 Pluviôse an VIII* (1800) gave competence to the *Conseils de la Préfecture* (which became the *Tribunaux administratifs* in 1953) to deal with disputes relating to public works. A wider interpretation of this provision allowed actions for damages relating not only to the building but also to the operation of public constructions. Despite the rapid development of the law of liability in tort of public authorities, the regime of liability applicable to public works remained a special one.

Strict liability has been widely applied by the courts in the field of public works. A number of claims for damage arise in connection with public works, either during their construction or their maintenance. However, a clear distinction has been made between their *usagers*, that is users, and third persons. For the latter category, liability is established as soon as a causal link between the work and the damage—which has to be exceptional—is proved. As to the former, they are expected to bear the burden of risk when they use the structure concerned. A fault will be therefore required but there is *présomption de faute*, that is a fault is presumed. In the case of *défaut d'entretien normal* (lack of proper

[69] *"l'Etat doit garantir ses ouvriers contre le risque résultant des travaux qu'il leur fait exécuter"*. See *Cames* (C.E.) June 21, 1995: [1995] Rec. Lebon 509.

maintenance), it is for the administrative authority to give evidence to the contrary. For instance, dangers on roads must be properly signposted.

The courts have recognised that users of public structures may rely on strict liability when a structure is "exceptionally dangerous". However, the *Conseil* restricted the scope of application of its case law by excluding from the category of exceptionally dangerous structures certain public works such as roads, when rock-falls or avalanches are very likely.[70]

Unlike accidental damage, permanent damage, that is that which lasts for a certain period of time (for example a street being blocked off owing to alteration, or devaluation of property resulting from noise, or various nuisances or pollution) is made good, whether the victim is a user or not, provided that it is exceptional and specific to the victim.

Dangerous things and activities

Strict liability is accepted in three cases. First, when one lives near dangerous substances or things, there is an abnormal risk for the neighbourhood or *risque anormal de voisinage* (see *Regnault-Desroziers* (C.E.) March 28, 1919: [1919] R.D.P. 239, which involved the explosion of ammunitions stored in a fortress in La Courneuve; see also *S.N.C.F.* (C.E. Ass.) October 21, 1966: [1966] Rec. Lebon 557, which was concerned with the explosion of a wagon full of ammunitions in the train station of Sézanne). However, the *Conseil d'Etat* did not follow the view of the lower administrative courts, that fireworks presented the same danger as ammunitions in order to justify strict liability (see *Moisan* (C.E.) March 30, 1979: [1979] Rec. Lebon 143).

Secondly, in 1949, the *Conseil* ruled that the use by the police of firearms and other objects "presenting exceptional risks for people and property" would entail strict liability (see *Consorts Lecomte* and *Franquette et Daramy* (C.E. Ass.) June 24, 1949: [1949] Rec. Lebon 307: in the first case, a pub owner, whilst sitting peacefully in front of his pub, was accidentally shot dead by a police constable who was chasing a fleeing motorist; in the second case, a bypasser was shot dead by a police

---

[70] See *Ministre de l'équipement et du logement v Dalleau* (C.E. Ass.) July 6, 1973: [1973] Rec. Lebon 482 and *Payet* (C.E.) November 3, 1982: [1982] Rec. Lebon 367, where the *Conseil* ruled to the contrary. Both cases were concerned with a coastal road "*la route du littoral*", on the island of Réunion. Throughout the year this was exposed to falls of rocks. *Vissicitudes Récentes de la Notion de Service Public* [1948] Rev. Adm. 23; J.-L Corail, *La Crise de la Notion Juridique de Service Public* (L.G.D.J., Paris, 1954).

In the first decision, the *Conseil* ruled that strict liability should apply owing to the exceptionally dangerous character of the road, even though there was no intrinsic defect or lack of maintenance. Ten years later, important consolidation works were carried out—notably a second carriage way was constructed—so that the road could no longer be regarded as being exceptionally dangerous (second decision).

constable who was chasing the assailant of a taxi-driver). Strict liability is justified only in cases where the damage is suffered by a person who is not connected to a police operation, as in *Dame Aubergé et Dumont* (C.E. Sect.) July 27, 1951: [1951] Rec. Lebon 447) which involved the death of a motorist shot dead by a policeman whilst forcing his way through a police cordon. In this case, the liability of the police was based on a *faute simple* because the cordon was not sufficiently visible.

Finally, strict liability has been extended to cases involving risks arising from dangerous activities, such as the escape of prisoners, liberal penal measures and medical treatment of mentally sick people who have permission to leave the hospital as part of the treatment, etc.[71]

Social risks

A special regime of liability, based on the idea of social risk and national solidarity, has been created by statute. For instance, the Acts of 1919 and 1946 provide for compensation for war suffering.

Under the Act of April 16, 1914 *communes* may be held liable for any damage resulting from meetings and gatherings. This gave competence to ordinary courts and provided for shared liability between *communes* and the State. This statute was amended by two Acts of January 7, 1983 and January 9, 1986. Article 92 of the former Act provided that

> "the State is liable for destruction and damage resulting from serious crimes and major offences committed by open violence, by armed or unarmed people in gathering and meetings, against persons or property."[72]

Victims of such offences must sue the State which can then sue the *communes*, where the damage was suffered, by way of an *action récursoire*. The latter Act provides that disputes are to be dealt with by administrative courts. Here liability rests on the concept of risk and not that of fault. This means that the victim need only prove a causal link between the acts of violence and the damage suffered.

The Act of January 3, 1977, amended by the Acts of 1983 and 1990, guarantees compensation to victims of crime who suffer personal injury. The State is held liable.

---

[71] In *Thouzellier* (C.E.) February 3, 1956: [1956] Rec. Lebon 49, the *Conseil* took the view that, although these are legitimate, modern methods of supervised education in specialised institutions for young offenders presented a special risk for third persons and, therefore, that any victim of damage caused by a young offender who had escaped from such an institution, entailed the strict liability of the State.

[72] "*L'Etat est civilement responsable des dégâts et dommages résultant des crimes et délits commis à force ouverte ou par violence, par des attroupements ou rassemblements armés ou non armés, soit contre les personnes, soit contre les biens.*"

Compensation for victims of acts of terrorism is provided for by the Act of September 9, 1986 on the Prevention of Terrorism and Acts against State Security, and the implementation *décret* of October 15, 1986. These provisions create a special regime of liability and a Guarantee Fund against acts of terrorism (financed by a tax on property insurance contracts). Victims of acts of terrorism must send their claim to the Fund. The criminal courts of Paris are the only competent courts to deal with related litigation.

Under the Act of December 31, 1991 a special scheme of compensation, together with a Fund responsible for the award of damages, was created for people who have been contaminated with the AIDS virus through blood products. The decisions of the Fund are appealable before the Court of Appeal of Paris.

Finally under the Act of July 1, 1964 (amended in 1975) the State is liable for damage caused by compulsory vaccination, and the Act of November 12, 1965 created a mechanism of compensation for damage of a nuclear origin.

Damage suffered by temporary agents of the Administration

In *Cames* (C.E.) June 21, 1995: [1995] Rec. Lebon 509), the *Conseil* established the principle of liability of the Administration when one of its members was a victim of a work accident. This jurisprudence, which no longer applies to civil servants as they are now protected by specific legislation, has been extended to temporary agents of an administrative authority.

(2) Strict liability based on *rupture de l'égalité des charges publiques*

It may happen that a lawful action of the Administration performed in the public interest may result in an abnormal burden for an individual citizen. In such a case the courts may hold the Administration liable if the damage is abnormal and specific to that citizen. Two criteria are considered: the seriousness of the damage and the number of persons who have suffered it.

Most cases are concerned with administrative decisions taken on the ground of public order. In *Couitéas* (C.E.) November 30, 1923: [1923] Rec. Lebon 789), the *Conseil* laid down the principle according to which administrative authorities may refuse to give assistance to a citizen to have a judgment enforced if there is a serious threat to public order. However, if such decision is lawful, then the citizen is likely to bear an abnormal burden in the public interest and, as the principle of equality is breached, is entitled to damages.

(D) THE LIABILITY OF THE STATE AS A LEGISLATIVE, JUDICIAL AND EXECUTIVE POWER

Once recognised, the principle of the liability of a public authority has been gradually extended to the idea that the State may, under certain circumstances, be held liable for damage caused in the performance of its legislative, judicial or government functions.

Although, for a long time, the State could not be held liable when performing its legislative functions, the *Conseil d'Etat* soon established the principle of *responsabilité du faits des lois*—liability resulting from the application of statutes—through the application of the principle of *équalité devant les charges publiques*. In a number of decisions adopted in the first half of the twentieth century, in particular in the case of *La Fleurette* (*Société des produits laitiers La Fleurette* (C.E.) January 14, 1938: [1938] Rec. Lebon 25), the *Conseil d'Etat* ruled that the damaging consequences of a statute should be made good.[73] Later on, in 1944, the same court confirmed its first ruling in a case involving a statute which imposed a higher proportion of hop in the production of beer with the view to supporting the hop market. This caused damage to the business of *Caucheteux et Desmonds*, which was the only specialist manufacturer of glucose used in the production of beer (see (C.E.) January 21, 1944: [1944] Rec. Lebon 22).

State liability resulting from an Act of Parliament is confined within strict conditions. First, the *Conseil d'Etat* will examine whether the statute concerned or the preparatory works have intended to exclude damages. Secondly, it will be considered that, in most cases, damages are not justified because statutory provisions are intended to satisfy the general interest which includes the economic as well as the social interest. Thirdly, the damage suffered must not only be certain and direct (that is not merely probable) but also specific to the victim and abnormally serious.

The liability of the State exercising its judicial powers is also limited. An Act of July 5, 1972 abolished the principle of no state liability in the case of damage caused by maladministration of the services of justice. The State may be held liable only in the case of *faute lourde or déni de justice*—miscarriage of justice (Article 11). Until 1978, the principle of liability was applicable to ordinary courts only. The *Conseil d'Etat* then ruled in favour of a right to damages in the case of serious fault occurring

---

[73] In order to support the milk market, the production of a substitute for fresh cream was banned under an Act of Parliament. As a result of this legislation, the only dairy factory producing this substitute had to close down its business. This was a serious and special damage.

in the course of administrative justice. This clearly excludes any fault resulting from the merits of a court decision as this has *res judicata* (see *Darmont* (C.E.) December 29, 1978: [1979] R.D.P. 1742).

Although, in principle, the lawfulness of *actes de gouvernement* cannot be examined by administrative courts, the possibility that the State may be held liable for damage caused by such measures—which are, for this purpose, regarded as statutes—is not excluded. State liability was raised in *Compagnie générale d'énergie radio-électrique* (C.E.), March 30, 1966: [1966] Rec. Lebon 257). This case was concerned with the damage caused to a company running a radio station known as the "*Poste parisien*" which was requisitioned without compensation by the Germans in 1940. The damage was notably resulting from the fact that compensation was postponed to an unfixed date by an international convention. Although the *Conseil d'Etat* did not regard the State as liable, because of the damage not being specific to the plaintiff, it laid down the principle of awarding damages to make good the prejudicial consequences of the application of international treaties.[74]

(E) CASES WHERE PUBLIC LIABILITY IS DEALT WITH IN ORDINARY COURTS

There are a number of cases in which the liability in tort of public authorities is dealt with by ordinary courts.

The case of *S.P.I.C.s*

In Topic Two above, *services publics industriels et commerciaux* have been identified as public services being governed by both public law—with respect to their status, organisation, powers, use of public property—and private law with respect to their activities—which are of a commercial and industrial nature—personnel (apart from the director and the accountant), and relationships with customers.[75]

---

[74] This was confirmed in case *Dame Burgat* (C.E.) October 29, 1976: [1976] R.D.P. 213 in which Mrs Burgat, a landlady, could not expel her tenant who was married to an international civil servant of UNESCO. In effect, the latter was protected by an agreement known as "accord du siège" signed by France and the international organisation. As a result, Mrs Burgat was awarded damages by the administrative court on the ground of breach of the principle of *égalité devant les charges publiques*.

[75] As seen above under Topic Two, *Electricité de France*, *Gaz de France and the* S.N.C.F. are examples of *S.P.I.C.s*. With respect to *France Télécoms*, there was some uncertainty: the telephone customers were deemed to be party to an administrative contract. However, the Act of July 2, 1990, on the organisation of the public service of the Post and *France Telecoms*, provided that the relationship between those public services and the members of the public using them are of a commercial nature.

In the leading case "*Bac d'Eloka*" (1921), the *Tribunal des conflits* ruled that, where no provision had vested the administrative courts with specific powers, ordinary courts were competent to deal with liability cases involving a public service run under the same conditions as a private business.

The administration of public authorities' private property

In the administration of public authorities' private property, the liability of the public authority is similar to that of a private person and, as such, is dealt with by ordinary courts.

Damages resulting from a *voie de fait* or a *emprise irrégulière*

In the case of a private citizen being improperly deprived of his property as a result of an action of the Administration (*emprise irrégulière*), or of his private property or fundamental freedoms being affected by an unlawful administrative action (*voie de fait*), damages are to be sought before an ordinary court.

Private liability of civil servants

Cases involving the liability of civil servants who have acted as private persons, fall within the jurisdiction of ordinary courts. Faults committed by civil servants which are not linked to the performance of their duties are dealt with by these courts as they are said to be "*fautes personnelles détachables*" (*du fonctionnement du service*).

Statutory jurisdiction of ordinary courts

Some legislation has extended the competence of ordinary courts in the domain of state liability. The Act of April 5, 1937 on state liability for damage caused to school pupils, or by school pupils as a result of inadequate supervision, substituted State liability for that of the teachers and gave competence to ordinary courts. However, the State still has the possibility of bringing an *action récursoire* against the responsible teachers in the case of *faute personnelle*. On the other hand, the administrative courts are competent if the damage results from maladministration of the service (for example an insufficient number of supervisory staff) or from insufficient maintenance of the buildings.

Under the Act of December 31, 1957, ordinary courts have jurisdiction to deal with car accidents involving administrative vehicles.

Chapter Five
Criminal Law

INTRODUCTION

(A) HISTORICAL OUTLINE OF FRENCH CRIMINAL LAW

French criminal law before the codification

Originally based on Barbarian private laws (for example Visigothic laws, Salic laws, laws of the Riparians, etc.), criminal law in France was contrasting with Roman law which was developed in the form of public administration of justice.[1] It was not until the Middle Ages that criminal law became a customary law common to all French provinces and the product of the merger of existing legal rules.

From the twelfth century, justice was delivered by professional lawyers. However, in the thirteenth and even the fourteenth centuries, the noble still resorted to private justice despite the creation of a system of public administration of justice. Later on, from the sixteenth to the eighteenth centuries, French criminal law was characterised by the diversity of its sources.

Roman law provided criminal practitioners with fundamental sources of inspiration for the thinking of a codified system of criminal law. The *Digest*, the *Codex* and the writings of *juris consulti* were regarded as being still applicable, except where customary provisions or a written text prevailed. This gave a rather European flavour to criminal law since the same influence of Roman law through the works of the Glossators and Bartolus could be found in The Netherlands (Damhoudère, sixteenth century), in Milan (Julius Clarus, seventeenth century), in the Papal States (Farinaccius, seventeenth century), and in Germany (Carpzov, eighteenth century). The opinions of these writers exercised considerable influence on judges, whose rulings were subsequently commented

[1] For a historical background of French law, see Dadomo and Farran, *The French Legal System* (Sweet & Maxwell, 2nd ed., 1996) pp. 1–11; Imbert, *Histoire du Droit Privé* (PUF, Coll. *Que-sais-je?* No. 408). For a history of French criminal law, see Laingui, *Histoire Du Droit Pénal* (PUF, Coll. Que-sais-je?, No. 690).

upon by learned writers. They also influenced the most famous French criminal lawyers—such as Pappon and Tiraqueau, in the sixteenth century, and Jousse, Muyart de Vouglans, Rousseau de la Combe in the eighteenth century—who gradually established the general principles of French criminal law.

At the same time, accusation and punishments were deeply rooted in local custom while criminal liability was strongly based on Canon law. Criminal law was also characterised by the rigour of penalties which were determined by local custom. These ranged from the death penalty, whipping, humiliation (for example the iron collar, pillory, exhibition in public, etc.), custodial sentences (mainly sending to the galleys), to penalties restricting liberty (for example deportation from a province, a town or the country).

From the second half of the eighteenth century, the criminal system, together with the general political, economic and social organisation of society, was criticised by philosophers such as Voltaire—who wrote satirical tracts about famous trials such as those of Calas, Sirven and Chevalier de la Barre—Montesquieu—whose *Esprit des Lois* contains one chapter on criminal law—and Rousseau with his *Contrat Social*. Yet the criminal law was mostly influenced by the works of the Italian writer Beccaria (1738–1794) and those of the English philosopher and jurisconsult Bentham (1748–1832). In his *Treaties on Offences and Penalties*, Beccaria criticised the rigour of penalties and notably the death penalty and torture, and believed that a moderate penalty effectively applied was more of a deterrent than a rigorous but uncertain punishment. He also emphasised the need for rehabilitation of the convicted offenders in society and for determining punishments according to offences and not their perpetrators, thus advocating in favour of an equal application of the criminal law.

Like Beccaria, Bentham regarded man as being driven by his own interests. Therefore, the purpose of penalties should also be determined according to sex, age, social rank or wealth of the offender. Corporal punishments should be replaced by custodial sentences. He even imagined a model prison called the Panopticon. The works of Bentham and Beccaria have exercised an enormous influence in Europe. For instance, the Austrian Emperor Joseph II abolished the death penalty in the new Criminal Code of 1788; the bailiff of Gent, Vilain XIV, had a new type of prison built; the Prussian Emperor Friedrich II abolished torture; in France, the Minister of Justice, Lamoignon, tried to reform the judiciary and criminal justice system in a more liberal way but faced the opposition of the courts, the *Parlements*.

The *droit intermédiare* and the Napoleonic Codes

Article 8 of the Declaration of Rights of Man and the Citizen of 1789 established the principle of *légalité* of offences and penalties, that is that these must be determined by law. Under the *Constituante* period (1789–1791), two reforms of great importance, inspired by the work of Beccaria, were adopted: the Act of July 19–22, 1791 on local police and police for major offences (*pour la police municipale et correctionnelle*) and the Act of September 24–October 6, 1791 on police dealing with serious crimes (*pour la police criminelle*). Both codified and unified criminal law.

With respect to criminal procedure, a system based on the English system was created and adapted to the administrative organisation of the time. However, under the *Convention* period (1792–1795), procedural laws were amended by the Code of 3 *Brumaire an III* (1795) and created for individuals the right of accusation, and reorganised the police. Under the *Consulat* period (1799–1804), an Act of 7 *Nivôse an IX* (1801) created a *ministère public*—the prosecution service—and specialised courts were created to combat increasing criminality.

Under the first Empire, two criminal codes were adopted and remained in force for 150 years, one of them remaining in use until 1994. Prepared by a Commission appointed in 1801, they were examined by the *Conseil d'Etat* in 1804 and again in 1808–1810 after consulting the courts. The Code of Criminal Procedure or *Code d'instruction criminelle* was promulgated in 1808 and the Criminal Code or *Code pénal* in 1810. Both came into force on January 1, 1811.

Influenced by Bentham, the draftsmen of the Criminal Code put the emphasis on deterrence and intimidation: for instance, attempt was regarded as being similar to the perpetration of the offence itself; the accomplice was subjected to the same sentence as the main perpetrator, etc. However, the main reforms of the Revolution were kept, such as the division of offences into three categories, the principle of the legal determination of offences and penalties, the use of custodial sentences, equality under the criminal law, etc. Fixed penalties replaced maximum and minimum sentences, together with a set of numerous aggravating circumstances, a few *excuses atténuantes* (statutorily defined mitigating factors) and a limited number of extenuating circumstances.

The Code of Criminal Procedure organised procedure in three stages, each of them being conducted by different authorities: prosecution, investigation and judgment.[2] It established a balance between the inquisitorial aspects of the criminal procedure inherited from the

---

[2] See Dadomo and Farran, *op. cit.*, pp. 192 *et seq*.

pre-revolutionary regime and the accusatorial character of the *droit intermédiare* period, and introduced the institution of the jury composed of lay men.

French criminal law since the codification

Although the Criminal Code did not inspire as much enthusiasm as the Civil Code, this remained a work of reference which, after being amended and completed by subsequent statutes, was in force until 1994.

Along with the resurgence of liberal ideas around 1830 and during the *Monarchie de Juillet* (1830–1848), the Criminal Code was reformed by an Act of April 28, 1832 in a more liberal direction. For instance, the iron collar sentence and mutilation were abolished. Penalties created in 1810 were reduced. Penalties for serious crimes were downgraded to penalties for major offences. With respect to serious crimes, the power to determine extenuating circumstances lay with the jury and no longer with professional judges.

The exemplary force of sentences was put into question in the light of comparative law. The reform of the prison system became one of the main objectives of successive parliaments and debate took place on the purpose of repression of crime, the purpose of sentences and the most appropriate means to enforce them. Also the idea that rehabilitation of criminals in society was just as important as deterrence started to prevail. This was put forward by the so-called neo-classical school represented in particular by Guizot, Rossi, Ortolan and Lucas. The neo-classical doctrine can be summed up into this formula: "*Punir ni plus qu'il n'est juste, ni plus qu'il n'est utile*" ("Punish no more than is just and effective"). Their ideas influenced the legislator between 1830 and 1870: for example, the reduction of sentences for various offences (Act of May 19, 1863), the application of special sentences to political offences (for instance, the Constitution of 1848 abolished the death penalty for these), the abolition in 1854 of the sentence called "*mort civile*" (loss of all civil rights) enforcement of the penalty of hard labour in the Colonies under the Act of May 30, 1864, supposedly intending to improve the nature of man ("*améliorer l'homme par la terre et la terre par l'homme*"). These measures failed, however, to reduce crime notably that perpetrated by recidivists.

The positivist theorists—inspired by the positivist philosophy of August Comte—criticised the neo-classical doctrine and rejected its abstract conception of criminals, the presumption that criminals had a free-will and the principle of proportionality of penalties. They believed that repression of crime should be based on the personality of the offender which had to be analysed not from a moral perspective but from the point of view of the threat of the individual to society. Only this threat could justify and help determine the measures to be taken against the offender. How could this threat be determined and measured? Lombroso, an Italian professor of forensic medicine, found the answer in the anatomic examination of individuals and believed in the concept of a natural born criminal. Crime could, therefore, be explained by anthropology since it was the resurgence of primitive instincts of man. Types of criminals, such as impassioned criminals or insane criminals, could be scientifically portrayed. By contrast, Ferri, an Italian lawyer and professor of law, believed that criminal behaviour could be explained by sociology. The reasons for crime were to be found in the social environment of delinquents. Both therefore believed in—physiological or social—determinism and in the moral irresponsibility of delinquents.

This doctrine has known great success and helped criminology develop. It also influenced French criminal law. For instance the Act of May 27, 1885 created the sentence of *relégation* (life deportation) for incorrigible recidivists. *Interdiction de séjour* was established whereby criminals could be prohibited from residing in areas of France where their presence was deemed to be a menace. *Libération conditionnelle* (release on probation) was introduced by the Act of August 14, 1885 and *sursis à l'exécution des peines* (suspension of sentences) was authorised under the Act of March 26, 1891.

Pragmatists adapted the positivist doctrine by abandoning its philosophical principles and putting into practice some of its recommended solutions. In France, the draftsmen of the 1934 bill on the criminal law reform was clearly influenced by this school of thought, but Parliament showed less enthusiasm towards it. However, a number of penalties were adopted such as those entailing loss of rights or the prohibition against taking up professional activities, etc. These were more preventative than coercive measures. Administrative penalties, such as deportation or disqualification from driving, had the same purpose. Also, informed about the social causes of certain forms of crime, Parliament adopted preventative measures such as measures against alcoholism, drugs, poverty, etc. On the other hand repression of economic and financial offences—at a time when scandals multiplied—was increased. Another reason for the reluctance of Parliament to put into practice the ideas of the pragmatists lay in the risk of infringing of individual rights and freedoms for the sake of the protection of the social interest based on an uncertain and possibly erroneous scientific diagnosis.

Another doctrine, *défense sociale nouvelle*, appeared after the Second World War when the protection of individual freedoms and human dignity became regarded as the utmost value. For its advocates, the protection of society is best guaranteed by helping individuals adapt to their social environment and preventing them from becoming delinquents. These ideas were applied by the Commission for the Reform of Penitentiary Institutions in its innovative programme of 1944. This was implemented notably in Book Five of the Code of Criminal Procedure. Furthermore, the *Société Internationale de Défense Sociale* adopted in 1952 a "minimum programme" which widely influenced French law. This programme was then revised in the light of 30 years of social, economic, political and technical developments. Like the positivist school, the school of the *défense sociale* favoured of a thorough examination of the personality of delinquents. This was made compulsory for minors by the *Ordonnance* of February 2, 1945 and extended to perpetrators of serious crimes—for example under Article 81(6) the defendant could request a medico-psychological examination.

An extension of the judges' powers to determine and enforce sentences was also recommended. This led to the creation of the *juge de l'application des peines* (judge in charge of the execution of sentences). Also the idea of delinquents being assisted during and after serving a sentence was put forward. This materialised in the creation of the *sursis avec mise à l'épreuve* (also called *probation*), that is the conditional suspension of a sentence with supervision and social control; in the regulation of Probation Committees; and in the adoption of measures relating to those released on probation or those who were *interdits de séjour*, etc.

This movement became the source of inspiration for considerable legislation until 1975: for instance, the Act of December 24, 1953 on the use of a detoxification order by the investigating judge; that of April 15, 1954 on treatment for alcoholism; the Act of April 18, 1955 making the laws on *interdiction de séjour* more lenient; the Act of July 17, 1970 creating *contrôle judiciaire*, etc. Similarly, more liberal rules on imprisonment were adopted under *décrets* of 1959, 1971 and 1975.

Criminal legislation in the past twenty years

In 1976, a Commission was created with the task of investigating violence. It appeared from its report that violence was emerging in all classes of society (for example farmers, shopkeepers, employees, students, pupils, prisoners, etc.): 105 recommendations were put forward. These were directed at preventing violence. However, the government of the day preferred to put the emphasis on the repressive side of its policy against crime. The imprisonment policy was made more rigorous. In 1975 two categories of prisons were created for long sentences: detention centres with a liberal regime and the *maisons centrales* which were prisons with a stricter regime. Some of these prisons were even provided with a high security area called "*quartiers de sécurité renforcée*" and more commonly known as "*quartiers de haute sécurité*", for prisoners who were considered as being extremely dangerous (these were abolished in 1982). From 1976 the powers of the *juge de l'application des peines* were restricted. Notably judges could no longer mitigate sentences for certain offences within a certain period of time called *période de sûreté* (security period).

In 1980, following a trip to the United States, the Minister of Justice, Alain Peyrefitte, tabled a Bill called "*Sécurité et Libertés*" based on the repression of violent offences, thus reinforcing security, and on the protection of freedoms. Hence its title. The bill was passed in February 1981. This was soon replaced, after the coming into power of the Socialists, by the Act of June 1983 which abolished the newly created category of violent offences and replaced certain imprisonment sentences by a *jour-amende* penalty (fine to be paid daily) or by *travail d'intérêt général* (community service).

The first concern of the newly elected Socialist Government was to reduce the prison population by using the law on amnesty and the presidential granting of free pardon. Its second concern was to abolish the death sentence—this was done on October 9, 1981—and to abolish a number of courts of limited jurisdiction such as the *Cour de Sûreté de l'Etat* (State Security Court) and the *tribunaux permanents des force armées en temps de paix*.[3] An Act of July 8, 1983 aimed at reinforcing the protection of, and assistance to, victims of crime.

Between 1986 and 1988, stricter identity controls, summary judgments for petty offences and the extension of the security period were re-established. A Prevention of Terrorism Act was adopted in September 1986. However, the provisions of the "*Sécurité et Libertés*" Act were not re-introduced.

(B) REFORMS OF THE CRIMINAL CODE

The early attempts

All the above measures and reforms were primarily intended to address urgent issues of the time. However, public authorities were also aware of the need for deeper reform of the Criminal Code. A first Reform Bill was tabled in Parliament in 1934 but was rapidly out-dated by the evolution of society. In 1974, the Minister of Justice announced that a reform was being prepared, and a first draft reform of the Code (general provisions) was put forward by a Reform Commission. Its final draft was published in 1978 after all legal professions and bodies had been consulted.

[3] See Dadomo and Farran, *op. cit.*, p. 76.

Unaffected by the new Socialist Government, the Commission re-drafted the general provisions part of the proposed draft. This draft, together with that on special provisions, was adopted by the Cabinet in 1986 and tabled before the Senate. It was not however until the general elections of 1988 that the draft on the general provisions was examined by the Senate and adopted in 1989. The whole Reform Bill was finally adopted under four Acts of July 22, 1992.

The New Criminal Code of 1992

The original aim of the draftsmen of this New Code was to create a coherent and comprehensive set of criminal laws, including criminal laws applicable to economic, tax and environmental law. However, this proved to be an impossible task. It is therefore quite likely that the New Code will be complemented in the future.

The New Code deals with: (1) the general provisions on criminal law (first Act); (2) offences against the person (second Act); (3) offences against property (third Act); and (4) offences against the Nation, the State and peace (fourth Act). Unlike the Napoleonic Code, priority has been given to the protection of the person, which is reflected in the fact that offences against the person are dealt with before those against property. Furthermore, the New Code is rather innovative on criminal liability. For instance, the principle of liability of legal persons was introduced and the concept of insanity as a defence was re-adapted and modernised. This New Code is also the expression of a new policy which combines greater severity against major criminality—for instance, with the introduction of new intermediary penalties between life imprisonment and the 20 years' imprisonment penalty—and greater indulgence for petty criminals.

(C) GENERAL PRINCIPLES OF FRENCH CRIMINAL LAW

The principle of criminal legality

The principle of criminal legality, also referred to as principle of legality of offences and sentences, is notably expressed in the Latin adage "*Nullum crimen, nulla poena sine lege*" and in Article 111-2(1) of the New Criminal Code which stipulates that:

> "Serious crimes and major offences, and sentences which are applicable to their perpetrators are determined by law."[4]

[4] "*La loi détermine les crimes et les délits et fixe les peines applicables à leurs auteurs.*"

Articles 113-3(1) and (2) further provide that:

> "No one can be sentenced for a serious crime or a major offence which is not defined by law, or for a minor offence which is not defined by a regulation."[5]

and:

> "No one can be subject to a sentence which does not exist in law . . . "[6]

This principle establishes the pre-eminence of the law enacted by Parliament: that Parliament alone can make substantive and procedural criminal legislation. Neither the Executive nor the Judiciary have this power. In its decision of January 19–20, 1981 on the "Security and Freedoms" Act 1981, the Constitutional Court ruled that Parliament had discretion to create sentences in connection with offences it had defined. The principle also implies that Parliament has the obligation to pass clear and precise laws.

In procedural law, this principle guarantees the balance between the defense and the prosecution as expressed notably in Article 6 of the European Convention on Human Rights on fair hearing and protection of the rights of the defense, in the principle of presumption of innocence, in pre-trial detention being subject to strict rules, in a fair trial and right of appeal.

The principle of legality also has to be complied with by judges who must base their sentences on the relevant legal provisions. Judges are also prohibited from interpreting criminal laws broadly unless the interpretation is favourable to the defendant or is a means of adapting an old law to new circumstances. The principle of legality also limits the jurisdiction of courts as to the determination of the sentence. A sentence cannot be higher than the highest one determined by law, or lower than the lowest one, unless there are extenuating circumstances. Nor can a court create a sentence where Parliament has failed to do so, nor decide on the forms of enforcement of a sentence where these are not determined by law.

Sources of criminal law

Logically, Acts of Parliament should be the only source of criminal law if the principle of legality is to be strictly applied. Regulations, however, have also become a more important source of law. Furthermore, domestic legal sources are supplemented by international laws.

---

[5] "*Nul ne peut être puni pour un crime ou pour un délit dont les éléments ne sont pas définis par la loi, ou par une contravention dont les éléments ne sont pas définis par le règlement.*"

[6] "*Nul ne peut être puni d'une peine qui n'est pas prévue par la loi. . .*".

Sources of criminal law are:

the *loi* in its narrow meaning, that is by Act of Parliament;

- legal texts regarded as being equivalent to a *loi*: these are:
  * texts adopted by *de facto* or interim governments in exceptional circumstances (for example laws passed by the Vichy Government between 1940 and 1944 or those *ordonnances* adopted by the interim Government in 1944–1945 (see *ordonnance* of 1945 on juvenile delinquency);
  * *ordonnances* adopted under Article 92 of the 1958 Constitution within the four-month period following its promulgation (for example the second half of the legislative part of the old Code of Criminal Procedure and the first part of the Traffic Code have been adopted this way);
  * presidential decisions taken under Article 16 of the Constitution on emergency powers (this was used by De Gaulle during the events of Algeria in 1962);
  * foreign laws may be also assimilated to national legislation (Article 699(2) of the Criminal Procedure Code provides that a French national who has committed an offence in a foreign country cannot be prosecuted and sentenced in France if this offence is punishable according to the law of this country. Similarly, certain German legal provisions are still applicable in Alsace-Moselle after its return to France at the end of the First World War.)

Some other provisions are only partially equivalent to an Act of Parliament:

* Under Article 11 of the Constitution, any reform of the organisation of public powers may be passed by referendum (for example a military Court of Justice was created by an *ordonnance* of 1962 following a referendum of the same year);
* Under Article 38 of the Constitution, the Government has the power to ask Parliament's authority to pass an *ordonnance*, within a limited period only, for carrying out its programmes. Parliament must then ratify the *ordonnance* before the deadline set out by the enabling Act.

- regulations may complement statutes on serious crimes or major offences. On the other hand, minor offences fall within the scope of application of Article 37 of the Constitution and are therefore created and defined by regulations only.

- international conventions are also an important source of French criminal law since Article 55 established the superiority of international law over domestic legislation: *e.g.*, international conventions on extradition, Community law, and the European Convention on Human Rights.
- general principles of law such as the presumption of good faith, freedom of movement, right of property, equality before the law, the principle according to which the offence requires intentional conduct by the offender (*mens rea*), fair hearing, the principle according to which the defendant always speaks last in court, etc.
- custom has a negligible role in French criminal law since the main source of law is written law, but may be used by the courts occasionally.

Temporal application of French criminal law

The fundamental principle, which applies to substantive law, is that criminal laws are not retrospective (*principle de non-rétroactivité*). This principle is expressed in Article 7 of the European Convention on Human Rights, the Preamble of the Constitution and Article 112-2 of the new Criminal Code. This principle is the corollary of the principle of legality: how in deed could an offence be punishable or punishable more severely under a new law before its coming into force?

The principle of *non-retroactivité* is therefore twofold:

- stricter laws cannot be applied retrospectively. With respect to "immediate" offences, such as theft, the law to be applied is that which is in force at the time of their commission. This applies also to offences which are said to be "*permanentes*", that is the effects of which persist in time (for example bigamy, prohibited billsticking). On the other hand, a new law would apply to "continuous" offences, that is offences which are continuingly perpetrated even if they have been committed for the first time before the entry into force of the new law.
- more lenient laws are retrospective in principle. This is called *rétroactivité "in mitius"* since this benefits the accused. Amnesty is the most striking example of retrospective laws.

In procedural law, the principle is that new procedural rules apply immediately. This applies to rules on *prescription*—the time-limit at the expiry of which an action in court is barred—to procedures (time-limit, forms, evidence), and to rules on jurisdiction.

Territorial application of French criminal law

Three answers can be given to the question of the territorial application of domestic criminal laws. First, national laws may apply to all individuals, whatever their nationality, who have committed an offence within the limits of the State where these laws are in force. Secondly, domestic laws apply wherever offenders are: these can be applied to nationals of a State who have committed an offence abroad, or to offences committed against nationals of this State or against the State itself. Thirdly, under the principle of universality, competent courts are those where an offender has been arrested, wherever the offence has been committed, whatever the nationality of the offender or that of the victim.

French law applies mainly the first principle as derived from Article 3(1) of the Civil Code[7] and from Article 113-2(1) of the New Criminal Code:

> "French criminal law applies to offences which are committed within the territory of the Republic."[8]

However, the second principle is also referred to in the Code of Criminal Procedure (see Title X on offences committed abroad Articles 689–696) and in Articles 113-6 to 113-10 of the New Criminal Code.

---

[7] "Criminal and security laws are binding on those who reside on the (French) territory." ("*Les loi de police et de sûreté obligent tous ceux qui habitent le territoire.*")

[8] "*La loi pénale française est applicable aux infractions commises sur le territoire de la République.*"

TOPIC ONE
OFFENCES AGAINST THE PERSON IN THE NEW CRIMINAL CODE

Offences against the person are dealt with under Act 92-684 of July 22, 1992. This became the Second Book of the New Criminal Code. Although less innovative than the Act 92-683, which amended the general provisions of the Criminal Code, the provisions on offences against the person are presented in the New Code before those on offences against property and against the Nation and the State. The Second Book contains around 180 provisions, that is more than a quarter of the New Code. This reflects the priority given by the draftsmen of the New Code. Unlike the Code of 1810, which protected the State and individual property first, the New Code of 1992, inspired by concern for human rights, gives priority to the person against violations of life, freedoms, body, security, dignity and the environment.[9] Moreover, the protection of the person is not limited to that of the individual but also includes humanity in general.

Under this part of the New Code, old offences carry more severe penalties; new offences are created; non-intentional criminal liability is given a new impetus; and the protection of some victims is re-inforced.

(A) CRIMES AGAINST HUMANITY

The inclusion of *crimes contre l'humanité* clearly reflects the will of the legislator to incorporate humanist values in the New Code. This is symbolised by promoting crimes against humanity to the top of the list of offences against the person. The New Code now offers a coherent approach to such crime, which, previously was dealt with under international provisions, the case law of the Court of Cassation and an Act of 1964 which did not subject prosecution of such crimes to time-limits.

Genocide

Genocide is defined under Article 211-11 as any act which is part of the planned destruction of a group of people on the ground of race, religion or any other arbitrary criterion. Such acts include any intentional attempts against life, serious bodily and mental harm, subjecting people

[9] In 1986, R. Badinter, then Minister of Justice, insisted that the New Code should reflect the new values of our time and be in line with fundamental texts on the protection of human rights.

to conditions of existence so as to result in its partial or total destruction, the deportation of children and the restriction of births.[10]

Other crimes against humanity

Article 212-1 criminalises acts of persecution, such as deportation, enslavement, systematic executions, kidnapping, torture and other inhuman acts, which are based on political, philosophical, racial or religious reasons. Destruction or extermination is no longer limited in its meaning to just the aim but includes systematic persecution of a group of people. Article 212-2 applies to the same acts committed during a war and draws the distinction between war crimes—the prosecution of which is time-barred—and crimes against humanity, in line with the decision of the Court of Cassation in the *Klaus Barbie* case.[11] These latter crimes are not time-barred. Furthermore any conspiracy to commit a crime against humanity has been criminalised under Article 212-3.

These crimes carry *réclusion criminelle à perpétuité*, that is life imprisonment, together with loss of civic, civil and family rights, the loss of the right of residence in certain places, the prohibition to perform public duties and confiscation, in full or partially, of private property (Article 213-1). Expulsion from the French territory may also be decided against foreign citizens, either indefinitively or for a maximum period of ten years (Article 213-3). *Personnes morales*—legal incorporated persons—may also be held guilty of crimes against humanity in which case penalties listed under Article 131-39 apply, among which are dissolution and confiscation of property.

By way of exception to Article 122-4, the criminal liability of the offender and accomplice(s) may not be waived on the ground of lawful orders. However, this factor may be taken into consideration by a criminal court when determining sentence (Article 213-4).

(B) PHYSICAL AND NON-PHYSICAL OFFENCES AGAINST THE PERSON

Like the former Criminal Code, the New Code criminalises a number of *atteintes à l'intégrité physique et psychique* of a human being. The novelty lies in the fact that under the New Code, a distinction is more clearly made between intentional and non-intentional offences and that

[10] The French Act on Abortion does not amount to genocide however, as there is no planned destruction of a group of people (see Court of Le Puy-en-Velay, March 14, 1995: [1995] Gaz. Pal. 2, July 17, at 7).

[11] See Cass., December 20, 1985: [1985] Bull. no 407.

endangering behaviour, which constitute a threat to life, health or security, is more seriously criminalised.

(1) Intentional offences

The New Code clearly distinguishes between *atteintes à la vie* (threats to life), other bodily and psychological harm, sexual offences and drug trafficking.

Atteintes à la vie

Atteintes à la vie, respectively defined as "*le fait de donner volontairement la mort*" (Article 221-1) and as "*meutre commis avec préméditation*" (Article 221-3), *meurtre* (murder) and *assassinat* (assassination), are intentional killing. Except in the case of *empoisonnement* (poisoning),[12] the means used to cause death are irrelevant. Homicide may only consist in a positive act, thus excluding abstention which may be the cause of death.[13]

Murder usually carries 30 years of imprisonment, except where there are aggravating factors besides premeditation,[14] in which case the penalty is life imprisonment. Furthermore, a multiplicity of supplementary penalties are listed under Article 221-8 and 221-9.[15]

Atteintes volontaires à l'intégrité de la personne

Torture and barbarity, violent acts and threats,[16] that is offences which all cause bodily or psychological harm without an intention to kill, are grouped under the generic terms, *atteintes volontaires à l'intégrité de la personne*. The inclusion in the New Code of torture and barbarity as a specific crime was intended to ensure the compliance of French criminal

---

[12] See Art. 221-5. It is punishable with 30 years of imprisonment, or life imprisonment when committed under the aggravating circumstances of Art. 221-4 (see below).

[13] However, abstention is taken into consideration when other offences are involved, such as *non-assistance à personne en péril* (duty of rescuing) or *mise en péril de mineurs* (endangering the life of minors).

[14] Under Art. 221-4, this includes killing a minor under 15, a parent or grandparent, a particularly vulnerable person (*e.g.* a pregnant woman, an elderly or disabled person) or a person involved in the administration of justice (*e.g.* judges, jurors, lawyers, etc.).

[15] For instance, suspension or cancellation of a driving licence, the prohibition on exercising a social or professional activity during which the crime was committed, confiscation of firearms, cancellation of a hunting licence, loss of civic, civil and family rights, etc.

[16] Under Art. 222-17, repeated threats, be they verbal or in writing, are punishable with six months' imprisonment and a fine of FF50,000 or three years' imprisonment and a fine of FF300,000 in the case of death threats. Threats which are made with the view to exerting pressure on someone, carry the same punishments as a death threat: (Art. 222-18).

law with international conventions. Torture or barbarity need not be used in the commission of another offence, as was the case of Article 303 under the former Code.[17] Subjecting someone to such acts is now punishable in itself. The penalty for such crime varies from 15 years' imprisonment to life imprisonment according to circumstances and the status of the victim.[18]

Violences—which include not only physical assaults but also any violent acts intended to cause emotional shock to the victim[19] as well as malicious telephone calls,[20] anonymous letters, etc.—are dealt with under Articles 222-7 to 222-16. Punishments attached to violent action vary according to the seriousness of the harm caused. *Violences* which result in the victim being unable to work for up to eight days are, in principle, punishable with a fine of FF10,000 (Article R 625-1). This may lead to up to three years' imprisonment and a fine of up to FF300,000 if the victim is not capable of working for a period longer than eight days (Article 222-11).[21] Where mutilation[22] or permanent disability[23] are caused, the offence carries ten years' imprisonment and a fine of FF1 million (Article 222-9), fifteen years' imprisonment—if committed

---

[17] Under the former Code, this was simply an aggravating circumstance of a *crime* or *délit*.

[18] Under Art. 222-3, the punishment is 20 years' imprisonment when the crime is committed against a minor under 15, a particularly vulnerable person, a parent or grand-parent, a spouse or cohabitee, a person involved in the administration of justice, a witness, a victim or civil party (as a means of intimidation or as a punishment), or when the crime is committed by a person vested with public powers, by a group of offenders and accomplices, or with premeditation or with the use of a firearm. This crime carries the same punishment when committed in conjunction with a sex offence other than rape.

The same crime is punished with 30 years' imprisonment when it is regularly directed against minors under 15 and vulnerable persons (Art. 222-4) or has resulted in mutilation or permanent disability (Art. 222-5); and with life imprisonment when torture or barbarity are committed in conjunction with murder or rape (Art. 222-2), or has unintentionally caused death (Art. 222-6).

[19] For instance, threatening someone with a loaded firearm, shooting above someone's head, entering by force, with a group of people, into someone's home (see Cass., December 16, 1953: [1954] D. 129), steering a car towards someone, threatening a group of people with a chainsaw (Cass., January 6, 1986: [1986] Gaz. Pal. 2. 598), etc.

[20] These are specifically dealt with under Art. 222-16.

[21] Those punishments are perceptibly higher than under Art. 309 of the former Code (between two months' and two years' imprisonment and a fine of up to FF20,000). When those violent offences are committed under one of the ten aggravating circumstances of Art. 222-12, they are punishable with five years' imprisonment and a FF500,000 fine, and ten years' imprisonment and a FF1,000,000 fine if they are committed by a parent or a guardian against a minor under 15.

[22] This would include excision or infibulation (see Cass., May 9, 1990: [1991] Rev. Sc. Crim. 565) or castration.

[23] These would include deafness or blindness (see Cass., November 6, 1985: [1985] Bull. no 347), the impairment of mental faculties (Cass., March 25, 1980: [1980] Bull. no 101) as well as the loss of use of a limb, ear or eye.

under one of the ten aggravating circumstances of Article 222-10—or even 20 years' imprisonment if committed by a parent or a guardian against a minor under 15. Finally, if the *violence* has caused "*la mort sans intention de la donner*" (negligent killing), the offender will serve 15, 20 or 30 years in prison depending on the existence or not of aggravating circumstances under Article 222-8.

Under Article 222-14, any acts of violence which are regularly committed against a minor under 15 or a vulnerable person are punishable with 30, 20, 10 and five years' imprisonment when they have caused the respective four harms listed therein.

Article 222-16 also criminalised malicious telephone calls and *agressions sonores* (invasive intrusion of noise), which are punishable with one year imprisonment and a fine of FF100,000, when they are intended to "*troubler la tranquilité d'autrui*".[24]

As with poisoning, *administration de substances dangereuses* has been dealt with as a specific offence under Article 222-15 but carries no specific punishment.

Sexual offences

The New Code distinguishes between rape, other sexual offences, indecent exposure and sexual harassment.

Viol (rape) is defined under Article 222-23 as any act of sexual penetration, whatever its nature, committed by force, duress, threat or surprise. An offence will qualify as rape where there is sexual penetration, thus excluding, for instance, anal penetration with a stick.[25] This definition is wide enough so as to include rape by and on either sex[26] as well as sodomy[27] and fellation.[28] Rape between spouses is also widely recognised under French law.[29]

The basic penalty of 15 years' imprisonment can be increased to 20 years when there are aggravating circumstances such as mutilation, incest, abuse of authority, etc. (Article 222-24).[30]

Like rape, other sexual offences require violence, duress, threat or surprise.[31] Unlike rape, however, Article 227-22 does not define these

---

[24] This clearly indicates that such forms of violence need not cause bodily or psychological harm.

[25] This would be torture and barbarity (see Cass., December 9, 1993: [1993] Bull. no 383).

[26] See Cass., July 3, 1991: [1992] Gaz. Pal. 39, concerning the rape of a son by his father; and Cass., January 4, 1985: [1985] Bull. no. 294, about a daughter being raped by her mother.

[27] See Cass., July 3, 1991, *op. cit.*

[28] See Cass., February 22, 1984: [1984] Bull. no 71.

[29] See Cass., September 5, 1990: [1990] Bull. no 313 and June 11, 1992: [1992] Bull. no 232.

[30] The usual supplementary penalties can also be imposed under Arts. 222-44–222-48.

[31] Without this component of violence, there cannot be an offence (see Cass., October 2, 1991: [1992] Dr. Pénal, Comm. 58).

offences. They may, therefore, be defined as opposed to rape in the sense that they do not consist in sexual penetration. The case law provides a number of examples of such offences: for example fondling breasts (see Cass., July 11, 1989) or pinching a woman's bottom or forcing a woman into a car (Cass., April 15, 1992). In all those cases, a sexual offence requires physical contact between the offender and the victim, otherwise the offence will fall in the category of *exhibition sexuelle* (indecent exposure).[32] These offences are punishable with five years' imprisonment and a FF500,000 fine, seven years' imprisonment and a FF700,000 fine—in the case of aggravating circumstances (Article 227-28, 227-29) [33]—or even ten years' imprisonment and one million francs—in the case of abuse of authority, threat with a weapon, injury, etc. (Article 227-30).[34]

Harcèlement sexuel (sexual harassment) was also criminalised under Article 222-33. The offence requires three components: (1) the offender must be a person who abuses his or her authority; (2) he or she uses orders, threats or duress (promotion, pay rise, sacking); (3) he or she harasses in order to obtain sexual favours. Such an offence is punishable with the same penalty as for indecent exposure.

Drug trafficking

The criminalisation of *traffic des stupéfiants*[35] has been transferred from the Code of Public Health[36] to the New Criminal Code, thus better reflecting the concern that this crime causes in today's society and giving the legislator the power to criminalise new offences.

Articles 222-34 to 222-39 make a distinction between the different drug related offences and, consequently, attach different penalties. Leading an organisation especially created for the purpose of producing, manufacturing, importing, exporting, transporting, possessing, selling, buying or using illegal drugs is a new offence of the utmost gravity punishable with life imprisonment and a FF50 million fine (Article 222-34). Producing or manufacturing illegal drugs carries 20 years' imprisonment—30 years, when committed within an organised group—and a fine of FF50 million. Also punishable with imprisonment and very

---

[32] Under Art. 222-32, this is punishable with one year imprisonment and a fine of FF100,000.

[33] These are the same aggravating circumstances as those for rape.

[34] Besides, as in the case of rape, the same supplementary penalties apply.

[35] The term *stupéfiants* is defined under Art. 222-41, by reference to the Code of Public Health, as any substances or plants classified as drugs under Art L 627 of this Code.

[36] However, some offences such as the use of drugs or incitement to use or deal with drugs are still punishable under this Code (Arts. L 628 and L 630).

heavy fines are other drug-related offences such as importing or exporting (Article 222-36), transporting, possessing, supplying or selling (Article 222-37(1)), facilitating the use of drugs and delivering prescriptions for the unlawful use of drugs (Article 222-37(2) (10 years' imprisonment and FF50 million fine). Although they do not constitute a drug trafficking offence *per se*, lying about the origin of the income or the property of a drug trafficker (for example by issuing fake invoices, fake pay slips or fake bills of debt) and money laundering, are punishable under Article 222-38 with ten years' imprisonment and a fine of one million francs. Also supplying someone with drugs for private use carries a penalty of five years' imprisonment and a fine of FF100,000.

Not only natural but also legal persons can be held criminally liable for these offences. Apart from supplementary penalties applicable to both types of offenders (Article 222-49 to 222-51, for example closure of public establishments, withdrawal of a licence for the sale of alcohol, etc.), legal persons may also incur penalties provided for under Article 131-39, that is dissolution, definitive or temporary prohibition from exercising professional or social activities, prohibition from borrowing public money, judicial supervision for up to five years, confiscation of property used in the commission of the offence, etc. Fines applied to legal persons are five times higher than those applied to individuals (Article 131-38).

(2) Unintentional offences

The old expression of "*atteintes involontaires à l'intégrité de la personne*" used in the New Code was not the most satisfactory one. This could be interpreted as meaning that there was no original intention to commit the offence. This, of course, is not always true. For instance, an employer may deliberately fail to apply safety measures at work without having the intention of causing bodily harm to his employees; a car driver may exceed the speed limit without having the intention of killing or harming someone. Furthermore, the New Code refers to "*manquement délibéré à une obligation de sécurité* . . . ", which suggests that intention may be a component in this category of offences.

Three types of wrong-doing may amount to an unintentional offence: (1) *maladresse* and *imprudence* are any fault committed independently of unlawful conduct (for example a driver who loses control of his car); (2) *inattention* and *négligence* consist more in failing or omitting to do something (for example failing to implement safety measures on a construction site, etc.); and (3) *manquement à une obligation de sécurité ou de prudence imposéee par la loi ou les règlements* which consists in ignoring rules and regulations (for example ignoring traffic rules or work safety rules).

The harm caused as a result of an unintentional offence is either death—*atteintes involontaires à la vie* (article 221-6, 221-7) or injury incapacitating a person from working—*atteintes involontaires à l'intégrité de la personne* (Article 222-19 to 222-21). This therefore implies that the victim be a person not, for instance, an embryo.[37]

If the lack of causal link between the wrong-doing and the damage suffered automatically waives the liability of the person charged, it is not a requirement that there is an immediate, exclusive and direct link (see Cass., May 30, 1972: [1972] Bull. no 179). There are indeed, various situations where death or injury may result from the combination of the wrong-doing by the person charged and the acts of a third person, or of the charged person and the victim, or where the wrong-doing by a third person was facilitated by the person charged, or where the damage suffered is only the indirect consequence of the wrong-doing by the person charged.

The penalties attached to these offences vary according to the degree of harm caused. *Homicide involontaire* (manslaughter) is punishable with three years' imprisonment and a fine of FF500,000 in the case of *manquement délibéré* (Article 221-6, 221-7). Incapacitating a person from working for at least three months leads up to two years' imprisonment and a fine of FF200,000, which can be increased to three years and FF300,000 in the case of *manquement délibéré*.

Not only individuals but also legal persons can be held criminally liable for these offences (see Articles 221-7 and 222-21).

(3) Endangering behaviour

A numbering of old and new offences were grouped under the generic heading endangering behaviour. The offence consists in adopting behaviour which may endanger the life or health of a person. If the danger materialises, the punishment will be increased.

Mise en danger may consist either in deliberately exposing a person to danger of death or injury (Article 223-1) or in deserting a person who is incapable—by reason of age, or physical or mental ability—of protecting him or herself against possible dangers (Article 223-3).

---

[37] However, the Court of Douai ruled that there was homicide in the case of an unborn child being killed in a car accident at the end of the pregnancy (June 2, 1987: [1987] Gaz. Pal. 145). There will also be homicide if the death of a new born baby is caused by negligence before the umbilical cord is cut (see Court of Amiens, April 28, 1964: [1984] Gaz. Pal. 2.167).

The generic term of "*entraves aux mesures d'assistance et ommissions de porter secours*" includes offences such as obstructing the arrival of rescue services (Article 223-5), failing to prevent the commission of an offence against a person (Article 223-6(1)), failing to rescue (Article 223-6(2)), and failing to combat disasters endangering persons (Article 223-7).[38]

Under Article 233-8, experiments carried out on human beings without their consent have also been criminalised.[39] Similarly, abortion carried out without the consent of the mother is severely punished.

Finally, although committing suicide is not a crime, inciting someone to do so (Article 223-13), or advertising methods of committing suicide (Article 223-14)[40] is an offence against the person.

Apart from supplementary penalties under Articles 223-16 to 223-20, these offences carry severe sentences of imprisonment (between one and five years) or heavy fines (between FF100,000 and 700,000).

(C) VIOLATION OF THE MORAL INTERESTS OF A PERSON

In contemporary society, crime in the form of violation of the moral interests of a person have experienced particular development but could not previously be combatted under ordinary criminal provisions. For this reason, specific legislation aimed at protecting privacy, security, tranquillity or dignity of a person was passed over the last decades. It is, therefore, not surprising to find in the Criminal Code such a variety and multiplicity of provisions on the protection of the moral interests of the person. Far from fundamentally amending the existing legislation, the New Code created a few new offences relating to the dignity of the person.

These have been classified in the New Code under three headings: violations of freedoms, dignity and personality.

Crimes against individual freedoms

Article 224-1 makes it an offence to unlawfully arrest, abduct, hold in custody or imprison someone. These are all separate and distinct offences and need not be all committed at the same time or by the same person to entail criminal liability. These actions are unlawful when carried out without due legal authority, thus excluding the case of the arrest of an

---

[38] In the latter three cases, criminal liability is waived, however, if one's intervention would put one's life or someone else's life at risk.

[39] These provisions have been supplemented by the Act of July 29, 1994 on Bio-ethics (see Title I of Book V of the New Criminal Code).

[40] This provision allowed the Court of Paris to sentence the authors of the second edition of "*Suicide, mode d'emploi*" (April 11, 1995).

offender by a citizen—which is allowed under Article 73 of the Code of Criminal Procedure[41]—or confinement in a special medical establishment.

These offences are punished with 20 years' imprisonment[42] and with 30 years' imprisonment if there are aggravating circumstances (for example in the case of mutilation, permanent disability or where the victim has been held hostage). If the victim is a minor under 15, the offence may even lead to life imprisonment (Article 224-5).

Hijacking airships, ships and other means of transport are dealt with under Articles 224-6 to 224-8 and carry a minimum penalty of 20 years' imprisonment.

Crimes against the dignity of the person

Crimes against the dignity of the person, include discrimination, *proxénétisme* (procuring, pimping and living off immoral earnings), imposing bad working or housing conditions, disrespect to the dead.

Discrimination has been defined very broadly under Article 222-1 as:

> "any distinction made between natural persons by reason of their origin, sex, family situation, health, disability, traditions, political convictions, trade union activities, or their belonging or not belonging, real or presumed, to a given ethnic group, a nation, race or religion."

The same definition applies to legal persons when such discrimination is directed at all or some of their members (Article 225-1(2)).

Article 225-2 punishes with two years' imprisonment and a FF200,000 fine, three specific forms of discrimination: (1) refusing to provide goods and services[43]; (2) obstructing the normal exercise of an economic activity, that is boycott; and (3) refusing to recruit, sanction or dismiss a person, or making the offer of employment subject to a discriminatory condition.

However Article 225-2 provides for three categories of exceptions. First, discrimination may be justified on the ground of health, in life and

---

[41] However, if keeping a thief in custody for an hour while waiting for the police to come is not unlawful (Cass., October 1, 1979: [1979] Bull. no 263), catching a minor who stole goods, keeping him in custody for a few hours and assaulting him is, of course, an offence (Cass., February 16, 1988: [1988] Bull. no 75).

[42] This can be reduced to five years if the victim of unlawful custody or imprisonment has been released within seven days.

[43] This would include refusal to serve food or drink (Court of Nantes, March 1, 1990), refusal to rent rooms or flats (Court of Douai, June 25, 1974), and discrimination against a handicapped person, etc.

accident insurance contracts. Secondly, a refusal to recruit or dismissal may be based on health or disability in accordance with the provisions of the Labour Code or the status of public servants. Finally, sex discrimination is lawful where gender is the determining condition for the exercise of an employment or a professional activity.

Under the new heading "*conditions de travail et d'hébergement contraires à la dignité*", the legislator sought to criminalise the exploitation of illegal workers or the unemployed. Under Articles 225-13 and 225-14, taking advantage of a vulnerable person or a person in a situation of dependence with the view to obtaining unpaid or underpaid services or subjecting him or her to working and housing conditions contrary to human dignity, is punishable with two years' imprisonment and a FF500,000 fine. These broadly formulated provisions leave the courts with a wide margin of appreciation.

Following the anti-Semitic attacks on the cemetery of Carpentras in the South of France, the scope of application of former Article 360 of the Criminal Code, which criminalised the violation of graveyards, was extended and the sentences attached to the offence increased. Under Article 225-17, any assault on a corpse and any violation, by whatever means, of a burial site is punishable with one year imprisonment and a fine of FF100,000. The punishment can rise to five years' imprisonment and a FF500,000 fine when the offence is perpetrated in relation to the race, ethnic group, nation, or religion of the deceased person.

Since an Act of 1991, associations for the protection of moral interests and associations of war veterans may take court action as civil parties against any perpetrators of such offences.[44]

Attacks against a person's personality

Under this generic term, attacks against a person's personality, the New Code deals with a number of offences which already existed under the former Code: *atteinte à la vie privée* (breach of privacy)[45]; *atteinte à la représentation de la personne* (misrepresentation of a person's image); *dénonciation calomnieuse* (false accusation); *atteintes au secret professionel* (breach of confidentiality); *atteintes au secret des correspondances* (breach

---

[44] On the role and rights of civil parties in criminal proceedings, see Dadomo and Farran, *op. cit.*, pp. 199–203.

[45] This consists in recording or transmitting, without the person's consent, words uttered in private or image taken of him or her in a private place. This may also consist in keeping or disclosing to the public or a third person any information or document obtained by one of the means mentioned above (Art. 226-1, 226-2).

of the right to respect of correspondence); and breach of a person's right through databases.

TOPIC TWO
THE GENERAL DEFENCES OF *NECESSITE, LEGITIME DEFENSE* AND *CONTRAINTE*

Defences whereby the criminal liability of a person is waived, are traditionally distinguished between *faits justificatifs*, which are objective justifications exempting the accused from criminal liability, and *causes de non-imputabilité*, which are subjective defences or excuses. *Légitime défense* (self-defence), *ordre de la loi* (lawful orders), *état de nécessité* (necessity), and the victim's consent are *faits justificatifs*. On the other hand, *trouble psychique* (insanity), *contrainte* (duress) and error are *causes de non-imputabilité*. However the New Criminal Code does not make this subtle distinction, and defences are referred to and dealt with in the single category of "*causes d'irresponsabilité ou d'atténuation de la responsabilité* (Articles 122-1 to 122-7).

(A) *ETAT DE NECESSITE*

Although the concept of *état de nécessité* was not unknown in Roman, Germanic and even Canon laws, there was no general provision on *état de nécessité* in the original Criminal Code of 1810. It was, therefore, left to the courts to develop this concept into an effective defence on the basis of a few limited provisions of the Code (see Cass., June 25, 1958: [1958] D. 693). Necessity as a defence was originally justified by the courts and commentators either on the ground of moral constraint (see Courts of Paris, January 5, 1945: [1948] S. 2.88) or lack of criminal intention on the part of the offender (see Court of Chateau-Thierry, March 4, 1898). Later on, commentators preferred to justify necessity on a more objective ground, namely the interest of society in the sense that the offender, in a situation of necessity, was not behaving in an anti-social way. There was, therefore, no need for society to punish, which anyway would prove inefficient.[46]

Today necessity is expressly recognised as a defence in the New Criminal Code. Article 122-7 stipulates that:

> "A person who, facing a present and imminent peril which is a threat to him or her, another person or a property, performs an act necessary for the protection of that person or property, may not be held criminally liable, save in the case of lack of proportion between the means used and the seriousness of the threat."[47]

---

[46] See J. Larguier, *Les Limites de l'Etat de Nécessité* [1982] Rev.Sc.Crim. 765.

[47] "*N'est pas pénalement responsable la personne qui, face à un danger actuel ou imminent qui*

Etat de nécessité requires that the offender is forced to make a choice between enduring a peril or committing an offence to avoid this peril. For instance, there is necessity where a woman has to choose between stealing a loaf of bread from a bakery and letting her child die of hunger[48]; or where a mother has to choose between denying a visiting right to the father of her child (*délit de non-représentation*) and causing the child the embarrassment of visiting his father in a prison.[49]

Necessity, however, may be relied upon as a defence only if strict conditions are met. First, the danger must represent a threat to a person, including the offender, or property. Secondly, the peril must be a present and imminent one. A general atmosphere of insecurity is, therefore, not sufficient to justify an offence on the ground of necessity.[50] The peril must present the character of an emergency. This is, of course, a matter for the courts to decide upon according to their discretion. Can the offender rely on necessity if he has imperiled himself? Although it is required in other countries (for example under Articles 34. and 34-1 of the Swiss Criminal Code) that the accused has not imperiled himself, this does not appear to be the case under Article 122-7. However, the French courts made it a necessary condition in the past.[51] Academic commentators are more divided upon the issue.[52]

Thirdly, the offence committed must have been necessary for the protection of the person or property imperiled. There must be no other alternative for the person concerned than to commit an offence in order to avoid the peril. For instance, a driver who is forced to cross a solid white line in order to avoid an imprudent pedestrian may rely on necessity (see Court of Avesnes-sur-Helpes, December 14, 1964). On the other hand, a shopkeeper may not justify counterfeiting goods on the ground that he was out of stock as a result of his supplier failing to deliver. The Court of Cassation took the view that this difficulty could have been remedied by other means (see Cass., February 11, 1986: [1986] Bull. No.

---

menace elle-même, autrui ou un bien, accomplit un acte nécessaire à la sauvegarde de la personne ou du bien, sauf s'il y a disproportion entre les moyes employés et la gravité de la menace."

[48] See the case of Ménard (Court of Amiens, April 22, 1898).

[49] Court of Agen, May 22, 1985.

[50] See Cass., November 21, 1974: [1974] Bull. no 345, which concerned a jeweller who committed a parking offence in order to be closer to the place where jewels were delivered.

[51] See Court of Rennes, April 12, 1954: [1954] S. 2.185, which concerned a lorry driver who, in order to avoid an oncoming train, was forced to break through the barriers of a level crossing, which he imprudently attempted to cross.

[52] See J.-Cl. Soyer and J. Larguier who are in favour of this condition and Pradel who is against.

54). Similarly, necessity is no defence for squatters (see Court of Rennes, February 25, 1957: [1957] D 338).

Fourthly, the means used to avoid the peril must be in proportion to its gravity. For instance, it is evident that killing a person to save an animal would be out of proportion, while running into a car to avoid running over a pedestrian is not. In principle, the safeguarded interest must be superior to the sacrificed one. However, the problem arises where both interests are of equal value. For instance killing someone else to save one's own life may not be easily justified on the ground of necessity.[53]

(B) *LEGITIME DEFENSE*

In Ancient law, self-defence used to be justified on the basis of duress. Any act of self-defence was an offence in itself, but was not punishable because the offender was regarded as having acted under undue influence originating from an attack which deprived him of his free-will. Self-defence was therefore regarded as a *cause de non-imputabilité*. The draftsmen of the Criminal Codes of 1810 and 1992 favoured the concept of self-defence as a right and, consequently, a *fait justificatif*. Self-defence then becomes legitimate only in the case of unjust attack and because society failed to prevent it.

Under Article 122-5(1):

> "A person who, facing an unjustified attack against himself or herself, or another person, takes, at the same time, action imposed by the necessity to protect himself or herself or that other person, cannot be held criminally liable, save in the case of lack of proportion between the means used and the seriousness of the attack."[54]

Similarly Article 122-5(2) stipulates that self-defence is justified, under the same conditions, to stop a crime against property being committed.

Besides this general principle, Article 122-6 creates a presumption of self-defence in two specific situations: (1) when repelling, by night, anyone attempting to enter into one's home as a result of threat, trick or force; and (2) when protecting oneself against perpetrators of violent theft or looting.

Self-defence requires that the attack on a person or property be

---

[53] It is arguable that, in this case, *contrainte* is a more appropriate defence.

[54] "*N'est pas pénalement responsable la personne qui, devant une atteinte injustifiée envers elle-même ou autrui, accomplit, dans le même temps, un acte commandé par la nécessité de la légitime défense d'elle-même ou d'autrui, sauf s'il y a disproportion entre les moyens de défense et la gravité de l'atteinte.*"

imminent. The attack must be genuine and may not be simply imagined by the person claiming self-defence.[55] This raises the question of the so-called *légitime défense putative*. Either one could have reasonably believed that one was going to be attacked, in which case self-defence is justified, or one wrongly believed so, in which case factual error instead of self-defence may be relied upon.

The response to an attack must occur "at the same time" as the attack and not before—in which case there would be premeditation on the part of the person pretending to be acting in self-defence—nor too long after the attack—which would then be a case of revenge. This is even more relevant in the case of an attack against property as Article 122-5(2) unequivocally stipulates that self-defence is justified only to "stop the commission of the offence". The attack must also be unjustified in law or by law. As a result, someone injuring a police officer carrying out a lawful arrest is not acting in self-defence. Is this condition met when someone is beaten up by the police (*passage à tabac*)? The courts' response has been negative on the ground that one should not rebel against the police, provided the police act to enforce the law and under lawful orders. This view is supported by Article 433-6 of the New Criminal Code which regards it an offence to commit any act of resistance against police forces.[56] To be unjustified, an attack need not be unlawful. For instance, a response to an attack from a child or an insane person could be justified under self-defence.

It is irrelevant that the response to an attack comes from the person being attacked or a third person, who witnessed the attack. This clearly results from the provision of Article 122-5(1).[57]

Self-defence is not justified in the case of an unintentional offence (see Cass., February 16, 1967: [1967] J.C.P. 15034).

It is evident that, as Article 122-5 provides, there is self-defence only where the response to the attack is necessary and proportionate to it. This requirement is not met if the victim of the attack, or a third person, could have resorted to other means to protect himself or another person. In other words, the response to the attack must have been the only alternative available.[58] Regarding the protection of property, Article 122-5(2) refers to a "strictly necessary" act of defence.

---

[55] Court of Paris, October 9, 1979.

[56] Note, however, that police officers may be held liable for any unjustified act of violence against a person.

[57] It is less clear, however, from Art. 122-5(2) whether the same principle applies to the protection of property. This provision indeed refers to "a" property and not "one's property".

[58] The necessary character of the act of defence is always difficult to assess in the case of police officers chasing criminals. See Cass., April 20, 1982: [1983] J.C.P. 19958, in which

Furthermore, the act of self-defence must not be out of proportion to the attack. The proportionate character of the act of self-defence is a matter for the courts to decide upon. For instance, killing someone in response to being slapped in the face is obviously not a case of self-defence. In 1974, the Court of Cassation ruled that the owner of a public house who shot at drunk people who were committing violent acts did not act in self-defence (November 28, 1974: [1974] Bull. no 362). In the case of crime against property, this requirement of proportionality is even more strict. The protection of property, however legitimate, does not justify homicide or serious or irreparable injury. This notably raises the issue of the use of booby-traps.[59]

As a general principle, the burden of proof of self-defence is on the person charged. It is for him and not the prosecution to prove that all the requirements for self-defence are met.[60] Where there is a presumption of self-defence as provided for under Article 122-6 (see above), this may be reversed by contrary evidence (see Cass., February 19, 1959: [1959] D. 161).

(C) *CONTRAINTE*

Together with error and *démence* or *trouble psychique* (insanity), *contrainte* (duress) is a *cause de non-imputabilité*. Under Article 122-2 of the New Criminal Code:

> "Any person who has acted under the influence of an irrestible force or duress may not be held criminally liable."[61]

Any force or *contrainte* exercised on a person has the effect of depriving that person of his free will and of excusing the offender from criminal liability.

In French law, a traditional distinction is made between *contrainte physique* and *contrainte morale*. In each case, the origin of the *contrainte* is either foreign (*externe*) or inherent (*interne*) to the person concerned. *Contrainte physique externe* may result from natural events, such as black ice on a road—which can be the cause of a traffic accident (see Cass., December 18, 1978)—or another person's action, as in the case of a conscript who was kept tied up in his home by burglars and, as a result,

---

a police officer was deemed to be acting in self-defence when a person held in custody seized a firearm.

[59] For instance, see Court of Troyes, May 24, 1977 concerning the killing of a burglar by a booby-trapped radio left in a cupboard.

[60] See Cass., May 22, 1959 and January 6, 1966.

[61] "*N'est pas pénalement responsable la personne qui a agi sous l'empire d'une force ou d'une contrainte irresistible à laquelle il n'a pu résister.*"

could not return to his regiment thus committing the crime of desertion, or that of a cyclist, who being trapped in a group of cyclists, ran over a policeman and caused his death (see Cass., January 5, 1957).

Contrainte physique may also be *interne*, that is inherent to the offender. For instance, the Court of Cassation ruled that a train passenger who, because he fell asleep from great exhaustion, missed the station where he was meant to get off, was under *contrainte*.[62] On the other hand, it was held that a woman who, under the emotional distress caused by the news of the dismissal of her husband, wrote offensive letters to the Minister of Justice and judges, was not acting under *contrainte*.[63]

There is *contrainte morale externe* when one commits an offence under threats or incitement by others. In both cases, this will only constitute an excuse from criminal liability if *contrainte* is irresistible.[64] Threats must also have been wrongful and overwhelming so as to deprive the victim of his free will.[65] If an offence has been committed as a result of incitement, this will only be excused on the ground of *contrainte* if the accused has lost all criminal intention.[66]

Unless the mental faculties of the offender have been impaired under the influence of violent passions or emotions, which is a case of insanity, *contrainte morale interne* has never been recognised by the courts as an excuse.[67]

In order to be an excuse, *contrainte* must have been irresistible so as to deprive the offender of all criminal intention. The difficulty of proof of irresistibility then arises, hence the harshness of the courts when considering this component of *contrainte*. Furthermore, the courts require that the offender has not put himself in a situation of *contrainte* as a result of a fault. For instance, a sailor, who was prevented from rejoining his ship because he had been arrested by the police and put in custody for drunkenness, could not be excused, on the ground of *contrainte*, from the charge of desertion (see Cass., January 29, 1921: [1921] S. 1.185).

As can be seen, the concept of *contrainte* is used in a much wider sense than English duress which covers only wrongful threats of another.

---

[62] See Cass., October 22, 1922: [1923] S. 1.287.

[63] See Cass., April 11, 1908: [1909] S. 1.473.

[64] See Cass., June 15, 1965: [1965] J.C.P. 4.106.

[65] See Cass., December 28, 1900, which concerned a Corsican owner of forests who, under threat, was forced to give shelter to criminals and hide them from the police. He was, however, found guilty of *recel de malfaiteurs* (harbouring criminals).

[66] In the case of a policeman pretending to be a drug buyer, the Court of Cassation ruled that a drug dealer may not rely on this excuse if the role played by the police officer has simply allowed him to get evidence of the drugs-dealer's unlawful activities (March 2, 1971: [1971] J.C.P. 2.16.815).

[67] See Cass., April 11, 1908 (n. 63, above). It is to be noted however, that perpetrators of crimes of passion have been granted extenuating circumstances.

Index